Dec 27/02 **DATE DUE**

E  ng

D1263734

HIGH
interest
books

Children's Press®
A Division of Scholastic Inc.
New York / Toronto / London / Auckland / Sydney
Mexico City / New Delhi / Hong Kong
Danbury, Connecticut

Book Design: Michael DeLisio
Contributing Editor: Matthew Pitt
Photo Credits: All photos by Maura B. McConnell except pp. 5, 7, 17, 33,
42–48 © Artville

Library of Congress Cataloging-in-Publication Data

Fine, Jil.
Baby-sitting smarts / by Jil Fine.
    p. cm. – (Smarts)
Summary: Provides tips for teens on learning and practicing good
baby-sitting skills, getting baby-sitting jobs, preparing for a particular
job, handling emergencies, and duties after the children are asleep.
Includes bibliographical references and index.
ISBN 0-516-23926-0 (lib. bdg.) – ISBN 0-516-24011-0 (pbk.)
1. Babysitting–Handbooks, manuals, etc.–Juvenile literature. [1.
Babysitting–Handbooks, manuals, etc.] I. Title. II. Series.
HQ769.5 .F5 2002
649'.1'0248–dc21
                                    2002002073

Contents

Help Wanted:
Responsible teen who wants to make money while having fun! Good money. Call Sally at (555) 555-5555

Introduction

Want to earn a little extra cash? Are you good with kids? If you answered yes to both of these questions, baby-sitting might be the perfect job for you! Baby-sitting is a lot of fun, but it also requires a lot of knowledge and responsibility. The most important thing to know is how to keep the child you're caring for safe. This book will teach you basic first aid and important safety tips. This book will also prepare you for the world of baby-sitting. Everything from getting the job to tucking the kids in at night is discussed. If you follow the tips and instructions in the pages that follow, you'll be on your way to becoming a great baby-sitter in no time.

For busy parents, a responsible baby-sitter who is available for work is headline news.

Chapter 1

Jump into Sitting

There are many ways to get ready for your first baby-sitting job. One popular way to prepare is by taking a Red Cross baby-sitting class. Most local Red Cross agencies offer affordable baby-sitting classes for eleven to fifteen-year-olds. The Red Cross class teaches new baby-sitters important safety tips and life-saving skills. This class is highly respected and a great way to learn.

If you do take this class, let your potential clients know. If they're considering more than one person for the job, your extra knowledge may tip the odds in your favor!

If you cannot take a class with the Red Cross, try a different path. It helps to speak with family members or friends of your parents who have children.

Taking a Red Cross class is one of the best ways to improve your baby-sitting skills.

Ask if you can help them take care of their child while they're around. Use the time to ask them questions. You will be learning from people who know what it takes to care for a child. This will help both you and the parents. You'll gain some valuable knowledge, and they'll have an eager, extra pair of hands helping them out.

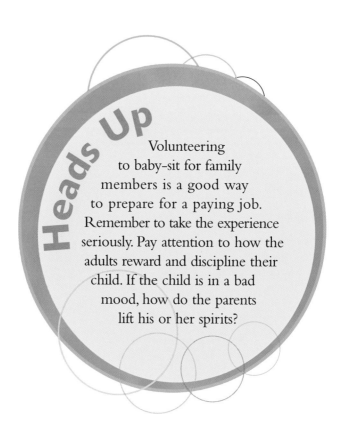

Heads Up

Volunteering to baby-sit for family members is a good way to prepare for a paying job. Remember to take the experience seriously. Pay attention to how the adults reward and discipline their child. If the child is in a bad mood, how do the parents lift his or her spirits?

Get Serious About Fun

Preparing to baby-sit also involves dreaming up fun ways to entertain children. Many baby-sitters bring along a bag of fun things to play with. The items you bring don't have to be expensive. Odds and ends that are lying around your house will do nicely. After all, they'll all be new to the child! Let your imagination roam—but keep the age of the child you're caring for in mind. Don't bring small things that a toddler or baby can swallow or choke on. Also, it's not wise to bring markers or pens with ink that can stain. Kids can be messy!

Heads Up

Here are some ideas of what to put in your bag:

- crayons
- paper lunch bags for coloring on or making into puppets
- glue
- big sidewalk chalk
- paper plates
- cheap construction paper
- old magazines, greeting cards, and scrap paper
- safety scissors
- nontoxic watercolors or fingerpaints
- an old shirt to use as a smock

Sally Chang

Baby-sitter Services
Caring and responsible.
I love children.
Rate: $5/per hour
      $1 more for each
      additional child
(555) 555-5555

Chapter 2

Getting the Job

Once you're prepared to baby-sit, you need to test your new skills. Baby-sitting is a business. The best and safest way to advertise in this business is by word-of-mouth. Talk to parents of young children in your community, school, or place of worship. Let them know that you are available to baby-sit. You may also want to make business cards to hand out to potential employers. Be sure to put your name and phone number on the cards. It's also a good idea to write down the rate that you plan to charge per hour. Never give your cards to strangers. Even though you may be anxious to start your new business, keep this rule in mind: You should only baby-sit for people you know.

Handing out your business cards to neighbors is a great way to get the word out: You're the right person for the job!

Sitting Pretty

Soon, the word will be out that a good baby-sitter is looking for work. When parents call, be prepared to discuss the rate that you will charge. A general rate is between three and seven dollars an hour. Sometimes, baby-sitters charge fifty cents to one dollar more an hour for each additional child. Baby-sitters may also charge more for an infant, since they need more attention and care. Before setting your rate, discuss the issue with your parents, along with any of your friends who baby-sit. This will help you figure out what the going rate is in your neighborhood.

Another issue to bring up when talking to your new employer is your schedule. Let him or her know when you are available and, if you have a curfew, at what time you must be home. Before agreeing to baby-sit, arrange your transportation to and from the job. Always have someone take you home at night. Never walk home alone.

Also, let your parents or guardians know about your baby-sitting plans. Be sure to tell them which

Some parents find it comforting to meet potential baby-sitters before offering them a job.

hours you are going to be working. Also provide them with the name, address, and phone number of the family you will be baby-sitting for.

Ask Away

Making a good first impression with a family is important. Call the family before the day of your

Heads Up

If your employers don't mind you having a snack, be sure not to chow down a five-course meal. They won't be happy if they return home to find an empty refrigerator.

job to ask some questions. (Be sure that they've got a minute to speak with you!) Take notes on each family that you baby-sit for. Many baby-sitters keep a file on each family, and then bring that file with them to each job. Creating a baby-sitting notebook will help keep all your information handy and organized.

Asking appropriate questions will make your baby-sitting experience safer and less worrisome. Doing this will show the parents that you are responsible. It will also let them know that you are truly concerned for their child's welfare. Before calling, write down the questions that you plan to ask. This way, you'll be sure not to forget anything important. If you get stuck trying to think of good questions, start with the following suggestions.

- Questions About Kids: Does the child have any special needs? Is he or she taking any medicine? If so, will you be responsible for giving it to the child? When and how much should you give?
- House Rules: How would the parents like you to deal with misbehavior? Are there any areas of the house where the child is forbidden to go? When is bedtime? Ask about rules concerning the use of the computer, the television, and the phone.
- A List of Duties: Do the parents expect you to take care of anything before they return? For instance, do you have to give the child a bath? Do they expect you to fix a meal for the child? If so, what does the child eat, and is there any food the child is allergic to? Are you expected to help the child with schoolwork? While on duty, are there house pets you will also need to care for?

Each family has its own routine. Asking questions ahead of time will help you understand just what that routine is—making it easier for you to follow.

Chapter 3

On the Job

The first time you baby-sit for a family, arrive a little early. Ask the parents to give you a brief tour of the house. As you stroll through each room, look around for possible safety hazards. Make sure that anything dangerous—like medicine, cleaning solutions, or alcohol—is stored in a locked cabinet. If the child is very young, look to see that stairways are gated and bathroom doors are shut. Swimming pools should also be gated or covered. Large objects that can fall or tip over need to remain out of a child's reach. Sharp objects should also be put away. If you see something unsafe, tell the parents. Think of possible fire exits and ask the parents if they have a family fire plan. Find out where emergency supplies, such as the first aid kit, flashlights, candles, and matches are kept.

Having baby-sitting smarts will help you turn a hazardous area into a safe one.

Number Crunching

Make sure to get emergency phone numbers. These important numbers should include the phone number of where the parents will be. If they have a cell phone or beeper, take down that number, too. You should also get the address and phone number of one of the family's neighbors. This could come in handy if the parents can't be reached. Also, be sure that you have numbers for the family doctor, the police and fire departments, and the poison control center. You should write down the address and phone number of where you are baby-sitting. If you need to call 911, it is important that you can tell the operator where you are. Keep all of this information near the phone. In the event of an emergency, you don't want to waste any precious moments.

Home Alone

You've gone through your safety check with the parents. Confidently, they say good-bye, leaving you in charge. Now you're ready for a fun evening with

Try to take a tour of unfamiliar homes. Have the parents point out any hazards or safety features, such as the latch on this cabinet door.

your young companion. Hold on—not so fast! Your little friend is screaming, upset to see her parents leave. What do you do? First, tell her that you are only going to be there for a little while. Then, assure her that you two are going to have some fun. Tell the child that her parents will be home that night. She will see them then, or first thing in the morning. Try to distract the child: Play with a toy or make funny faces. Your greatest ally is your imagination. Anything that makes the child laugh will get your evening off to a fine start.

Heads Up

Keep those house doors locked! Don't let a stranger in, and don't let anyone know that you are the baby-sitter. If you think someone suspicious is lurking outside, don't investigate. Call the police. It's better to have an officer check it out than to take the risk yourself.

Safety First

Children are extremely curious. Sometimes they do seemingly fun things that are actually harmful.

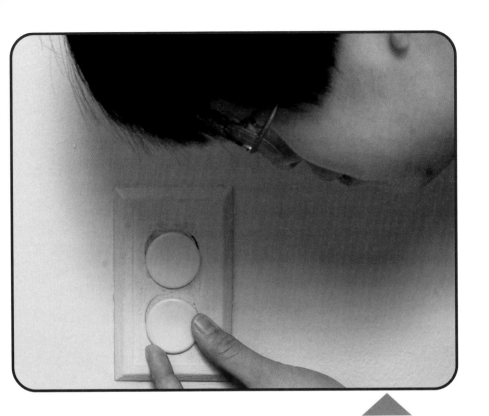

Kids tend to touch before thinking, which is why this baby-sitter is making sure the electric outlets are covered up.

No matter how hard you prepare and work to keep them safe, kids may still find a way to get into harm's way. Knowing some basic first aid steps can really help you out.

Let's say the child cuts his knee. The first thing you should do is wash your hands. After your hands are clean, wash the cut with mild soap or water. If the family has antibacterial ointment, put some on the cut.

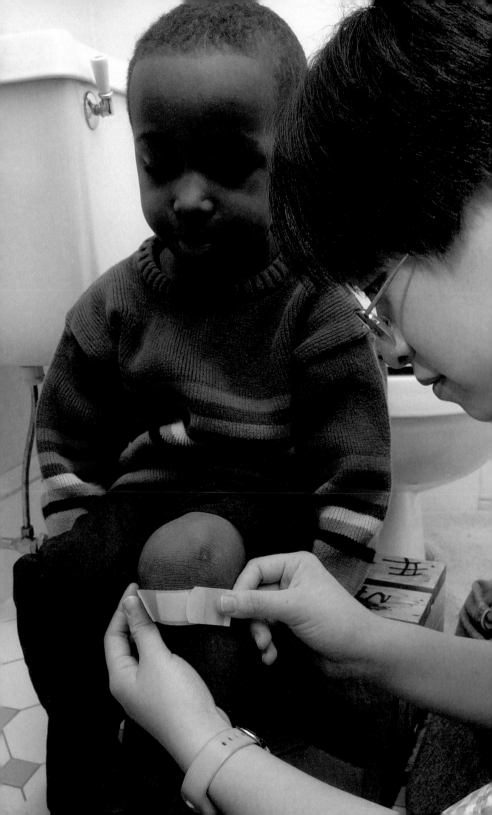

Then, apply a clean bandage. If the cut is deep and looks bad, make sure to wash your hands, but do not wash the wound. Washing a bad wound can make it bleed more. Instead, apply pressure just above the wound to slow the bleeding. Once the situation is under control—or if you can't get it under control—call 911. If there is an object in the wound, don't try to remove it. Let an Emergency Medical Technician (EMT) or doctor examine it. After calling 911, follow up with a phone call to the parents. Following these tips will lower the risk of infection and serious injury.

Fun for All Ages

Fun is an important part of baby-sitting. One way to make baby-sitting fun is by creating engaging activities for you and the child to do together. In addition to the items in your baby-sitting bag, you should know what kids of different ages can (and like to) do. Knowing the child's interests will make the evening a fun, relaxed, and safe one.

Tending to minor scrapes and cuts is part of a baby-sitter's job. But you should leave really serious injuries to the professionals.

23

Many kids love to show their creative sides to their sitters.

Infants

Babies like to be held, sung to, and rocked. They like to play with brightly colored toys and things that make noise, such as rattles. Babies are excited by the world around them and love to see new, colorful things. Take care to make sure that what they play with is clean, soft, and safe. Toys should not fit into a baby's mouth.

CPR Basics

CPR stands for Cardiopulmonary Resuscitation. CPR is a way to keep someone breathing when that person becomes unconscious, or passes out. If a child between the ages of one and eight passes out, follow these steps:

1. Check for any response or breathing. Check the child's pulse by placing your first two fingers under the child's ear, near the jawbone.
2. Tilt the child's head back and listen for breathing. Grunting, gasping, or snoring are signs of struggle and should not be considered normal breathing. If the child isn't breathing normally, pinch his or her nose and cover his or her mouth with yours. Blow until the child's chest rises. Give two breaths.
3. Listen for breathing. If the child doesn't start breathing on his or her own, press the heel of your hand on the child's sternum. The sternum is located between the nipples on the chest. Push down with the heel of your hand about 1 to 1 ½ inches. Push down five times. A good way to time your pushes is to count, "One and two and three and four and five."
4. Check for any signs of breathing. If there are none, give the child another breath.
5. Repeat steps three and four for one minute. Then, quickly but calmly, dial 911. Continue to perform CPR until help arrives.

Note: The instructions above should be followed only as a guideline. To receive proper training, be sure to complete a CPR course.

While it may be easy to entertain babies, they require lots of attention. You should always be alert when baby-sitting an infant. *Never* leave a baby unattended.

Older Children

Drawing is fun for kids of all ages. The best things for toddlers to use for drawing are fat, unwrapped crayons. Toddlers' hands are still very small, and big crayons are easier for them to hold. Try to tape down the paper that they are drawing on so that it doesn't move around. Older children like to draw, too. Another fun activity to try is writing a short story, then having the child draw pictures to match it. Or, create puppets from lunch bags and put on a play. With a little imagination, crayons and paper can provide hours of amusement.

Making music is another way to bring some joy and flair to the evening. Empty butter tubs or oatmeal boxes make great drums. You and the child can dance and sing, composing your own words. There are plenty of ways to have fun while baby-sitting.

If the child you're sitting for likes music, you can turn a few pots and pans into a smashing success!

Keep your eyes open for new ideas. From board games to reading to homework—keep the child amused, and the hours will fly by for the both of you!

End of the Night

You've had a great evening, and bedtime is approaching. If you were asked to give the child a bath, make sure you watch her the entire time. It only takes a few inches of water for a child to drown. The water should be warm, but not hot. A good way to test the water is by dipping your elbow in. If you are bathing a baby, always keep one hand on her so that she doesn't slip.

Sometimes, even for an experienced sitter, getting kids to go to bed is a monumental task. There are things you can do to save time and tears. Ten minutes before bedtime, give the child a warning. This lets him know what to expect and prepares him for it.

Many kids need to calm down before bedtime. Reading books or listening to soft music can help. Give your child a choice as to which activity she

Reading a child's favorite book at night helps calm him or her down before bedtime.

would like to do before bed. Say something like, "Would you like to read 'Little Red Riding Hood' or 'The Ugly Duckling' tonight?" This way, the child feels like she has some say in what's happening.

Once the child has fallen asleep, you should quietly check on her or him every 15 minutes or so.

Use the time before the parents get home to clean up any mess you made. Do the dishes and put away any stray toys. Try to leave things exactly as they were when you arrived.

When the parents return, give them a brief rundown of the evening. Let them know if their child got hurt, broke anything, or if anything else out of the ordinary happened. Figure out how many hours you worked and how much you are owed. If the parents appear to have been drinking and you are supposed to get a ride home from them, do not accept. Instead, call your parents or a neighbor to pick you up. Don't be afraid to stop baby-sitting for a family if you feel uncomfortable around the parents or don't get along with the child. There are plenty of families looking for a good sitter. You should not stay in a situation that makes you uncomfortable.

Just because the child is sleeping doesn't mean the baby-sitter's work is done. Always check in on the child after bedtime to make sure all is well.

Be sure that the parents you're working for are willing and able to take you back home.

Chapter 4

Are You Experienced?

The following story describes the first job of a baby-sitter named Sally. As you read, think about Sally's choices. Are they all good decisions? Think about what you might do differently if you were in the same situation.

Sally's Sitting Experience

Sally arrived at Mr. and Mrs. Marshall's house at 5:45 P.M. to baby-sit for their two-year-old son, Jack. Mrs. Marshall wrote down her cell phone number on a slip of paper, then handed it to Sally. Sally put the number into her pocket and went over to play with Jack. As the parents were leaving,

Providing the child with a few fun activities can help make your sitting experience go much more smoothly.

they asked Sally if she had any questions. Sally shook her head no and continued playing.

After a few minutes, Jack didn't want to play anymore and started to get upset. Sally remembered that she had brought along markers and a coloring book. She and Jack went into the kitchen and sat at the table. Jack scribbled all over the pages of the coloring books. Soon, his artwork was also all over the table. When Sally tried to take the markers away, Jack even drew on her new shirt.

Now, Jack was screaming and crying. Sally took him into the living room. She picked up one of Jack's stuffed animals and started making funny animal noises. After a few minutes, Jack was smiling again.

Jack had calmed down, but his cheeks were still red. Sally felt his forehead and face. He felt very warm. Sally decided to take his temperature. She looked in the bathroom for a thermometer, but couldn't find it. After a few minutes of frantic searching, Sally found the thermometer in the kitchen. When Sally returned to the living room. Jack was lying on the sofa, playing with a toy.

Some children are better than others at reporting when they feel ill. If you have a hunch that the child you're sitting for is sick, follow it up.

Sally took Jack's temperature. It was 100 degrees Farenheit (38 degrees Celsius). Sally decided to call Jack's parents and let them know that their son was running a fever. However, the piece of paper with the Marshalls' cell phone number wasn't in her pocket!

She looked everywhere, but couldn't find it. Sally called her mom. Sally's mom told her to give Jack some water. Since the two families were friends with each other, Sally was able to get the Marshalls' cell phone number. As soon as Sally hung up the phone, she gave Jack a glass of water. Then, she called the Marshalls. They told her that they were in the middle of dinner and would come home as soon as possible.

Sally helped Jack into pajamas and had him choose a book to read before bed. Soon, Jack was asleep. After trying, and failing, to wash the stains out of her shirt, Sally went into the kitchen. She worked hard to clean the marker stains from the table. By the time the Marshalls got home, Sally had cleaned most of the stains off. Mr. Marshall paid Sally and drove her home.

Another Look at Sally

Sally did many things right, but she also could have made some better choices. What would you have

It's important to keep contact information, such as telephone numbers, in one place. That way, you won't have to scramble in an emergency.

done differently? Let's consider her decisions from the beginning.

To start, Sally should have written down the parents' cell phone number, along with other important numbers, and left them by the phone. Luckily, her mom was home and was able to help her out.

It was great that Sally brought along activities to share with Jack. She shouldn't have brought markers, though. Those are too difficult, and messy, for a two-year-old to play with. Sally learned the hard way that markers stain clothes. Crayons would have been a better choice.

Sally made the right decision to take Jack into the living room when he started misbehaving. She knew to take him away from what was making him upset. Making him laugh with the stuffed animal was also a good move. Sally was able to take control of the situation and keep Jack from getting more upset.

When Sally saw that Jack looked feverish, she did well in acting quickly—maybe too quickly. A baby-sitter should never leave a child alone, especially a child as young as Jack. Sally was lucky that

A responsible attitude and a fun outlook are the building blocks to many successful baby-sitting jobs.

Jack didn't wander off or get hurt. She could have avoided her long search for the thermometer if she had asked the Marshalls where their first aid supplies were kept before they left.

When Sally read the thermometer and saw that Jack did have a low fever, she did the right thing by calling her mother. She acted quickly to help Jack by notifying his parents. Most of the time, a fever is not a big enough emergency to call 911. However, a high fever can be very dangerous. It's important to let the parents know as soon as possible that their child is ill.

Sally did a good job managing bedtime and getting Jack to sleep. She also proved how responsible she was when she cleaned the table before the Marshalls returned. Sally made mistakes but, in general, was a good sitter. She acted quickly and calmly when things went wrong. If you learn from Sally's mistakes and follow her good examples, you'll be on your way to becoming a prepared, responsible—and well-paid—baby-sitter.

> Don't forget: You're not alone. In an emergency, you have firefighters, doctors, and police officers all within your reach. They're just a few digits away.

allergic a physical reaction to things like pollen, food, or plants

antibacterial something that kills bacteria, which is a microscopic living thing that may cause disease

Cardiopulmonary Resuscitation (CPR) a method of reviving someone using mouth-to-mouth breathing and chest compressions

curfew a rule that dictates a specific time when you have to be home

entertain to amuse and interest someone

hazards dangers or risks

life-saving done to save someone's life

New Words

ointment a thick, often greasy substance put on the skin to heal or protect it

rate a charge or fee

responsible to be trusted and have important duties

suspicious a concern that something is wrong or bad

thermometer an instrument used to measure temperature

transportation a means of getting from place to place

word-of-mouth to speak about someone's talents or character; to give a reference

For Further Reading

American Red Cross Staff. *American Red Cross Baby-sitter's Handbook.* St. Louis, MO: Mosby–Year Book, Incorporated, 1998.

Brown, Harriet N. *The Babysitter's Handbook.* Middleton, WI: Pleasant Company Publications, 1999.

Kuck, K.D. *The Babysitter's Handbook.* New York, NY: Random House Books for Young Readers, 1997.

Vavolizza, Christine and Mark. *Every Baby-sitter Needs This Book.* White Plains, NY: Peter Pauper Press, Incorporated, 1998.

Zakarin, Debra Mostow. *The Ultimate Baby-Sitter's Handbook.* New York, NY: Putnam Publishing Group, 1997.

Resources

Organizations

American Red Cross Headquarters
Attn: Public Inquiry Office
1621 North Kent Street, 11th Floor
Arlington, VA 22209
(703) 248-4222

Safe Sitter
5670 Caito Drive, Suite 172
Indianapolis, IN 46226
(317) 355-4888

Web Sites

American Red Cross—Babysitter's Training Course
www.redcross.org/services/hss/courses/babyindex.html
Find out about the baby-sitter's training course on this Web site. You can also learn some important baby-sitting tips and find your local Red Cross chapter.

Resources

CBC4Kids Baby-sitting Guide

http://www.cbc4kids.ca/general/kids-club/babysitters/started.html

This Web site has a detailed baby-sitting guide. It includes tips on getting started, fun activities to do on the job, and other important information.

The Nemours Foundation: TeensHealth—Baby-sitting Basics

http://kidshealth.org/teen/mind_matters/school/babysit.html

Learn lots of important information about baby-sitting on this informative Web site.

Index

About the Author

Jil Fine spent many a night baby-sitting her younger brother—and he turned out just fine.

JAMES GANDON AND HIS TIMES

JAMES GANDON
AND HIS TIMES

———

BY HUGO DUFFY

Gandon Editions, Kinsale

JAMES GANDON AND HIS TIMES

© Gandon Editions and the author, 1999.
All rights reserved.

ISBN 0946846 286

Designed by John O'Regan (design © 1999)
Produced by Nicola Dearey
Printed in Ireland by Betaprint, Dublin

GANDON EDITIONS
Oysterhaven, Kinsale, Co Cork – *tel* +353 (0)21-770830 / *fax* +353 (0)21-770755
e-mail gandon@eircom.net / *visit our web-site* www.gandon-editions.com

cover / frontispiece
Tilly Kettle with William Cuming, *James Gandon, Architect*
n.d., oil on canvas, 123 x 98 cm
(courtesy National Gallery of Ireland)

back cover
James Gandon and Henry Aaron Baker, *Inns of Court*
c.1800, ink, sepia ink and wash, 44 x 56 cm
(courtesy Irish Architectural Archive – RIAI Murray Collection)

All uncredited illustrations by the author

––––––––––

AUTHOR'S ACKNOWLEDGEMENTS

With particular gratitude to Tegral Building Products, without whose generous support this book would not have been published. They also conceived of and sponsored the formal launch of the book at Gandon's Custom House.

Also in gratitude to the Minister and the Department of Health and Children, and to the Minister and the Department of the Environment for their generous sponsorship of the book.

In addition to the above, I wish to thank Scott Tallon Walker, Ove Arup & Partners, the Royal Institute of the Architects of Ireland, Radley Engineering Ltd, and John Sisk & Son Ltd, for their assistance towards the publication.

I wish to thank the many people who helped me over the years while I was putting this book together and are too numerous to mention here. My particular thanks to Dr Edward McParland for his unfailing help and support, to Mrs D'Arcy-Harte of London, to the late Frank McCauley, to Niall Meagher, to my late partner and friend Louis Peppard, to Irene Tyrrell and Moira O'Brien for typing my various attempts at texts, and commenting on them, and, of course, to my wife Jeanie and my family for their generous help and advice.

DEPARTMENT
OF HEALTH
AND CHILDREN

DEPARTMENT OF THE
ENVIRONMENT

SCOTT TALLON WALKER
OVE ARUP & PARTNERS
THE ROYAL INSTITUTE OF THE ARCHITECTS OF IRELAND
JOHN SISK & SON LTD
RADLEY ENGINEERING LTD

This book has been sponsored by

FOREWORD

SHANE O'TOOLE

James Gandon shaped Dublin as no other architect, before or since. His monumental buildings define the popular image of our capital city even today. In their time, they helped create the impetus for the city's expansion to the east, signalled the decline of the medieval city, and confirmed the ascendancy of 'Georgian' Dublin.

Hugo Duffy's biography of Gandon brings the man – and his times – closer to us. We can see that the professional architect's life has changed little in two hundred years. We recognise Gandon's alarm at the difficulties to be contended with in laying the foundations of the Custom House, his regret in being compelled to start building before the plans had been completed, and the public controversy and 'planning' difficulties surrounding the project. Human nature is constant. Here, in the form of the Malton letters, is professional jealousy on a grand scale. There is scandal, in the shape of John Beresford, the 'king of Ireland', whose development of the Custom House opened up his brother-in-law, Luke Gardiner's lands for fashionable redevelopment. We are reminded, too, of the surprising fragility of heroic architecture. As Maurice Craig pointed out fifty years ago, all Gandon's major work has been bombarded, burnt, rebuilt or at best added to: the nearest approach to work as he left it is the restored exterior of the Custom House, and the Benchers' Dining Hall in the King's Inns.

Above all, this is a human story. Of great triumphs matched by equal disappointments. Of the fragile character of Gandon, a man constantly on the edge, often resentful, and troubled by gout. Of his enduring friendships. And of the decisive difference particular individuals – patrons, such as Beresford, the Wide Streets Commissioners and the Duke of Rutland – can make to the carrying out of the great works that determine the futures of cities. It is a lesson we should not overlook in our own times.

SHANE O'TOOLE FRIAI
Company Architect
Tegral Building Products

INTRODUCTION

EDWARD McPARLAND

Even if he had not been a great architect, James Gandon's eventful life would be worth studying. His father was a bankrupt and alchemist; Gandon was offered employment in Sumatra and St Petersburg; his personal circumstances – nervous collapse, perhaps in the late 1770s, and a wife who seems to have survived her reported death by many years – were colourful enough to invite speculation; his London was that of developing artistic institutions such as the Royal Academy in the 1760s and '70s; his Dublin intimates were those most closely involved in making Dublin one of the most brilliant cities of Europe at the end of the century; he fled the rebellion of 1798. As one who witnessed, and was involved in, the fast-changing world of late Georgian Britain and Ireland, James Gandon had a fascinating life.

Gandon's interesting story is made attractive by his personality. We can follow him impetuously throwing his father's books out the window. We join him shooting snipe in Oxford Street, and on boating trips handing out 'Wine and Punch to all who would accept it'. We read his affectionate (and indecorous) correspondence with the affectionate (and indecorous) Paul Sandby. And the conviviality of Gandon's company is conjured up by the inscription on the slab which covers the tomb he shares with the antiquary Francis Grose: 'To the Memory of Captain Grose FRS Who whilst in cheerful conversation With his Friends Expired in their Arms Without a Sigh'.

But an interesting and attractive story is made great by Gandon's genius, to which his Dublin buildings are the monument – the Four Courts, King's Inns, the Custom House, the extensions to Parliament House for the House of Lords. These are the buildings of a great European architect, and they are all (except the Inns) bound inextricably together by the outrageous conspiracy to move the centre of Dublin in the late eighteenth century from its medieval to its present site. It was a conspiracy involving the Revenue Commissioners, the Wide Streets Commissioners and parliament. Its purpose was the enrichment of the private Gardiner estate, and its architectural agent was James Gandon.

The opportunities offered to Gandon in Dublin in that brilliant decade, the 1780s, were immense. He rose to the occasion spectacularly. And the integrated account of his life and his architecture which follows stimulates many thoughts.about the fortuitous nature of architectural development.

Why Gandon? Why invite this architectural nonentity (as he was in 1780) from London to execute the greatest buildings of the late eighteenth century? Why not employ the resident Thomas Cooley, whose recently completed Royal Exchange was the most radical and thrilling public building in Dublin since Edward Lovett Pearce's Parliament House?

Extraordinarily, one of the most important reasons for choosing Gandon seems to have been that John Beresford, then looking for an architect for his new Custom House, was a friend of Lord Carlow, who went to the same parties (Paul Sandby's) as Gandon in London. Beresford needed an architect from outside Ireland, since the whole new Custom House affair was so cloak and dagger (literally, if Gandon's story of his need on the building site of a 'good cane sword' is to be believed) that the building had to be designed abroad. Thomas Cooley, in Dublin since beating Gandon into second place in the competition for the Royal Exchange, had reason to be piqued: recent work is making it increasingly clear that, if offered the scope, Cooley was as great an architect as Gandon.

Such an evaluation of Cooley is likely to be supported, for instance, by the work soon to be completed by Dublin Corporation in restoring the Royal Exchange (now City Hall) to something very close to Cooley's original intentions. The nineteenth-century internal partitions are being removed, and from the Victorian chrysalis is emerging a building of extraordinary quality, fit to rank with the Custom House and the Four Courts, or with the Ecole de Chirurgie and the Bagatelle. Cooley's building will be seen to be good enough to demand a reassessment of his place in architectural history, a reassessment already prompted by his pre-Gandon plans for the Four Courts. These are recorded in the Caledon album, which reveals him as messenger of radical neoclassical news to Dublin in the late 1760s: Chambers' Casino at Marino was then rising, and indeed Cooley learned from it in designing the Exchange. But the Casino was a little bit out of town; the Exchange was a flamboyant, and even aggressive public statement by the merchants of where they wanted the centre of Dublin to stay.

In 1780, in other words, Cooley would have been a much better bet than Gandon for Dublin patrons looking for a great architect. But, as architect to the merchants, Cooley was on the wrong side, and could not be trusted. He even gave evidence to a parliamentary enquiry, advising against moving the Custom House downstream. He had to be sacrificed. And having begun the buildings on the Inns Quay for a record office as part of a complex which he planned at one stage to include the King's Inns and Four Courts, he had to suffer the frustration of its long-drawn-out progress, and the posthumous indignity of the Inns and Courts job going to Gandon.

With the plots, bribes and cliques, the high stakes and the venomous attacks on him in the press, there is much more to Gandon than the bricks and mortar he contrived so fastidiously. The mid-nineteenth-century *Life*, published by his son, is unshapely in construction and unreliable in details. My own study of Gandon is focused on his bricks and mortar, and their implication for town planning. What follows is a more rounded picture, with new and unpublished research, of a great architect who comes alive in a way not seen before. We learn a great deal about James Gandon as an architect by learning about him as a man.

DR EDWARD MCPARLAND
Dept of the History of Art
Trinity College Dublin

AUTHOR'S FOREWORD

———————

James Gandon's work is well documented. There is the original *Life*, edited by Thomas J. Mulvany, and composed of excerpts from Gandon's own writings, together with items of information, or misinformation, provided by his son. It was published in Dublin in 1846, and its purpose was to dignify Gandon's life and works and to endow him with that status of gentleman so dear to the hearts of the Victorians. Few factual statements in *The Life* can be trusted.

Then there is the definitive work on Gandon's architecture, *James Gandon, Vitruvius Hibernicus* by Edward McParland. It is a work of true scholarship. The sources of Gandon's work are expertly traced and explained, and few architects have been so well served.

But Gandon's personality, his personal life, and the background, both historical and social, against which he acted have so far been ignored. Here I have attempted to supply this dimension of his life. The first part of his career in London lay very much in his own hands, and a poor job he made of it. The second part, in Ireland, depended largely on external forces against which he was helpless, but these, nonetheless, forced him to display that genius he believed he possessed, but which he himself was unable to bring to maturity.

His personal character is less easy to determine. There are few clues, and those there are may have been given greater significance than they deserve.

HUGO DUFFY
Dublin, November 1999

Hugo Duffy was born in Clontarf, Dublin, in 1918. He was educated at Blackrock College and University College Dublin, where he graduated in architecture in 1942. Having spent some time in the office of WH Byrne & Son and in the Office of Public Works, he entered into partnership with his friend, the late Louis Peppard, and together they carried on a practice in architecture until they retired in 1983. He married Jeanie Smyth from Galway, and they have five children and eighteen grandchildren.

James Gandon, Architect, by unknown artist
(courtesy The Royal Collection, London)

PART I – GANDON IN ENGLAND

THE EARLY YEARS (1742-1758)

In 1846, *The Life of James Gandon, Esquire, MRIA; FRS, &c. Architect* was published by his son. It is generally known as *The Life*. It was, in greater part, edited by Thomas J. Mulvany RHA, who died before the work was completed. The book includes a considerable amount of autobiographical material, which appears to have been written by Gandon during his retirement. Here are the opening lines of *The Life*:

> The distinguished architect whose life we now commence was born in London on the 29th of February 1742, Old Style, in New Bond Street, at the house of his grandfather...

It is a date which has been copied into a number of works of reference, including the *Dictionary of National Biography* (DNB), but 1742 was not a leap year. In addition, the England of that time followed the Julian calendar, so that an error of eleven days had arisen between the English and the greater part of Europe by 1752. An act was passed (24 Geo. II) correcting this error and also changing the start of the year from 25th March to 1st January. Dates after this were said to be in the 'New Style'. Gandon's birth, as recorded at St George's, Hanover Square was on 20th February 1741, 'Old Style'.[1] This becomes 20th February 1742, 'New Style'. Mulvany was not the first to have been confused by the change. Mulvany continues:

> ...his grandfather, who was a native of France and had emigrated from Blois during the reign of Louis XIV, on the revocation of the Edict of Nantes ... other members of the Gandon family became planters in Jamaica; but he had brought with him quite enough of wealth to enable his family to live in respectable independence. His son Peter lived with him he married a Welsh lady by the name of Wynne, by whom he had two children, James, the subject of these memoirs, and a daughter who married Captain Handyside. She died but left no issue.

In these two paragraphs, Mulvany manages to include quite a few items of misinformation. No doubt he put down whatever Gandon junior told him without question, but since the Edict of Nantes had been revoked for the second time in 1685, we find the years before this date were years of persecution for the Huguenots, so the majority of them had left France by this time, and Gandon's grandfather, Peter Gandon, who was born on 9th April 1682,[2] had already left France. Gandon's great grandfather, also Peter, who was born about 1660, was twenty-five in 1685. The great-grandfather had married a Gloriante Jolly in 1681.[3]

The Huguenots were, in general, skilled tradesmen and relatively prosperous, but refugees rarely succeed in taking with them much of value. Against this, Mulvany paints a pleasant picture of Victorian respectability – settled comfort, inherited wealth, independence. The colonies and the army are mentioned. However, the grandfather's son, also named Peter, and the father of James (if we have not gone astray among the various relationships), was apprenticed on 4th April 1728,[4] and on 1st April 1736 was admitted to the Gunmakers' Company, and sworn, and paid his fee of 13s 4d.[5] On the same day, at the Court of the Gunmakers' Company, Peter Gandon, presumably the grandfather, was charged with having six pairs of foreign pistols in his shop.[6] They had been found there on 24th March, and his defence was that two pairs were the property of another person. He appeared again before the court on 1st July, and was fined 10s 'apiece for each of said six pistols', but for some reason the fine was mitigated to 30s.[7]

It is a curious incident about which we would like to know more. Presumably the family, still French-speaking, had kept up some sort of business connection with their European friends, and may have grown careless in the carrying on of some kind of illegal trade. At this time, they appear to have been living in relative comfort, perhaps through hard work subsidised by the sale of smuggled arms to even-up the disability they must have suffered through local prejudice against foreigners. We might wonder too if James inherited a trace of a French accent in his speech.

Peter (the younger) married Jane Burchall, a widow (whose maiden name may have been Wynne), on 25th November 1739 at St Martin in the Fields,[8] and for some time they appear to have lived in the grandfather's house, for James refers to his early childhood there and to the fact that the house was fitted with casement windows.[9]

Over the years, the younger Gandons appear to have abandoned their Huguenot faith as well as their Huguenot friends, and it is only on the bankruptcy of Peter (the younger) that we find the old ties revived. Curiously, the branch of the family mentioned as being planters in Jamaica is unrecorded in the lists of landowners in 1754, and also in the return of slaves on estates for 1810 and 1811.[12] That other community in Jamaica, the pirates of Port Royal, kept no records.

We are also told that at the age of seven, James was sent to a boarding school at Batfield in Herefordshire.[13] At first sight it would seem strange that his parents should have chosen to send him to a place so remote from London. The English authorities are definite that no such place as Batfield exists;[14] it is suggested that the school may have been at Coldbathfields in London, an area now ill-defined. Mulvany goes on to say that James was next sent to a boarding school at

Kensington Gravel Pits when he was about nine, and stayed there for five years, a period which we shall see cannot be reconciled with his being recalled from school at the age of eleven. There are now no records of any such school, but it might have been one of the private ventures of this kind which had sprung up around London during the eighteenth century, and ceased with the death the headmaster.

Gandon seems to have been happy at school, and here for the first time he shows promise of what was to come. Mathematics and drawing, we are told, engaged his interest It must have been a remarkably good school, for the students presented their own plays, and Gandon became sufficiently skilled in landscape drawing and painting to prepare the scenery and stage decorations for them. He was addicted to sketching sieges and fortresses on his slate, and this is of particular significance when we come to examine his architectural style, although the psychologists would, no doubt, be tempted to attribute this preference to a feeling of insecurity. They could also point out that Gandon must have been made aware of the character of civil commotion, when, at the age of ten (in 1752), disturbances took place due to a belief then current that the change in the calendar would deprive everyone of eleven days of his life. That Gandon, in later years, displayed a more than normal aversion to public disorder may well have had its roots in this occurrence.

Gandon's parents had by now moved into their own home, a circumstance which seems to have released his father from some inhibiting factor in the family home. The little we know of Gandon's father, Peter (the younger), suggests that he was one of those who realised, at an early age, that honest work is not sufficient to make a man wealthy, and who, believing themselves to be worthy of better things, begrudge the daily round, and look to fortune to provide success. Peter Gandon, unfortunately, fixed his eye on the dream of alchemists – the philosophers' stone – and, untroubled by his moderately profitable occupation, was soon absorbed in the practice of alchemy; becoming, as Mulvany remarks: 'quite a proselyte of this most seductive science'. He took over one of his wife's kitchens, and fitted it out with furnaces, crucibles and retorts, and here, with an audience of the idle and of professional parasites, settled down to his experiments. His patient wife was forced to watch helplessly as good money went up in smoke. As his apparatus proliferated, he attempted to encroach on her main kitchen, but here she put her foot down and circumscribed his activities. Gandon writes:

> I perfectly recollect the appearance of my father's residence on my return from school at holiday times; although now upward of seventy years ago, yet are the impressions as strong in my mind as of any recent occurrence; that after descending to the lower departments among furnaces and various other apparatus for experiments I was quite in fear, during my

approach to headquarters, of committing some injury among the combustibles. But my chief object was to find out my father's station as he was always infinitely more indefatigable in his occupations than the others. On these subterranean visits, I had to encounter a variety of personages, most of whom were dressed in the costume of the day, with large flowing wigs, holding gold or amber headed canes, and awaiting with solemn composure the results of the different experiments.

On my return from these visits I was frequently required by my mother to describe the persons who were thus intruding on the cook's premises. This suggested the idea of making a few pencil sketches, imperfect certainly, but sufficiently characteristic to give an idea of the persons; several of these juvenile representations I retained and, having improved both the outlines and costume, gave them to Captain Grose who, having made further improvements on them, published them in his Olio.

When these chemical experiments were concluded, and neither gold, silver nor any other metallic substance was produced among the ashes, sufficient to defray the expense of even heating the various apparatus, these learned personages were allowed to depart, as my mother was resolved to have no more intrusion in the other parts of the house.

The parties generally adjourned their meetings for the evening, to Old Slaughter's Coffee House, in St Martin's Lane, which the wits, the artists, the literary and eccentric characters of all descriptions have frequented for more than a century past.

We are told that a French ex-soldier, who called himself Chatellain, attended these sessions. His significance may lie in the fact that he possessed some books dealing with alchemy. Whatever role these may have played in prompting Peter Gandon's aberrations must have excited him to further excesses. Chatellain, said to have originated the broad manner of engraving, was also original in the manner of his passing, when, after a heavy supper of lobster, being further tempted, he succumbed to a surfeit of asparagus. Gandon continues:

> Another remarkable person who attended these alchemic experiments, was Baron Swanveldt, by birth a German; he was professionally a physician; his appearance and manner evidently bespoke him to be a man of education and station; he was the inventor of those celebrated powders, now known as James's Powders. Swanveldt, having fully established their merits as a medicine, induced Doctor James to purchase the receipt, for which James was to pay him ten thousand pounds. A portion of this purchase money was paid before Swanveldt's death, but when his widow demanded from James the remainder, he refused to pay, alleging that his

composition for the fever powder was different from that prepared by Swanveldt, in as much as his powder contained a portion of calomel, which did not form a part of Swanveldt's composition, The result was that the widow commenced an action for the recovery of the sum due, and the verdict of the jury being in her favour, James was constrained to pay the amount demanded.

I have frequently seen the receipt for these powders, they were in my father's possession, but I was then too young to pay much attention to such matters. If, however, my recollection is accurate, antimony and hartshorn formed two of the principal ingredients in the preparation; at all events, the composition is now so well known, that I am inclined to believe any chemist can make them.

It is ironic that Gandon's father, during his search for chemical wealth, had the receipt for Dr James's Powders in his pocket, and if he had turned over his apparatus to their production, his future would have been assured. The powders became very popular during the latter half of the eighteenth century. They were quite potent, producing tremor, hallucinations, nausea, antimony poisoning and other effects, depending on the metabolism of the victim, and they crop up from time to time as the apparent cause of the deaths of not a few historical characters. (They polished off Oliver Goldsmith.)

Finally, the father's resources came to an end. At about the same time his wife died, and without her, his affairs became hopelessly involved. He became a bankrupt on 23rd April 1754, when Gandon was twelve years old.[15] Gandon has this to say about his mother's death:

My mother's death was most unfortunate for my expectations; I have every reason to believe that the declining state of my father's affairs at this period must have contributed to depress her usually good spirits. But her truly affectionate solicitude in promoting every object connected with my education and her anxious care of me during my youthful days can never be effaced from my memory.

She had for many years previous to her death used every exertion in regulating my father's establishment, by which she had often preserved his affairs from entanglements.

Very shortly after this calamity, I was ordered home from school at Kensington, and I was soon afterwards informed that my return to school was quite impractical; the embarrassed state of my father's affairs being the cause. In addition to a variety of difficulties, resulting from a total inattention to domestic management, my father had imprudently become security, to a very large extent, for a person of the name of Brooks, a native of

Ireland, who at this period had an extensive manufactory at Battersea, near London. Brooks became an insolvent, which so involved my father, in addition to his other difficulties, as wholly to put an end to any expectations I might have indulged in, as regards my advancement in life. On my return home from school, I found my father's property, of every kind, in the hands of his creditors.

It is difficult to reconcile Gandon's account with the facts as they are recorded. It is a fact that Brooks became a bankrupt in 1756, when Gandon was fourteen years old. Brooks had left Dublin early in 1746 and established himself as an engraver in London. Here he perfected a method of printing in enamel on china. This was taken up by Sir Stephen Theodore Janssen, later a Lord Mayor of London, who, with some others, backed Brooks to the extent of setting him up in a factory in Battersea. Brooks, a chronic inebriate, mismanaged the business, and an Order in Bankruptcy was issued against him on 27th January 1756. This was nearly two years after Peter Gandon became a bankrupt, and on the face of it there is no apparent connection between the two occurrences. However, there must have been some relationship if we are to explain the intrusion, into Gandon's account of the Brooks affair. It is possible that Peter Gandon had some interest in Brooks' business, perhaps a speculation on borrowed money which did not work out, and which dealt a second and final blow to his hopes at a time when he was perhaps beginning to find his feet again.

Neither Mulvany nor Gandon himself mention the bankruptcy of Peter Gandon. Mulvany may not have known about it, but Gandon's motives are not quite so simple. We have to keep in mind that Gandon is writing some sixty or seventy years after the event, now long suppressed. But at the time of the bankruptcy it was no secret, for the *London Gazette*, (9367, April 27/30 1754), carried the following notice:

Whereas a Commission of Bankrupt is awarded and issued forth against PETER GANDON of the Parish of St James Westminster Middlesex Gunmaker, and he being declared a Bankrupt is hereby required to surrender himself to the Commissioners in the said Commission named, or the major part of them on the 3d and 15th Days of May next and on the 11th day of June following at 3 of the clock in the afternoon on each of the said days at Guildhall London and make a full Discovery and Disclosure of his Estate and Effects, when and where the creditors are to come prepared to prove their debts and at the Second Sitting to chuse assignes and at the last Sitting the said Bankrupt is required to finish his examination and the Creditors are to assent or to dissent from the allowances of his Certificate. All persons indebted to the said Bankrupt or that have any of his effects are not to pay or deliver the same but to whom the Commissioners shall appoint but give notice to MR NORTON of the Middle Temple Lane.

To appreciate Gandon's position, we must remember that in the eighteenth century, and until 1861, there existed a legal distinction between bankruptcy and insolvency. The term bankrupt applied solely to those who were traders. Their property and possessions were sold and the money divided according to certain rules between all the creditors. A certificate was then issued confirming the completion of this process, and this certificate protected the bankrupt, should he become prosperous again, from all further demands by his creditors, and from prison, which might well follow such demands. On the other hand, the term 'insolvency' was more respectable, applying as it did to all those not in trade – noblemen, gentlemen and vagabonds alike. Although they went through much the same process, they were not protected against future claims should they come into property later. The distinction may be regarded as involving both status and honour. Thus, Gandon's father is represented as an innocent victim of Brooks' collapse, and we notice how careful Gandon is to refer to Brooks as an insolvent, avoiding the taint of trade.

This was a matter of serious concern for Gandon. The days when he was the son of a bankrupt gunmaker were long past, and he was now a gentleman of property. His long career was at an end, and his family were grown-up, with a daughter married into the nobility. Any hint of a connection with trade was to be avoided, and so he constructed a seamless account of his early years with the professional care he brought to his art, hiding his real disaster behind one a little later (and quite well known), while projecting the picture of an eccentric father sharing a financial loss with no less a personage than the Lord Mayor of London, and, at the same time, covering over the hopeless period between his twelfth and fourteenth years. But in reality we know little of what went on during that time, and can only resort to plausible speculation to reconcile fact with the fiction of Gandon's account. He continues:

> I had just then completed my fourteenth year, possessing great liveliness and spirits: but when I reflected on the altered state of the dwelling, and on my own reception, and looked at the melancholy prospects then before me, so different to those to which I had been accustomed, a deep depression came over my spirits which nothing but time could remove. Of my father's influential friends many were dead, and others, in embarrassed circumstances had retired to various places. I, therefore, regarded myself as thrown on the world's vast stage with no guiding star to lead me to any path; while darkness and dismay appeared like clouds gathering round me, I felt that I had neither rudder to steer by, nor compass to guide my way.

The depression of my spirits it would be impossible to describe.

Just at this moment I got access to my father's room, the one in which his books were deposited, and I recollect, as perfectly as though the occasion were but of yesterday, the feelings I experienced on encountering several of his Rosicrucian books, 'Ah!', I exclaimed, 'those books have been my ruin.' I no longer controlled my feelings, but opened the window and threw many of them into the street; but my career was stopped by the interference of some friends. I afterwards regretted this act, as many of the books were both scarce and curious.

Here is a striking incident, even more so since details of extravagant actions on the part of Gandon are rather sparse in *The Life*. Gandon's outburst seems, as he describes his mood, to have had its roots in deeper and more permanent feelings, and reminds us that character is revealed mainly by significant action. Here we have an action which can be classed as one of total preoccupation with self.

At that time there were, broadly speaking, two classes of individuals: those who were by birth or possessions in a position to dominate others, and those who worked and served. A small number fell into an intermediate class: merchants, lawyers, and those who practised an art, such as painting, sculpture, music or architecture, which was in demand to enhance the status of the dominant class. These artists partook of something of the status they helped to promote, and even at the age of twelve, Gandon seems to have fixed his ambition on such a career, apparently finding within himself, even at that early age, the urge towards such activities. He continues:

My father's embarrassments were now very great, and after making the best arrangements in his power with his creditors, his income was scarcely sufficient for his own support in his declining years; nor yet could he hope by any personal exertions of his own to to increase it, afflicted as he was by hereditary gout. It was therefore quite evident to me that the period had now arrived when it became my duty so to exert myself as to encroach as little as possible on his very limited means'.

How, in these circumstances, the Gandon family managed, we do not know. Did they return to the grandfather's home? Was it here that James spent the two years before he began his art education? There is an entry in the burial registers of the parish of St James, London, of a Peter Gondow who died on 25th January 1756, when Gandon was fourteen years old. Spelling, especially of names, was somewhat erratic at that time, so it is possible that this entry may mark the death the grandfather. Then, perhaps, the grandmother, Ester Gandon, became possessed of sufficient funds to send James to Shipley's Drawing School. Gandon merely notes:

I was soon after blessed with sufficient fortitude, (for which I have ever been thankful) to make these exertions successfully, by an introduction to a profession in which, by great application, I have been enabled to support myself respectably in life, which has ever been my most desired object.

My predilection for the study of the Fine Arts occupied all my thoughts. I availed myself of every opportunity of improvement in the several departments of the arts, particularly architecture, ornament and perspective. The early part of the mornings was principally devoted to reading the classics, and after these, mathematics, and such other works as might contribute to my acquisition of knowledge generally. In the evenings I drew at Shipley's Drawing Academy where I became a regular attendant. This school was at that period the first in London in general estimation. Many of the most eminent painters and architects of the day received their first instructions there.

William Shipley was a quiet man of reserved manner and slow and deliberate speech, with something of the bulk and appearance of Dr Johnson. In his youth, among many other abstruse researches, he had studied drawing. He too was a patron of Old Slaughter's Coffee House, where he was in the habit of sitting to one side by himself, writing or drawing in a book. His withdrawn manner led to the suspicion that he was a French spy, or worse still, a Roman Catholic priest. Eventually he was arrested, and had great difficulty in convincing the magistrates of his innocence. In 1754, Shipley was appointed registrar of the newly founded Society of Arts, and set about turning to good account the drawing classes at the Society's office. The *Public Advertiser* of 25th June 1757 carried this notice:

Drawing in all its branches taught by William Shipley, Registrar of the Society for the Encouragement of Arts, Manufacture and Commerce, and other Masters at the above Society's office.

As it will be Mr. Shipley's endeavour to introduce Boys and Girls of Genius to Masters and Mistresses in such manufactures as require Fancy and Ornament, and for which the knowledge of Drawing is absolutely necessary; Masters or Mistresses who want Boys or Girls well qualified for such manufactures may frequently meet with them at this School, and Parents who have Children of good natural abilities for the Art of Drawing, may here meet the opportunities of having them well instructed and recommended to proper Masters or Mistresses, by applying to Mr. Shipley, at Mr. Bayley's, the corner of Castle Court, opposite to the new Exchange Building in the Strand.

A genteel apartment is provided for the reception of Young Ladies of Fashion, who are attended every day from eleven till one.

Gandon concludes:

> I had every opportunity of acquiring at Shipley's a theoretic knowledge of
> architecture, and my drawings of this period obtained some notice, partic-
> ularly my architectural drawings. My portfolio was occasionally inspected
> by a few friends, who patronised my early efforts with encouraging appro-
> bation. During this time I attended a course of lectures in anatomy, which
> I have ever considered essential to the formation of a correct judgment
> and pure taste, in the arts of painting sculpture and architecture.

Gandon met many of his future friends during his two years at Shipley's, and his
acquaintance with the majority of English artists of the eighteenth century had
its beginnings here. It was a time of new things, when young men of talent were
turning their attention to the arts. It was a vigorous and exciting time when the
harsh outlook of the seventeenth century was softening, and the roots of the
modern world were already tentatively spreading beneath the surface.

THE TIMES

In England, during the early part of the eighteenth century and up to the time
of Gandon's birth, the influence of the owners of large estates was paramount.
Robert Walpole, the most influential of the Ministers of Government, was in
sympathy with them, and his policies were based on the belief that the interests
of the land-owning classes, generally Tories, were best served by a stable peace.
His influence was directed towards the preservation of this peace, and he and his
government, which had the support of George II, avoided any entanglements
with the European conflicts then current. However, manufacturing and merchant
classes, mostly Whigs, were growing in wealth and influence, and during the thir-
ties, came to regard the French as their greatest rival. They desired an expansion
of their overseas markets, particularly at the expense of the French, and a conse-
quent increase in trade. They became convinced that their ends would be best
served by force. They wanted war, and in 1742, the year of Gandon's birth,
Walpole was forced to resign, and Pitt, or Chatham, as he is otherwise known,
joined the Government, and England was firmly on the way to empire.

At first there were some frustrations. The Jacobite invasion of 1745 was
the cause of much consternation, then the European allies ate up money and
men, and by 1756, when Gandon was fourteen and about to enter Shipley's, the

war party, faced with the start of the Seven Years War, was forced to admit that the situation had got out of control. There was gloom in the country, and defeat seemed near.

Pitt now obtained sole control of affairs, and having first blockaded the French fleet and then destroyed it, in a remarkably short time he secured a series of victories which gave the English not only French Canada, the Sugar Islands, and a firm foothold in Africa, but entry to the Indian sub-continent. Pitt's successes generated great popular enthusiasm, and it was probably at this time that Gandon choose to forget his French ancestry and his Huguenot origins, and to share in the excitement of the English victories during his last year with Shipley and his early years with Chambers. It may not be too fanciful to infer that the various victory celebrations would have suggested to him one of his favourite architectural motifs: the triumphal arch. The accession of George III in 1760 and the increasing war debt brought Pitt's influence to an end. But he left behind a pattern which would endure for now the Industrial Revolution had begun, and, fructified by the markets stolen from the French, gathered pace and direction.

So, Gandon's birth coincided with a new era of progress and expansion in England, which was, within his lifetime, completely to change the climate of society. However, the great difficulty in our approach to the terms of his daily life is in our inability to visualise the conditions of the average person of that time, to taste the flavour of life as it was lived, to feel the sullen desperation of the poor, and the inordinate desire to attach oneself to the aristocratic classes, such as possessed Gandon.

In 1742, the population of England was probably six million. Most people lived at or below subsistence level, and as the century progressed, many became impoverished, for they were deprived of access to the common land following its enclosure by the local landlords. Under Elizabethan law, the parish was responsible for its poor, but the numbers of indigent persons became so great that the parish could no longer cope. Parliament provided for the union of parishes to build workhouses, thus the term 'union workhouse'. The inmates were hired out to any manufacturer who would keep them alive, and to preserve this reservoir of cheap labour, the inmates were at times manacled to prevent their escaping. The fear of the workhouse drove thousands into the larger towns and cities.

In the cities, and particularly in London, conditions became unbelievably insupportable. The most notable feature of London was the stench. There were no sanitary systems, refuse was dumped in the streets, with sewage and butchers' offal rotting in the alleys. Every corner and recess was used by the public to relieve itself. There were about half a million people in London at that time, the majority living in squalid circumstances, infested with lice, fleas and other parasites, diseased and continually hungry. Typhus, typhoid, smallpox and dysentery were endemic, interspersed with virulent influenza epidemics. Death was a nor-

mal occurrence, with low life-expectation; probably one out of four children survived to adulthood. The people were rickety, deformed by toil, wizened by
hunger, and pockmarked; clothes were filthy and seldom changed, water for
washing a luxury. It is understandable that the poor turned to gin and crime for
survival. Riots, looting, burning and destruction were common.

The centre of London, however – that territory of the gentry, the nobility
and the rich merchants – was experiencing a renaissance. The landlords were
clearing away slums, and elegant squares and terraces of tall town houses were
going up. Resident justices had been installed to read the Riot Act: a legal pre-
caution before the troops were called in to deal with civil disturbances. A parliament of property owners promulgated harsh laws for the protection of property.
Some of these were extreme: a child convicted of stealing an article worth more
than a shilling could be hanged.

John Wesley began his work in 1738, four years before Gandon was born,
and his progress continued during Gandon's lifetime. It was Wesley who brought
religion to the poor and the lower classes in the towns, people who had been
ignored by the Established Church. Towards the middle of the century,
Methodism had become highly organised and was probably the most powerful
force in the country. The Methodists were disciplined, and their remarkable
attachment to honesty and duty gave the English a sense of moral superiority
which has been a perennial source of annoyance to other nations. Wesley died in
1791, and he himself, and at the end of his life, with his unique respect for truth,
tells us that:

> The Methodists in every place grow diligent and frugal; consequently they
> increase in goods. Hence they increase in pride, in anger, in the desire of
> the flesh, the desire of the eyes, and the pride of life. So, although the
> form of religion remains, the spirit is swiftly vanishing away.[17]

WILLIAM CHAMBERS

Gandon had spent about two years at Shipley's when he had the good fortune to become apprenticed to William Chambers. Chambers had, but a
short time previously, completed the rigorous course of study he had
planned for himself, and must have found in Gandon and his work qualities to
which he could respond. For Gandon the association was crucial. Nowhere else
could he have found so excellent an introduction to contemporary architecture,

William Chambers by Sir Joshua Reynolds
(courtesy National Portrait Gallery, London)

and a master so familiar with the art both ancient Rome and of modern Paris. He was also to acquire an attitude and a style of living which would lead him in his future career to near failure and to sufficient success.

William Chambers was born in 1723 in Sweden to a Scottish family which ran a shipping business in Gothenburg. He was nineteen years older than Gandon. He was sent back to Ripon in Yorkshire to be educated, and at the age of sixteen he returned to Sweden and entered the service of the Swedish East India Company. For ten years he acted as 'supercargo' on a number of voyages to the East. During his visits to China, he took the opportunity to study Chinese art and architecture, of which he took extensive and detailed notes. He also managed to amass a respectable amount of money by availing of his privilege to bring back a certain amount of personal cargo. This, in general, took the form of tea and silks, which proved to be quite profitable. By 1749, at the age of twenty-six, he had decided to become an architect and to apply the fortune he had accumulated to this end. He wisely made a start by spending nearly a year in Paris in the office of J.F. Blondel, one of the new and progressive architects of the capital, and here he became familiar with many of Blondel's students, men who would make names for themselves as practitioners of the emergent neoclassicism.[18]

Rome, however, was his goal, where the young noblemen of Ireland and England came together to complete their education. These were the future patrons of architecture and the arts, and the professional student who could attract their interest was assured of patronage and a practice when he came home. Chambers came here in the autumn of 1750, and put himself under the tuition of Clerisseau, then regarded as the leading authority on architectural draughtsmanship and taste, and credited, however doubtfully, with no small influence on the course of architectural development over a wide area. It was not in Chambers' character to neglect any opportunity, and he embarked on a number of expeditions to other centres of the arts of Italy, carefully studying and recording the best examples of antiquity then available.

In 1751, Chambers was back in Paris. Here he met Joshua Reynolds, the painter who was completing his own studies of classical art. They quickly recognised in each other a mutual ambition, and became cronies, if not quite friends. They spoke freely of their plans and hopes, and mutually agreed that they might need each other in the future. They were to torment each other for the rest of their lives.

This second visit of Chambers to Paris had a special purpose, for Catherine Moore, his future wife, joined him here. Farrington, the gossip, says she was a milliner's girl who followed Chambers to Paris. She seems to have been a beauty, and before Reynolds left in October, he painted her portrait. Chambers took Catherine with him back to Rome, and here he committed a grave blunder: he quarrelled with Clerisseau. Robert Adam immediately snapped up Clerisseau, for not only was Clerisseau himself indispensable for his purpose, but he would provide Adam with a first-hand account of the progress and activities of William Chambers. It was a portentous reversal of fortune, for, from then on, Robert Adam began seriously to rival Chambers and later to supplant him with potential clients, and, in time, to deprive him of the clear leadership in his profession towards which all his efforts had been directed. Adam's name is still current both for an architectural style and, chiefly, as the progenitor of a fashion in furniture, while that of Chambers is only vaguely remembered.[19]

Thomas Telford's impressions of the two men are interesting. In 1782 he was working at Somerset House, and he says:

> I became known to Sir W. Chambers and to Mr. Adam ... the former haughty and reserved, the latter affable and communicative, and a similar distinction of character pervaded their works: Sir William's being stiff and formal, those of Mr. Adam playful and gay.[20]

Once more in Rome, Chambers' freedom of manoeuvre was further curtailed by the necessity for an early marriage to Catherine. The wedding took place on 29th March 1753, and they lived in the same house as Piranesi. Their first daughter, Cornelia, was born on 5th July 1753, and then Selina in 1754 or 1755, just before their return to England. The baby was too young to travel, so it was left behind in Rome for a time with a nurse, and the parents and Cornelia arrived in London in the spring of 1755.[21] Here they took rooms at 16 or 18 Russell Street, Covent Garden, beside Tom's Coffee House. It was not an impressive address for an architect who had his eye on noble clients. Friends of Robert Adam wrote to him in Rome to this effect, and he dryly remarked, '...as I hear from England that Chambers is not doing great things, I may hope to come in for my share of the pock-pudding with the rest.' Later, in 1756, Chambers toured Scotland with Lord Bute. The news alarmed Adam, but he comforted himself with the remark that the visit showed 'he cannot yet be in high demand', and that 'If he were well employed he would never have found the time',[22] a shrewd assessment of affairs, for Chambers was disappointed at his progress. Not untypically, Adam said of Chambers, 'You must know Chambers has a set of spies here at Rome to enquire what I am about, what my intentions are, and what progress I have made.' Thus, even before they may be said to have begun their professional careers, a thin fog of paranoid distrust and suspicion had arisen between them.

But Chambers' Scottish tour was the symbol of something more. He was already the tutor in architecture to the Prince of Wales, a position to which, as Gandon tells us, 'he was recommended for his experience and knowledge ... which combined with his accomplished manners rendered him the most eligible person to be selected for the purpose.'

Chambers' 'accomplished manners' are comprehensively described by Robert Adam when he says:

> All the English who have travelled for these five years are much prepossessed in his favour, and imagine him a prodigy of genius for sense and good taste. My own opinion is that he in great measure deserves their econiums, though his taste is more architectonic than picturesque – as for grounds and gardens Boucher can't be more Gothic. But his taste for bas-reliefs, ornaments and decorations of building he both knows well and draws exquisitely. His sense is middling but appearance is genteel and his personage good, which are most material circumstances ... he despises others as much as he admires his own talents which he shows with a slow and dignified air, conveying an idea of great wisdom which is no less useful than all his other endowments, and I find sways much with every Englishman: nay, he is in such esteem so intimate and in such friendship with most of the English that have been in Rome, that they are determined to support him to the utmost of their power, among whom are Tylney, Huntingdon and others of great consequence and even reckoned of great taste. Were I conscious to myself of having superior genius for drawing as well as being provided in good hints for designing, and as many great designs finished, finely drawn and coloured as he had to show away with, it would be a different thing. But that can only come with time.[23]

There can be no doubt that Chambers took himself very seriously, and his self-important utterances, backed up as they were by a unique experience and a real competence, would take him far in the eighteenth century; these qualities made noble gentlemen feel at home with him. Any real touch of humour would have soon destroyed him, for they too regarded themselves with a grave complacency.

He was still in Russell Street at the end of 1757, for Adam, back from Rome, visited him here to find him 'drawing in a poor mean lodging up a long dark stair which is wretched'. But Chambers soon changed his style of living. He moved into a house on the west side of Poland Street, no. 58, adjacent to Oxford Street, and in 1758 he took on Gandon as his first apprentice. Gandon tells us:

> In a very short time after he settled in London he required an assistant, a sort of office clerk, or pupil, to make the necessary working drawings required for the various works in which he was then engaged. Some friends of mine advised me to wait on him, at his house in Poland-street; I did so, and on producing my portfolio, he appeared to be satisfied with my early drawings. In a very short period afterwards, I was regularly indentured to him as a pupil, and at a very modest fee.

Gandon was indentured to Chambers in 1758. His fee for his apprenticeship he describes as 'a very moderate fee'. He continues:

> My daily occupations a Chambers' office did not interfere with my atten-
> dance at the different schools in the evenings; but more particularly with
> that of Shipley's an establishment most superior in its arrangements; it was
> attended by the most respectable students in London.[24]

So Gandon went to live with William Chambers and his family. He was sixteen years old, and Chambers was now thirty-five, and for the first few years they appear to have got on well together. Here he met Lord Charlemont, who conde-scended to interest himself in the young man and to exhort him to 'the cultiva-tion of a pure taste in architecture'. It is hardly an exaggeration to say that this meeting was eventually to change the course of Gandon's life.

Those days cannot have been idle ones. Chambers was in the midst of composing his great work, his *Treatise on Civil Architecture*, and an examination of the plates shows Gandon's name on a few of them. Gandon's drawing is excel-lent, surprisingly so for so young a man, and it was unfortunate that one of the plates he drew was the subject of future criticism: he had halved a metope at the corner of an entablature. It was a mistake Chambers would not have made, and which he should have seen in the work of an assistant who could scarcely pretend to an equal experience in the refinements of Classical architecture. Clearly it is evidence of the trust Chambers must have already placed in him.

Apart from the *Treatise*, work included the Arch at Wilton, the Casino at Marino, and the premises for the Society for the Encouragement of Arts, Manu-facturers and Commerce. There was Goodwood House and Castle Hill, and all the usual minor works of an architect's office. Working drawings had to be pre-pared for all these projects, and the future would show that the ambitious Gandon, in turn, took full advantage of the opportunities offered to him for the practise of work, which was both excellent and scholarly.

The group of architects which served the government and the nobility was small and select, and like any such specialised body, its members came to know each other fairly well. Trained assistants were scarce, and the amount of work which each could conveniently carry out was limited, so it was not unusual for a potential commission which could disrupt a steady practice to be passed from one to another. It was John Carr, an architect from York, who introduced Chambers to Augusta, the Dowager Princess of Wales. Carr, born in 1723, was of an age with Chambers. He was admitted a Freeman of York in 1757, being described as a 'stonecutter', but in fact he practised as an architect, doubling in future years first as Sheriff and later Lord Mayor of York.

The Princess of Wales was anxious to lay out and embellish her grounds at

James Caulfield, 1st Earl of Charlemont, by Richard Livesay
(courtesy National Gallery of Ireland)

George III, King of England, by B. West / E.Fisher
(*courtesy National Gallery of Ireland*)

Kew, and Chambers was appointed. The undertaking forced Chambers to take a house near the gardens, and he brought Gandon with him. Chambers' work at Kew, like his work in Paris and Rome, could not be left behind until he had extracted its full value from it. Back in Poland Street, he and Gandon were busy preparing the drawings of the buildings at Kew for publication. By now, Gandon had a companion apprentice, for Edward Stephens was articled to Chambers in January of 1760. The work at Kew was published in 1763 as *Plan, Elevations, Sections and Perspective Views of the Gardens and Buildings at Kew in Surrey*.

On 25th October 1760, George II died unexpectedly, and his grandson, the Prince of Wales, succeeded as George III. He had no liking for those in office under his grandfather, and set about getting rid of them and bringing in his own favourites. The difficulties borne by Chambers during his tutorship now paid off, for George held him in high regard and Chambers found himself with convenient access to the centre of power and patronage.

George III was stubborn, obtuse and, at first, only a little mad, qualities enhanced by his determination to have his own way. He ousted Pitt from office, and to please his friends, the Tories, brought the Seven Years War to a close in 1763, with a disastrous treaty. By mixing blunders with acts of arrogance, he destroyed the favourable position of his country which had been created by Pitt, and then lapsed into insanity. He had married a German princess, Charlotte, on 8th September 1761, and a fortnight later they were crowned in Westminster.

An early appointment of the king was that of Chambers to be one of the 'Architects of the Works', at a salary of £300 a year. Perhaps Chambers experienced something of the feelings of a suitor to a rich and ancient widow who becomes aware of a lover installed in the back room, when he found that his companion Architect of the Works was to be Robert Adam. Gandon, however must have welcomed this opportunity to enlarge his experience.

Adam had the Earl of Bute to thank for this appointment, for, in spite of their junketing in the Highlands, Adam remained the Earl's favourite. Bute, by repute the lover of the Queen Mother, was brought into the government by George III, but his period of office lasted only eleven months. He was succeeded in turn by Greville, Rockingham, Grafton and North, for periods varying with the king's moods, until Pitt took over. During this time, no further royal favours were received by Adam, a circumstance due, we can suspect, to Chambers' influence with the king.

As Architect of the Works, Chambers was responsible for the temporary seating, the stalls and other arrangements of this kind for the coronation of George III. Chambers gave Gandon a ticket for the ceremony, and although he does not mention it, no doubt he was a witness of the various odd incidents which took place. As, perhaps, a fitting portent of the years to come, the arrangements were haunted by a recurring element of farce. The marshal's horse refused to enter the hall in any position except backwards. There was much confusion of an unexplained character, and inexplicable delays. Horace Walpole has left a short description of the scene, in which the Duke of Newcastle exercised his habit of getting himself into the wrong place:

> The Coronation is over: 'tis a more gorgeous sight than I imagined. I saw the procession and the Hall; but the return was in the dark. In the morning they had forgot the Sword of State, the chairs for King and Queen and their Canopies. They used the Lord Mayor's for the first and made the last in the Hall; so they did not set forth till noon, and then, by a childish compliment to the King, reserved the illumination of the Hall till his entry; by which means they arrived like a funeral, nothing being discernable but the plumes of the Knights of the Bath which seemed the hearse ... of all the incidents of the day, the most diverting was what happened to the Queen. She had a retiring chamber with all conveniences prepared behind the altar. She went thither – in the most convenient what found she but – the Duke of Newcastle.

Perhaps much of the trouble was due to the tradesmen prematurely drinking to the health of the King, quite apart from the reputation then held by the Office of Works for gross inefficiency.

The work in Chambers' office was now considerable. Over the next few years, Styche Hall, Coleby Hall Temple, alterations to Walcot House and Duddington House, a bridge and gateway at the Hoo, and other works for the nobility in London were in hand.[25] Certainly Gandon could hardly complain that his apprenticeship lacked variety. Indeed, as assistant to one of the two leading architects in England, each of whom had had a unique training on the continent, he would have been a poor pupil if he did not profit from it. In the event, Gandon had the gifts which go to produce an architect of quality. He had the energy to apply himself, and it can be shown that at the end of his apprenticeship, he was, in all but experience, basically the superior architect of the two (as can be seen from his work on the Casino and Wilton Arch). He seems to have left Chambers as soon as his seven years contract was completed,[26] probably some time early in the year 1765, when he was twenty-three years old and Chambers was forty-two. At that time, Chambers was in the process of moving his family into a Palladian Villa at Whitton, formerly owned by the Duke of Argyll. With the Tory landowners now under the protection of George III, he saw before him a long and prosperous practice. At the same time he was also moving his office over to no. 13 Berners Street, one of a row of houses in which he owned an interest.[27] The previous year, in August 1764, Chambers had taken on another articled pupil, John Yenn, who became his favourite.[28] Some or all of these changes may have had their influence on Gandon's decision. They seem to have parted amicably and with mutual respect, but the suspicion remains that they been getting on each others' nerves towards the end. Gandon, like the sorcerer's apprentice, had, perhaps, by this time absorbed much of Chambers' self-importance, a trick which could hardly have endeared him to his master.

STYLES

James Gandon's professional life coincided with the second half of the eighteenth century, a time of exceptional architectural change when the Romantic concept of art had already diffused itself throughout northern Europe and was greatly to influence the designs of buildings. Architectural styles had always been in the process of change, but only through a logical development of what had gone before. Now, for the first time, change came to be influenced by factors other than those dictated by structural developments and by alterations in social conditions.

To those who never had the inclination to pursue the history of architecture, most of the buildings previous to this century, especially from the Renaissance onwards, look very much alike. Their original features, striking when first displayed, are now dimmed and diminished by time, and confused by the aesthetic anarchy of the nineteenth century. But to enter more fully into Gandon's life, it is desirable to have some appreciation of the ideas and problems which exercised his mind, and to be able to recognise where he stood in the shifting architectural values of his time.

Generalities in this matter can be grossly misleading in particular instances, but broadly speaking, it can be said that the Renaissance had run its course in Italy in the sixteenth century. In France too, although to a lesser extent, this was true, while in Ireland and England the influence of the continent was only becoming apparent in a tentative manner early in the seventeenth century. The main sources of inspiration were carried home by the younger members of the nobility who began to visit the countries of Europe at this time, following the fashion of the 'grand tour'. Italy attracted those on whom a Classical education had made some impression, and Rome became the centre to which they gravitated. Here they soon monopolised the best accommodation, set up a social life to their own pattern, and eventually went home with paintings and sculptures and, where their resources were sufficient and sometimes even where they were not, with the urge to rebuild or reconstruct their town and country houses. This quiet

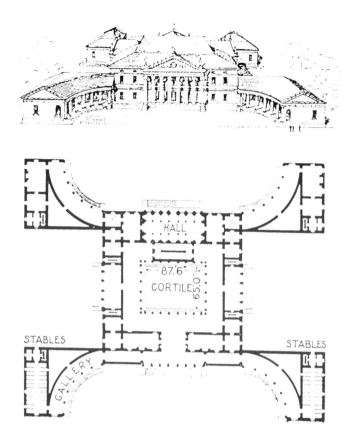

Palladian Architecture
top House for Sig. Mocenigo in the Brenta (*unexecuted*)
bottom Villa Capra, Vicenza

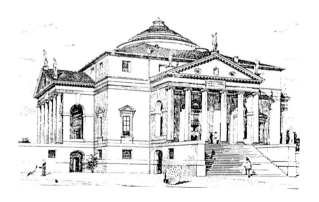

development of Classical taste was rudely accelerated by the plague and by the great fire of London. After 1670, the genius of Wren made familiar his own conception of the Baroque in the London churches, and particularly in St Paul's.

To go back a little, we can say that the Renaissance proper was largely represented by the palaces of the ruling urban Italian families. These buildings exemplified the principles laid down by Vitruvius, the author of an ancient Roman work on the principles of architecture, but within a generation or so, the lively Renaissance imagination grew tired of such academic restraints, and very startling innovations, now defined as Mannerist, were introduced by Michelangelo and others. Of these others, Palladio appealed to the taste of the Irish and English nobility, mainly because his work was popularised by Inigo Jones, and also, perhaps, because he did not affront their natural conservatism to the same extent as Michelangelo. In addition, Palladio originated designs for two classes of buildings with which the nobility were personally concerned: the town house and the country villa.

In the town house, Palladio, using the ground floor as a base, united the first and second floors by means of external columns, carrying their proper architrave, frieze and cornice. He emphasised the first floor, or the *piano nobile*, which accommodated the main social rooms, and these were punctuated by the smaller windows of the second floor. Occasionally, an attic storey was added when his methods were later adopted by the Georgians.

The innovations displayed in two of Palladio's country villas had particular significance for his admirers: firstly, his design for the Villa Capra, the country house planned on a square, in which a central area rose through the full height of the internal floors (as seen in Chiswick House in England), and secondly, his house on the Brenta set the fashion for a more common composition, where the central mass was linked with flanking pavilions by curved colonnades. Examples of this type are the Bluecoat School in Dublin and Russborough House in Co Wicklow, as well as Kedleston Hall and many others in England.

Palladio's Mannerism consisted in a number of departures from the classical canon, such as the use of supporting columns, not on the ground as was normal, but either on piers or resting on the ground floor, using it as a base. He would introduce subsidiary columns to a smaller scale than the main columns. He also gave his name to the Palladian window, which became the basis for the design of a number of Dublin doorways (for example, those on Merrion Square). He popularised the fashion of punctuating a design vertically with small square windows on the top floor, as in many Dublin houses.

Palladio's introduction of curves on plan heralded the Baroque. While the High Renaissance and Mannerism still adhered to rectilinear design, the Baroque was characterised by the introduction of curves, first in plan and then in elevation. It can be said that whereas Classical Renaissance architecture dealt in pro-

left to right Palladian town house, London town house, Dublin town house

portion, elevational patterns, and the contrast of solid and void, the Baroque was more concerned with the contrast of curve against curve and mass against mass. Ornamentation became of greater importance, firstly to emphasise significant detail which reinforced the design, and later for its own sake, although this was never a prominent feature of the Baroque in England, and less so in Ireland.

At about the time of Gandon's birth, a new factor began to make its appearance: Classicism became infected with Romanticism. Although both qualities are nearly always intermingled in the arts, so far Classicism was dominant. To be clear about what we mean by each example, one must, of necessity, be extreme. The Classical quality is concerned with order, proportion and harmony, as viewed from a purely intellectual standpoint – such as the contemplation of a perfectly cut diamond. On the other hand, the Romantic apprehension is enlivened by the emotions and the feelings: gloom, joy, nobility, idealism, and the curiously pleasant sense of loss evoked by the contemplation of the ruins of a supposedly perfect civilisation. A passion for these emotions was generated at that time by a number of circumstances: the publication of drawings of ancient classical ruins from the remoter countries about the Eastern Mediterranean; the monopoly of Classical education by the noble and governing classes which led them to feel that they were the inheritors of the mantle of the Roman senator and the Roman lawgiver; the appearance of a quasi-historical fiction with a strong vein of melancholy, such as the Gothic novel; and the growth of the empire. In painting, Romanticism took the form of a desire to depict the nobler moments in Roman history; in sculpture, the representation of the more mythical classical figures; and in architecture, a determination to return to the pure classical forms of the Augustan age, while discounting, or believing themselves to discount, the developments of the Renaissance. This new architectural style, known as neoclassicism, was embraced with enthusiasm by the French and with a certain reserve by the English.

Gandon had the good fortune to have served his apprenticeship with William Chambers, who in turn had spent some time in Paris and was familiar with the French neoclassicists, as well as having studied the original remains of the Augustan age in Rome. Gandon readily absorbed both streams during his time with Chambers, and there is reason to believe that he had access to the latest designs from Paris, as well as the sketches made by Chambers during his Roman visit. Chambers had also been in China, and this fact alone made him the recognised authority on Chinese art and architecture, but Gandon does not appear to have shown any interest in this area.

Gandon developed, however, a wide and more historical vision, declaring his interest in the works of Wren and Hawksmoor, and in the more dramatic compositions of Vanburgh – all seventeenth-century practitioners of the now-despised Baroque. In fact he was eclectic, gathering principles and motifs from a wide variety of sources, and integrating them with unmistakable genius into the buildings he designed, while at the same time, quite sincerely, he was prepared to express his taste as being guided by the pure stream of the ancient classical architecture of the Roman world. Greek architecture – which many of his contemporaries declared to be 'of a purer well than Rome' – he ignored, maintaining to the end that the Roman style was faultless. He made a few brief excursions into the Gothic, but what he thought of the other historical styles which were resurrected during the Romantic revival is unclear.

MARINO AND WILTON

The Casino at Marino in Dublin can only be described as a shrine devoted to the Classical arts: the arts of the eighteenth century and of the Age of Reason. Lord Charlemont was one of the more cultured men of his time, and he devoted many years of his life to the creation of a perfect building to enshrine the works of art he had collected during his travels abroad. The outstanding architect and artists of the day were sought out and brought together to contribute to this essay in perfection. Expense was not considered and no detail was neglected in the achievement of his dream. William Chambers, who was both friend and architect for Lord Charlemont, gave the work his full attention. During the building, Charlemont was often short of money to keep it going, so progress was slow. The work started about 1759, but as late as the 1770s some details were still unfinished. The special furniture, much of it made by Dublin craftsmen, has disappeared, as have the works of art, sold off during the nineteenth century as the Charlemont estate became impoverished, and the building itself suffered severely from neglect. But now, after a number of years of careful work, it has been restored almost to its former state.

The Casino is of special interest to us in that Gandon came to Chambers' office in 1758, and it is almost certain that he made the working drawings for it as building started, as already noted, in the following year. How far the main elements of the design had been decided before Gandon's arrival we cannot say, but it is not unusual for an architect whose time is taken up by prospective clients to appoint an assistant to take over the development of the plans to save him time, and it is in certain aspects of the Casino which are not prominent in the mass of Chambers' work that we may, perhaps, find something of Gandon's hand.

Naturally, the first thing which strikes us is the dearth of windows. There are fifteen windows in the building, but generally only one or two are visible at a time. Then the entrance is at the narrow end, and the internal tight planning could only have been achieved by weeks of patient work, which was not in Chambers' character. There is also a curious difference between the external scale and that of the interior. Although the Casino has three floors and numerous rooms, it appears from outside to consist of only a single storey. It might be that Gandon acquired such preferences from Chambers' directions to him, but they are not found in Chambers' other works. The placing of the urns on heavily decorated plaques and the statues on flat cornices and over columns reoccur frequently in Gandon's work.

That Gandon had a hand in the design of the Casino (and no superficial hand) is attested to by the friendship which sprang up between him and Lord Charlemont. Charlemont had a very genuine appreciation of Gandon's talents, which led him to recommend him firstly to his Irish fellow noblemen, and through Lord Carlow, to Beresford. It was not an appreciation which could have developed from the casual meetings at Paul Sandby's (a native of Nottingham, and an artist who held a Crown appointment), but only through the discussion of the design of a concrete proposal such as that of the Casino while he was in Chambers' office.

The Casino is unique both in Ireland and Europe. Dr Edward McParland cites the Palladian Villa Rotunda at Vicenza, and Inigo Jones's Queen's House at Greenwich as its peers. Throughout the nineteenth century and well into the twentieth century, the Irish authorities seem to have been unaware of the trea-

Sir William Chambers
The Casino at Marino, 1758

Sir William Chambers, The Casino at Marino, 1758
Survey by Alfred E Jones, 1917-18
top Elevation
bottom left Ground Floor   *bottom right* First Floor
opposite Sections
(*photos: Michael Blake for Gandon Archive, Kinsale*)

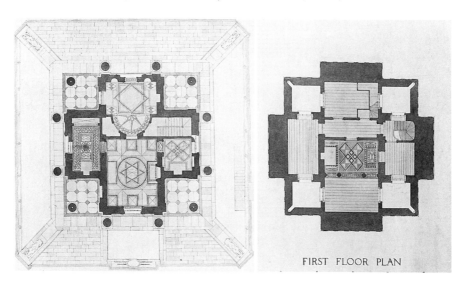

FIRST FLOOR PLAN

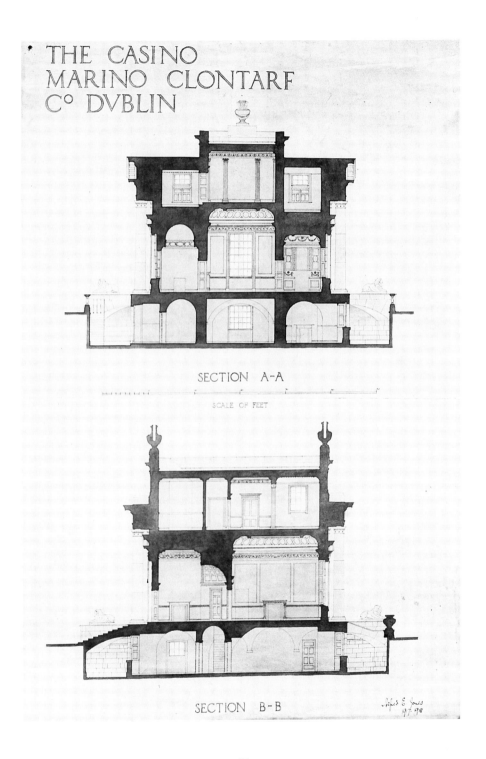

THE CASINO
MARINO CLONTARF
Cº DVBLIN

SECTION A-A

SCALE OF FEET

SECTION B-B

sure they had inherited. The beautiful parkland which was its setting has been invaded by other buildings. In any society conscious of cultural matters, these would have been cleared away and a proper entrance devised. At present, access is from a narrow side road which is difficult for visitors to find.

Looking at the Wilton Arch (at Wilton House in England) we are immediately conscious of the quality of its proportions, which could only have been acquired by careful and persistent designing. It was designed during 1758/59, when Gandon had just joined Chambers' office, and it has the character of his design work, as shown in later features and not generally found in Chambers' work. These features include the use of a subsidiary order, the twin pilasters at the front corners, the central plaque over the arch, and the build up for the position of the sculptured horse and rider. The plates with their uneven husk ropes on the spandrels are practically a Gandon trademark. We can also note the balustrade over the lodges, hiding the roofs.

The Wilton Arch, 1758/59

IN PRACTICE

In 1765 James Gandon was twenty-three years old. During his time with Chambers, he could scarcely have avoided contact with many of his clients. What little evidence we have shows that he gained their respect as a competent designer and architect, and a secure and active career with Chambers was open to him.

It is hard to believe that he did not give this option some consideration, for he was always concerned for his own advancement. But he decided to terminate his association with Chambers, and he moved into lodgings above Mr Babb's bookshop in Oxford Street, which at that time extended only a short distance beyond Bond Street, and it was so remote from the activity of London that he was able to pursue, we are told, the gentlemanly occupation of shooting snipe in the adjacent fields. We are given no hint of the sources from which he drew financial support. Any professional man setting up in practice on his own must be in a position to maintain himself for several years, especially so in the practice of architecture where fees are notoriously tardy. He is silent too about his father and sister; indeed there is no further mention in his writings, or at least that portion of them which we have, of his family or indeed of his numerous uncles and aunts.

He had, however, quite a few friends, and not all of them from the penurious artistic circles in which he liked to move. One of these, Barry Hutchinson, was solicitor to several of the London companies or guilds,[29] and he introduced Gandon to them. They had halls and other properties which required maintenance from time to time, and would provide a welcome income, small but steady, for a young architect. We are told that one of these, the East India Company, offered Gandon the appointment of architect and civil engineer to Fort Marlborough in Sumatra.[30] Possibly it was a position for which there was little competition, as the colonial powers, and particularly the Dutch, which had set up garrisoned trading posts were forced to keep up a regular supply of men to replace the desperate wastage by disease.

Sumatra lies on the equator. To the east, the land is flat and the rain forests only stop at the coastal swamps. At that time, several thousand men died each year due to the severe living conditions. Gandon, cautious as ever, went to some of his Quaker friends for advice, and fortunately turned down the offer.[31] It is surprising that he should have give the invitation any serious consideration, for he was one of the best equipped younger architects in London, and had every reason to take an optimistic view of his professional future. Perhaps the example of Chambers' Chinese travels may have tempted him, but this is unlikely. The occasion may have been confused by Mulvany; it would be more comprehensible some fifteen years later when Gandon was in low water.

As far as we know, Gandon's first private client was Sir Samuel Hillier (or Hellier), a gentleman from Staffordshire who lived at the Wodehouse, Womburne, a few miles to the south Wolverhampton. Sir Samuel was a man who was culturally alert. He was captivated by Handel, whose music was, to a large extent, based on either the ideas of others or his own earlier works. Oddly enough, the works of Gandon show a similar trait. At any rate, he was commissioned by his new friend to design a memorial to Handel which would grace Sir Samuel's estate. Gandon says:

> I have passed many pleasant days at my friend, Sir Samuel Hillier's seat in Staffordshire. He was musical, and particularly admired Handel. He was very much attached to me; brought me to several musical parties in his neighbourhood and supplied me most amply with venison and game.[32]

The memorial was constructed probably during 1767, and Gandon's design for it

Handel memorial, 1767
(courtesy The Royal Collection, London)

was exhibited by the Society of Artists in 1768. When we look at the rather imperfect sketch which has survived, we are reminded of the Temple of Bellona which Chambers erected at Kew. There is nothing inherently original about this design – it should be possible to find a similar building in most parts of Europe – but in Gandon's time it was something new to the English countryside. Only traces of the foundations now remain.

Gandon's practice grew slowly and remained small. Mulvany tells us that in 1767, a Sir Henry Oxendon engaged him to carry out alterations to his residence, Broom Park in Kent. Perhaps he meant Sir Henry's father, Sir George Oxendon, who was still very much alive in 1767, having inherited the property, curiously enough, from his second son. Sir George was an enterprising character, notable for his 'extremely handsome' appearance and for his profligacy.[33] He married an heiress, the daughter of Edmund Dunch, and then proceeded to seduce her sister, Bell Dunch, the wife of the MP for York. In addition, he enjoyed the reputation for being the real father of Horace Walpole, the 3rd Earl of Orford. When he died in 1775, Sir Henry inherited Broom Park.

We do not know precisely what Gandon did here, but it has been suggested it was no more than some internal alterations and a small extension. If any of his work survives, it is now unrecognisable, for the house fell into the hands of Lord Kitchener, a compulsive renovator. When Kitchener left for Egypt in 1911, he had already pulled out the interior and was engaged in rebuilding it to a different plan, in much the same way as he had destroyed the interior of his official residence in India.

The first considerable activity of Gandon was directed towards the production of a continuation of Colin Campbell's three volumes of *Vitruvius Britannicus*, which had illustrated the outstanding public and private buildings of the day. For too long the English had subscribed to similar volumes of architectural drawings dealing exclusively with Italian and French architecture, so Campbell's work, being a new experience, proved very popular and added greatly to his prestige. No doubt, this was a factor Gandon had in mind when he decided to have himself associated with that work. Perhaps his experience with Chambers had given him an exaggerated expectation of the value of architectural publications in promoting private practice, but Chambers had been in a position to publish his own works and not those of competing architects, so, to be fair, we must attribute to Gandon the desire to advance the quality of contemporary architecture.

He choose as a companion and partner for this work an architect in the Office of Works, one John Woolfe, an Irishman from Co Kildare. They were already friendly, possibly from business dealings after Chambers became one of the architects of the Works. Woolfe lived in Scotland Yard and, no doubt, had plenty of time to spare from his official duties.

It was an ambitious undertaking, and the cost of paper and engraving would have been high. The first volume, volume IV in Campbell's series, was published in 1767, and the sale was in the hands of J. Taylor of the Architectural Library at no. 59 High Holborn. Some thirty buildings were illustrated on ninety-eight plates. The standard of drawing and engraving was excellent, and the presentation pleasing. The uneasy Gandon felt, however, that he had been put upon in some way by Woolfe, and Mulvany, while admitting that Woolfe bore his share of the expenses and was 'a man of high honour', alleges that Woolfe was 'not of very active habit; hence the whole of the labour of preparing and bringing out the book rested on Mr. Gandon.'

An examination of the plates in volume IV does not bear this out: of the ninety-eight plates, nineteen are double-page so there are seventy-nine full-page plates. Of these, Woolfe drew forty and Gandon thirty-four, while five plates are unsigned. However, Gandon engraved nine of the plates, as well as drawing them, so it must be admitted he did more work than Woolfe, but not to excess. Nonetheless, it is an interesting piece of information from Mulvany, which looks as if it had its origins in Gandon's writings and from a part of them now lost.

Evidently, volume IV was successful, for we find them collaborating once more for the production of volume V, which was published three years later in 1770. Their choice of buildings is interesting: of all the buildings illustrated in volume IV, only one is by Chambers while two are by Adam, and of the twenty-six in volume V, one is by Gandon himself, one by Chambers, three by Adam, and four by Carr of York, a circumstance we will have to look at later. That Gandon was in a position to include a work of sufficient importance of his own was due to his friendship with Paul Sandby.

Paul Sandby was Gandon's closest and most loyal friend. He and his brother Thomas were born in Nottingham, Thomas in 1721 and Paul in 1725. This leaves Sandby seventeen years older than Gandon, so that in 1769, when Gandon was favoured for the work of designing a new Shire Hall for Nottingham he was twenty-seven and Paul Sandby was forty-four. The Sandby brothers appear to have been self-trained draughtsmen. They engaged the interest of a Mr Plumptre, MP for Nottingham, who secured positions for them at the Tower of London in the ordnance mapping department. Thomas became private secretary and draughtsman to HRH William Augustus, Duke of Cumberland, and was with him in his campaigns in Flanders and Scotland. He married (secondly) Elizabeth Venables on 26th April 1753, and they had ten children.[34]

Meanwhile, Paul had become draughtsman for the survey of the Highlands after the rebellion of 1745. Their involvement in this lead to further advancement: Thomas became Deputy Ranger of Windsor Great Park in 1746,[35] and, in time, an informal friend and adviser to George III; Paul was appointed by the Duke of Grafton to be Head Drawing Master to the Military Academy at Woolwich at £300 a year, for which he had to attend on only one day a week.

Paul Sandby was indefatigable in the pursuit of his art throughout his life, spending most of each week in drawing and sketching. In 1760, when Gandon was with William Chambers in Poland Street, he was living at Mr Pow's Dufour Court, off Broad Street. He had married a Miss Anne Stogden,[36] for, it was said, her personal charm, on 3rd May 1757, and they had three children. She was painted by Francis Cotes as Emma or The Nut-brown Maid. In 1766 he moved to Poland Street to the house just vacated by William Chambers, and in 1772 he bought no. 4 George's Row, Oxford Road, where he lived until his death in 1809. Curiously, Thomas Malton and his family later occupied the house in Poland Street.

Paul Sandby's sketches and watercolour work attracted many of the young artists in London (such as Mortimer and his friends), including Gandon. There was also another group of people who began to visit Paul Sandby about this time, and, strangely enough, they were members of the Irish nobility and gentry: Lord Carlow, Frederick Trench, and Joseph Deane Bourke, who was to take up Gandon's interest with the competition committee for the Royal Exchange in

Paul Sandby by Sir William Beechey
(courtesy National Portrait Gallery, London)

Anne Sandby (née Stogden), mezzotint by Edward Fisher after Francis Cotes
(courtesy National Portrait Gallery, London)

Dublin. Thus, quite fortuitously, Gandon found patrons who would ensure his future work in Ireland. The interest of the artists in Sandby's circle seems to have waned as the numbers of aristocratic visitors grew, and Sandby's house became a regular meeting place for those of the group who happened to be in London.

Gandon's friendship with Paul and Thomas Sandby was a considerable asset. As favourites of the king, the Sandbys were in a position to advance Gandon with potential clients. It illustrates the lack of serious political divisions at the time that Sandby's circle included Lord Charlemont, Lord Carlow and others, as well as William Mason and Sir George Savile, who were not in favour with the Court. Paul Sandby's influence probably worked mainly through his brother Thomas, who was closer to the king.

Apart from Paul Sandby, Gandon enjoyed two other lifelong friendships, as much as or perhaps more than many people can claim. They were John Hamilton Mortimer ARA and Captain Francis Grose. Each in his own way seems to have satisfied a different facet of Gandon's character, in so far as we can interpret it. Mortimer was a man of dubious reputation and extravagant lifestyle. Strong minded, unscrupulous and adventurous, a frequenter of the drinking clubs and coffee houses of Covent Garden and its environs, his appeal, to some extent, may have been to the disappointed and resentful part of Gandon's personality. However, Mortimer's mastery of his craft remained an essential factor in his attraction for Gandon, who, throughout his life devoted himself to the pursuit of aesthetic ideas and ideals. Perhaps it would not be going too far to say that every other area of human activity held little interest for Gandon, and as a consequence, any sort of friendship, or even close acquaintanceship, was difficult for him if a common interest in the arts was lacking. The only other quality which in any way attracted Gandon was strength of character. We shall see how his future patron, the Hon John Beresford, who was an egregious exponent of this principle, secured Gandon's loyalty, although his appreciation of aesthetic matters was minimal.

Mortimer and Gandon were of an age, Mortimer having been born in 1741 at Eastbourne.[37] They met at Shipley's Academy, where Mortimer attracted Gandon's interest and respect through his talent for drawing. Gandon tells us 'he was, as to originality, a Shakespeare in the Arts: many convivial hours we spent together', and 'I have a beautiful drawing by him, of an Academy figure from life, which he executed in about one hour and a half. I have another drawing of his, which represents one half of the skeleton, the other the nude, with all the muscles most truly expressed. This drawing was finished one evening when we were together.'

That tight little company of London artists were well acquainted with each other, their main area of professional contact lying within the Society of Artists. In 1763, the Society offered premiums of one hundred guineas and fifty

John Hamilton Mortimer and pupil by Mortimer
(*courtesy National Portrait Gallery, London*)

guineas for the best historical painting. This was Mortimer's specialty, and his picture secured the second prize. Whitley tells us that Romney was, in fact, awarded second prize, but that Reynolds, who was jealous of him, had the decision set aside and the award given to his friend Mortimer. Mortimer, in turn, is reported as having said that Romney deserved the prize, not because of the merits of his painting, but because Romney, at that time poor and friendless, 'painted it in a room so small that he could not examine the effect of the whole at a single view and at a proper distance, and that under this disadvantage his performance was surprising'. The painting in question was Romney's *The Death of General Wolfe*.

Gandon had formed most of his friendships at Shipley's. Many were of an age with him, and they included Charles Churchill, Francis Wheatley, 'Nat' and Marchant, Evan Lloyd and Thomas Jones. Thomas Jones was a Welshman, a painter and a member of the Society of Artists. They spent convivial evenings together in places such as the Devil's Tavern and other coffee houses in the vicinity of Covent Garden.

In 1775, Mortimer surprised his friends by marrying Jane Hurrell, a farmer's daughter. He became a reformed character, and left London to live in the country. In 1778 he was elected an Associate of the Royal Academy, and returned to London, Three months later he caught a fever, and died on 4th February 1779.[38] His death must have been a profound shock for Gandon, and he can scarcely have failed to mention it in that part of his writings lost to us. It was to be one more unsettling factor at a crucial stage of Gandon's life.

SHIRE HALL

As early as 1742, the need for a new Shire Hall was felt at Nottingham. This need was underlined by the partial collapse of the floor of the old hall, but beyond some repairs, nothing was done for over forty years. There is a lively description of the accident in the *Nottingham Courant*:

On Friday last, March 17th 1742, Sir Lyttleton Powis, Judge of Assize, came in here, being met as usual by the High Sheriff, attended by a good number of gentlemen on horseback, though a very rainy day.

On Saturday was Commission Day for the County of the Town but there was no business worth mentioning.

On Monday morning, after the Judge had gone into the County Hall, and a great crowd of people being there, a tracing or two that supported the floor broke and fell in and several people fell with it, about three yards into the cellar underneath Some were bruised, but one man named Fillingham was pretty much hurt, one leg being stripped to the bone. This caused great consternation in the Court, some apprehending the Hall might fall, others crying out fire etc. which made several people climb out of the windows. The Judge being also terribly frightened, cried out: 'A plot, a plot!', but the consternation soon being over, the Court proceeded to business. However the Judge told the Grand Jury and Gentlemen he would lay a fine on the County of £2,000 for not providing a better Hall, no doubting that if they built a new one, or got the old one well repaired, but on their petition His Majesty would remit the fine. At the request of the Foreman of the Grand Jury the fine was suspended.

Later it was decided to apply for an Act of Parliament to rebuild the County Hall, and at a meeting of the Gentlemen, Clergy and Freeholders of the County at the

Swan, Mansfield, on 23rd June 1768, it was decided to ask the grand jury to give directions for the Act. At the end of the draft resolution is a list of persons who brought plans: 'Mr. Gandon of London, Mr. Opsdell of Sandbeck, Mr. Simpson of Budby, Mr. Roberts of Nottingham, Mr. Stanley of Chesterfield'.

Gandon had lately been introduced to the poet Mason, who, in turn, introduced him to Sir George Savile and 'other influential gentlemen in the town of Nottingham'. The presentation of plans for similar works was at that time by personal patronage, and here there was no competition, as such. Gandon, thanks to the influence of his patrons, was in a position to command an interest in his designs above that of his fellow architects. Gandon's plans were favourably received, and we find him writing to the justices on 15th October 1768, and discussing the plans which he had shown them at Mansfield, 'which seemed to meet with your approbation with regard to their conveniency but thought to be too magnificent'. He sent them a new plan with the comment that 'the expense of this design will amount to about the sum of £2,500'.

The prudent public servant is inclined to confuse money with value. Certainly the gentlemen of Nottingham made a poor bargain when they rejected Gandon's first design. There are many examples of this facet of public economy where money is saved and value lost, but a few buildings, which are works of art in themselves, embellish the cities in which they stand – a pleasure for the citizens and monuments to the enlightened spendthrifts who erected them.

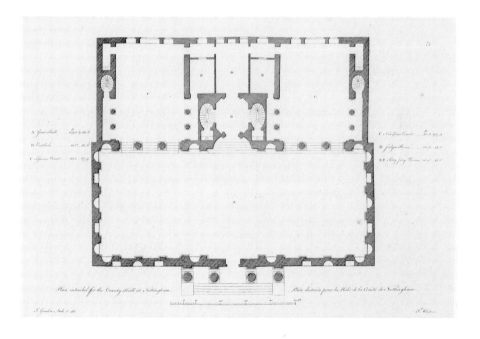

Shire Hall, Nottingham, 1772
top Façade *bottom* Cross-section *opposite* Plan
(*courtesy National Library of Ireland*)

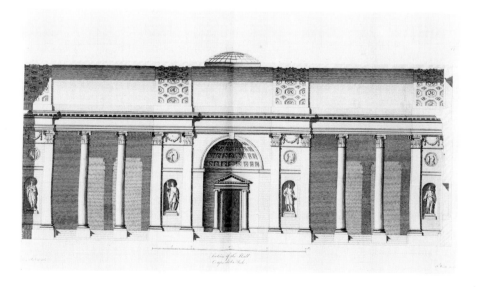

It was Gandon's first major work, and the job proceeded well. The grand jury at the Lammas Assizes in 1768 resolved to apply for an Act of Parliament, and called another meeting at Mansfield. At this meeting, the details of the business were decided, and were confirmed by the local courts. The Act of Parliament was passed without opposition, and the commissioners appointed by the Act held their first meeting on 15th August 1769 at the Swan in Mansfield. Gandon's plans were approved at this meeting, and the commissioners' clerk, Mr Hurst, was instructed to invite tenders.[39]

Building started, probably about the new year, and the commissioners met again on 6th March 1770, at the sign of the Black Moor's Head in Nottingham to appoint a clerk of works. They appointed William Roberts, a Nottingham builder, to supervise the erection of the building by a Mr Pickford of Derby, and to report any neglect or default by the contractor to the Clerk of the Peace. For this he was to be paid £60 when the building was complete. At that time, this seems to have been a reasonable amount.

Keeping this in mind, it is of interest to examine the cost of the Act of Parliament which preceded the building of the new Shire Hall. The bill was passed through its various stages by the Clerk of the House of Commons, a Mr George White, obviously a man of some experience. His account for the cost of this process came to £181.5.8, or something over £20,000 in today's currency. Some of the details are notable:

> Making several copies for committees, £10.
> Paid House Fee, £29.18.8.
> Paid Committee Clerk's Fee, £3.0.0.
> Paid Housekeeper's and Messenger's fees, £3.0.0.
> Paid Doorkeepers for delivering prints £1.0.0.
> Paid Gratuities to Housekeeper and 4 Messengers £2.0.0.
> Lords' Fee, £54.
> Committee Clerk's fee and Gratuity £5.0.0.
> Yeoman Usher and Doorkeepers' fees £5.0.0.
> Paid Porters, coach hire and small gratuities to 2 servants
> at both Houses, £2.0.0.
> Solicitation fee, £21.0.0.[40]

So Mr White had £45.7.0 left over for himself.

The commissioners incurred the first serious extra by deciding 'that all the apartments of the new Shire Hall have rounded arches of brick' instead of timber, and the roof to have 'stone columns' instead of wood. At their next meeting on 21st August 1770, they ordered the erection of iron palisades in front of the hall, new walls for the gaol, and a lead covering for the cornice of the hall. They also allowed a payment of £60 to Gandon, 'on account of the money due to him'. As he was now scarcely a month married, this would have been welcome. The erection of the building seems to have proceeded without incident, but on 12th December 1770, a wall fell and wrecked some houses in the 'Narrow Marsh'. Gandon is not mentioned in the enquiry which followed, but the wall was some distance from the hall and outside his area.

The last meeting of the commissioners was held in the grand jury room of the new hall on 10th March 1772. No doubt Gandon was in attendance. The task of extracting his fees would have been uppermost in his mind as the nobility was notorious for the tenacity with which it clung to moneys due to the deserving commoner.

In this, the first considerable building designed by Gandon, our interest lies naturally in his original and considered plans for Shire Hall, and not in those modified to meet the wishes of his clients. At that time, and in that part of England, the fashion was for a settled type of Baroque architecture, best displayed through the works of John Carr of York. The style of Gandon's original design would be new to the gentlemen of Nottingham, and they did not like it. Gandon, apart from the reduction in floor area, had further to modify his plan in a number of ways, and Shire Hall, as built, is not an impressive work of architecture. Its proportions are awkward, and are not helped by the elaboration of the feature over the portico. There are window cases with pediments on the ground floor, and the plain faces of the recessed flanking walls have been breached. Shire Hall has been extensively altered since Gandon's time, judging by the alternative plan in *Vitruvius Britannicus V*.

However, when we look at the rejected design for this building, we find it to be, as Sir John Summerson remarks, a surprising design for its time, and he finds in it evidence of Gandon's familiarity with the latest French work. It has weight; it is shorn of unnecessary ornament; the columns stand on a grounded plinth; and the conventional portico, or void, in the centre of the building has been strengthened by the heavy attic storey. But perhaps the most striking detail we notice is the absence of windows. This is not a usual feature of a courthouse, nor is it an environmental necessity, as would be natural in a country with strong sunlight. It appears to be a personal preference, one which we shall come across frequently, and, indeed, a factor deeply ingrained in Gandon's design instincts. The deep niches, unencumbered by architraves, emphasise the mass of the walls, and the portico is given interest by the central plaque and by the statues between the outside columns, all typical Gandon features, but none of these explains the excellent proportions, which are Gandon's claim to mastery.

When we look at the plan and section, we can pick out Gandon's preference for certain features, a preference he was to retain for the rest of his life. There is the difference in levels between the public space and the court proper;

there is the use of the classical screen of two columns; there are the oval staircases in the thickness of the walls; and, of course, the lighting of the most important apartments from above in order to avoid the use of windows. There is restraint: the richness of the decoration is controlled and nicely graduated to emphasise the judges' central entrance from the public space. There is prudence in the manner in which the central apse, with its ornament and its doorway, its inviting apsidal shape, which at the same time gives weight and depth to the centre of the composition, is in happy contrast to the voids of the flanking screens, while in contrast, these screens tend to exclude the observer. The inner wall design is in full contrast to the façade of the building, and would have been a delight to the observant visitor, as would the long segmental vault over the public space, with its central lantern and Diocletian windows at the ends.

The planning of the courts themselves is ingenious for that time, when faint regard was paid to such practical details by architects struggling with the Classical discipline. It appears simple at first sight, but on examination we find the courts so arranged that one may approach them in several ways, depending on the part of the court to which one belongs. The judges, too, have a choice. No sectional drawing of the courts appears to have survived, but it would be interesting to know if the circular stairs at the external walls lead to galleries, and what form these galleries would have taken.

THE ROYAL ACADEMY

The years 1767 and 1768, exciting as they were for Gandon, held a wider interest. George III had pursued an erratic course since his coronation: ministers had come and gone, and now John Wilkes was back from his exile in France to torment him again. The king had not long to wait. Soon Wilkes was standing for Parliament, and on the second attempt, he was elected for the County of Middlesex. There were deplorable scenes of public satisfaction. Then he was taken before the King's Bench as an outlaw, fined and imprisoned. Even this was no brake on his capacity for creating scandal. He wrote that the Secretary of State was responsible for the massacre of St George's Fields. For this he was expelled from Parliament, a course which failed to subdue him.

Another and more private row was also in progress, and here Gandon was involved. This was the rumpus in the Incorporated Society of Artists. At this time he was working on his designs for the competition for the Dublin Royal Exchange.

Perhaps the highlight of the year 1769 for James Gandon was his success in a competition for the first gold medal for architecture to be offered by the new Royal Academy. Gandon describes the occasion:

> As soon as I read the advertisement for the distribution of the premiums, I was like a person electrified. I hurried to my friend, Paul Sandby, who soon assured me that I could have no chance of success as a competitor for the gold medal in architecture, in as much as I was not eligible to be a candidate: the advertisement requiring that all the candidates should be students of the Royal Academy. This restriction certainly appeared a formidable obstacle to my becoming a competitor on the occasion ... I had not much time for reflection, and the temptation was great but I soon determined how I should act: I immediately entered my name as a student of the Academy, and attended all the lectures given by each professor. This was my only alternative.

It is hard to resist the suspicion that there is something more here than just the ambition to win a medal; where Chambers is involved, Gandon seems to be under some compulsion unknown to us. Gandon continues:

> The Academy gave ample time for the candidates to prepare their respective productions. I commenced instantly to arrange my ideas on the subject given which was a triumphal arch commemorative of the Seven Years War.
>
> The day at length arrived when the candidates were to send in their designs, and I was soon informed, to my great gratification, that my design was declared the best, and that consequently I should obtain the Gold Medal.
>
> On the day fixed for the distribution of the medals, but before they were actually delivered, the architectural class were required to attend a Committee of the Academicians in a private apartment in order to test their respective powers in impromptu composition. The different subjects were deposited in a vase out of which each candidate drew his envelope in which the subject was written. That which came to my hand was a park-gate, or rather, an ornamental entrance to a park. Having first arranged my ideas, I then sketched out my design, and it was more admired by the Committee than my triumphal arch.
>
> When the medals were being distributed I was congratulated by many of the members, but particularly by Sir William Chambers, who expressed the pleasure he experienced on finding his pupil so early distinguishing himself.[41]

This simple sentence, so typical of Gandon, covers an incident during which both must have suppressed rather mixed feelings. Gandon, originally an associate of Chambers and an intimate of his household, was now a professional rival, albeit a minor one. More immediately, he was one of that body of minor artists which had driven Chambers out of the Incorporated Society of Artists. Chambers had then engineered the setting up of the Royal Academy, from which he was determined to exclude all those who had previously opposed him. Yet, here was Gandon, who had somehow managed to obtain the first gold medal for architecture offered by Chambers' academy! But there were other Academy competitions for which Gandon had entered, as Edward McParland has noted, in which he was not successful, but no mention is made of these.

If we are fully to appreciate the incident, we must go back a few years. In 1765, the year Gandon set himself up in practice, George III granted a charter to the general body of English artists under the title of the Incorporated Society of Artists. Ever since their first public showing in 1760, this loose association of painters, sculptors and architects had mounted an annual exhibition which had grown in prestige and unexpectedly shown a profit. Now with a corporate identity confirmed by royal signature, one would have expected, as Gandon puts it,

> ...that the Society would be placed in a very desirable situation ... but unfortunately they were not long connected together, when dissensions arose among them, which continuing, produced in the course of three years an irreparable breach, and eventually a total dissolution of the Incorporated Society.

The Incorporated Society was designed to be what we would call a democratic institution, although the term 'democratic' had overtones of anarchy at that time. Many of the artists came to resent the autocratic conduct of Chambers and some of his fellow directors. One would think they were within their rights by deposing these by election, but Chambers and his colleagues were not of a disposition to bow to such demands. As it happened, they comprised the more gifted and well-established members of the Society, and Chambers' influence with George III was worth more than the combined influence of the rest. The outcome was never in doubt, but it is interesting to see what Thomas Jones, an acquaintance of Gandon had to say about the meeting on the feast of St Luke.

> The meetings of the Society at the Turk's Head had been for some time very much agitated with these jarring sentiments, nor could all the good humour of our jolly and facetious President, Fran. Hayman persuade the disputants to lay aside their mutual bickerings and drown their heartburnings in bumpers of wine – Things had now almost come to a Crisis – Sir

William Chambers headed the Directorial party, and the Popular Party, which consisted of some of the most turbulent, joined by the Junior Members, were supported by Mr. Payne. It was to be owned that the Directors managed their Affairs with great address – they had by a very ingenious Artifice, contrived to have that unique Anatomical figure and the other effects which were the joint property of the general Subscribers to the Old Academy in St Martin's Lane, removed to Pall Mall and so laid the foundation of a new exclusive Academy of their own – some of the most eminent as well as the most moderate Members of the Society were rather neuter during these Commotions – Nor were they, I believe, let into the whole of the secrets of the junto, for after a most tumultuous meeting at the Turk's Head (on the feast of St Luke) where I was present, one of them put a stop to all the Disputes at once by declaring to our astonishment and mortification that His Majesty had given his sanction to the establishment of a Royal Academy, and under whose patronage they meant to open an exhibition in Pall Mall. Several members of the first consequence at the time inveigh'd in the strongest terms against the measure who afterwards joined them and Reynolds himself in my hearing declared that from that day forward he never meant to exhibit, but that if he did he should exhibit with the original Incorporated Body but even Reynolds in the course of time was seduced by Titles and Honours. Thus was brought about this great Schism in the arts and which originated in the private feud of two rival individuals and in that alone, but which insensibly involved the whole Society within its vortex, after a series of some years spent in wrangling, gave birth to the Royal Academy.[42]

Gandon's notice of the Incorporated Society of Artists is kind to Chambers and to the Royal Academy, and the reader would not suspect that Gandon was a supporter of the rebel party, while maintaining his friendship with Paul Sandby and, it seems, Richard Wilson. Contemporary opinion was nearer to that of Thomas Jones. It seems that the Society had held an exclusive exhibition for the King of Denmark in 1768, at which Gandon's design for the Handel memorial was on view. In spite of stringent control over the admission tickets, William Chambers was able to secure twelve tickets for his friends. This brought to a head the resentment of the Society towards the directors and led straight to the final breach.

Nevertheless, the exhibitions of the Royal Academy were not without their embarrassments. The seeker of oddities will find entertainment in its records, such as the resolution excluding all persons except members of the royal family from the Academy while the female model was sitting. But it was the exhibition of 1780 which perhaps attracted the widest attention. It was the first exhi-

Gandon's design habits

1 This sketch of the Nottingham
   Courthouse illustrates
   Gandon's aversion to the
   introduction of windows and
   his preference for top lighting,
   where possible. He would also
   omit the architrave from his
   entablatures, externally and
   internally, and never use it on
   his niches.

2 This feature, the triumphal
   arch in its various guises, was
   Gandon's favourite motif, as
   in (1) above, where it forms
   the basis for the portico.

3 The panel, either flush or
   recessed, with a medallion, a
   band and a niche, and with or
   without flanking columns or
   pilasters, is another common
   motif in his repertoire.

4 The simple Classical screen
   flanked by (3) above, as at B,
   or the triumphal arch as at A,
   will be found in the court
   houses. He was fond of
   creating overlapping, double
   readings (see south front of his
   Custom House).

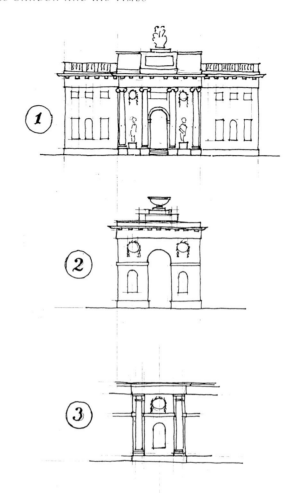

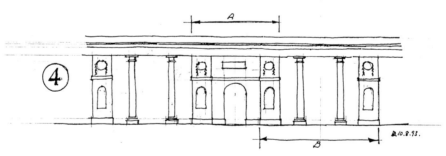

Gandon's design habits

opposite *Joseph Deane Bourke* by *Sir Joshua Reynolds*
(courtesy National Gallery of Ireland)

bition in the new Somerset House. Those who attended were deeply shocked, and a series of violent letters appeared in the newspapers. The Antique Room was stocked with casts of the more famous statues of the pagan world, and some were displayed on the staircases. A personal appeal to Sir Joshua Reynolds begged him to remove these statues, which were 'the terror of every decent woman'. A painting by William Peters was attacked on the grounds that any husband with his wife and children would, for decency's sake, have to keep away from that part of the room where the painting was hanging. The outcry against Peters came at an unfortunate time, for he was then preparing for ordination. Northcote was also strongly attacked, but the statues were the chief target of the majority of the complaints. One correspondent makes the typical remark 'that for a woman to have the pleasure of studying the royal portrait she must forfeit her claim to delicacy'.[43]

THE ROYAL EXCHANGE

The first fruits of Gandon's meeting with Lord Charlemont during his early years with Chambers were gathered when Lord Charlemont recommended him to the Rev Joseph Deane Bourke, then a dean of the Established Church who may be identified as a subsequent Archbishop of Tuam and Earl of Mayo. Mulvany says Deane Bourke had first consulted Gandon about some alterations he proposed for the Palace and Deanery at Ferns. Here Mulvany is again mistaken, for, as John O'Donovan has pointed out, it was unlikely that a dean would be allowed to meddle with the Bishop's Palace. On going further into the matter, O'Donovan identifies Mrs Scanlin's house at Killaloe as the original Deanery where the Rev Joseph Deane Bourke was living in 1768, for he was then the Dean of Killaloe and not of Ferns. The house as it stands has little or no relationship with any designs Gandon may have drawn up for the Dean of Killaloe. No drawings are known to have survived, and there is no evidence of any work resulting from their association.[44]

The dean, however, encouraged Gandon in his next Irish venture. This was the preparation of a design for the competition for a new Royal Exchange for

Dublin. Like many Irish affairs, this competition had its genesis in circumstances typically remote from their outcome. We must go back to 1763, when a Mr Thomas Allen was appointed Taster of Wines in Ireland. This was one of many sinecures in the gift of the government, and the appointment was by patent. Whatever the position may have been worth, Mr Allen decided to augment it by requiring a fee of ten shillings per ton on all imported wines. He might have succeeded in his bluff had he followed the custom of the age and offered some measure of compensation to the more influential of those concerned. However, the overbearing manner in which he made his demand alarmed the Dublin merchants, who formed an association against him. They appointed a committee of twenty-one to represent them, and having by subscription raised a large sum of money, they took Mr Allen to court. Much to their surprise, they won their case without any great delay or expense. Perhaps Mr Allen had also neglected those lawyers who were concerned in the affair. The merchants were now left with a considerable sum of money on their hands, and were not too sure what to do with it. But the elation of their victory had somewhat enlarged their self-esteem, and in the end they decided to build a commercial exchange for themselves. The money in hand was to form the nucleus of a fund for this purpose, and during the next few years they added considerably to it by running lotteries. In 1765 they received a gift of £8,000[45] towards the project from George III, and by November 1766 the sum at their disposal amounted to £55,173.13.0.[46]

They now proceeded to look for a site, and settled on a plot of ground on Cork Hill. Here had stood Cork House and Lucas's Coffee House, but these buildings had been demolished, and there was a scheme in mind at that time to erect here the statue of George I which used to stand on Essex Bridge. The merchants had some precedent, for their choice as the gardens of Cork House had been used by them as an exchange around 1760. It had been an open exchange, with colonnades under which they could shelter in wet weather. The arrangement was not very suitable for the Irish climate, and the merchants remembered this when they came to draft their advertisement announcing a competition for plans for the new exchange. By November 1767, they had obtained a grant of the ground, and in July 1768 they published their invitation to architects to compete for the new building. It was an excellent advertisement, setting out their minimum requirements and one likely to ensure the greatest variety of designs. It ran:

> Dublin, July 17th 1768
>   The Trustees of the Royal Exchange, intent on obtaining the most elegant and commodious plan, of which the Ground appropriated for that purpose is capable, and disposed at the same time to take this opportunity of exciting a laudable Spirit of Emulation among persons of Genius in architecture, do hereby promise the following Premiums for the three best

Plans which shall be approved of, viz. For the Best, One Hundred Guineas. The Second, being the Performance of a different Artist, Sixty Guineas. The Third, on the same condition, Forty Guineas.

The Trustees are of opinion, and find it to be the general sense that all Circumstances considered, a covered Exchange will be preferable to one open in the centre.

It is meant that the Building shall have two grand Fronts, the Principal one to Parliament Street, the other to Castle Street, and it is wished to be so contrived to accommodate the Merchants with a very fine large Room to assemble in, distinct from the great Hall, for the Purpose of the Exchange, a Room or two of moderate Size for Committees to meet in would also be desirable.

The Trustees do not mean to have Shops, or any Rooms in the Building to let, unless vaults, which might open to Exchange Alley without Inconvenience. There is a map of the Ground and Avenues leading thereto, in the Hands of Christopher Deey in Crampton Court which any person, who has occasion may view and take a copy of.

The Plans intended for this Competition must be delivered to him on or before the 29th. September next.

Signed by order of the Trustees, CHRIST. DEEY, Reg.[47]

This advertisement may have been published in the London papers also, but it is more likely that Gandon became interested in the competition through his client, the Rev Joseph Deane Bourke. Gandon, with his predilection for competitions, would have been anxious to take part, particularly as this one seems to have aroused great interest in the compact society of architects and artists in London. The closing date left them little time because of the uncertainties and delays in communication between Dublin and London, and some protest must have been made, for very soon the date for the presentation of the plans was put forward. Early in September, this notice appeared in the Dublin papers:

Dublin, August 31st 1768

The Trustees of the Royal Exchange have resolved to prolong the Time for receiving the Plans to the 1st. January next, after which day they will not admit any to the Competition for the Premiums offered in their Preceding Advertisement. It is intended to exhibit all the Plans to public Inspection, from the fifth of January to the first of February, when the Trustees will proceed to a Determination of their Merits, in which due Regard will be had to the Sense of Persons of the most universally acknowledged Taste in Architecture, and unquestionable Impartiality and Honour.

A Map of the Ground will be immediately forwarded to London and fixed up in the Royal Exchange there.[48]

At this time, Gandon was designing Shire Hall, so the promise of an additional contract must have coloured his hopes. When we remember the efforts he made to qualify himself for the first gold medal offered by the Royal Academy, it seems clear that he was convinced of his competence to take it, should he be presented with the opportunity to do so.

The impression which comes across the centuries is that of a man who believed himself to be master of the art of architecture as it was then practised, who saw his grasp of the elements of this art as superior to that of his colleagues, and who was thoroughly at home with the current conventions. Many of us have come across practitioners of the arts whose belief in the superiority of their own vision seems to run ahead of their performance. Gandon was that rare phenomenon: an artist who, with reason, was assured of his own merit.

The autumn of 1768 must have been, for Gandon, a period of calmly savoured and well-merited success, and he appears to have made full use of the extended time. He kept in touch with the Rev Joseph Deane Bourke, and, on his advice, refused to trust his designs to the post, but sent them over through a forwarding agent in Chester. They arrived in Dublin on 1st December, and were presented to the committee of the Exchange by his influential friend in person. No time was lost in letting Gandon know how things were going, as that evening the Dean wrote to him.

Dear Sir, – I received your letter yesterday, as also one from Mr. Smith of Chester with advice of the case containing your drawings and designs, which I received this day, and taking the earliest opportunity of acquainting you of their safe arrival.

I have already shown your designs for the Royal Exchange to some friends of mine, good judges, but not of the Profession who approve extremely of your plans, &c.,&c. Your front to Castle-street is elegant, and that to Parliament – street is not less to be admired; yet by one it was thought that some of the figures and ornaments in the latter might have been spared, as, by that means the general beauties and proportions of the whole would strike the eye to greater advantage.

This is a matter in which I do not take upon myself to determine, but as you have communicated this affair to me as a friend, I thought you would not take it amiss to acquaint you of these observations, that, in case any alterations should be required you may take your measures accordingly.

Your disposition of the ground is highly approved of. It cannot be enlarged notwithstanding any plan for that purpose. You have lighted it extremely well, which was a very difficult point to gain considering how much you were hampered on all sides. Upon the whole, I must say, without any compliment, that you have shown great judgment in your designs, and displayed true taste and genius in the construction of it.

One observation more I should make, which is, that it was thought that you had not taken sufficient notice of the declivity of the ground.

You see how I write to you with the candour of a friend: I have now enclosed a map of the ground, with the particular falls marked, which you will accordingly note.

The letter goes on to welcome Gandon's observations, and mentions his plans for the Deanery House. It concludes:

Some other plans for our Exchange have come to hand, one from Mr. Ivory of Northwitch, but none, I think, which should occasion uneasiness.

I remain, your obedient servant, Joseph Deane Bourke.[49]

Gandon's reply was clearly intended for the eyes of the committee, and he appears to have taken pains with its composition to make it as complimentary to the merchants as possible. The Rev Joseph Deane Bourke was away from Dublin, and it was only on his return, perhaps towards the end of the month, that he received it and then mislaid it. He was, however, prompt to find out how the competition was going, and to pass on to Gandon the criticisms of his designs.

Dear Sir, – I have been the greater part of my time in the country since I addressed you last, or you should have heard from me long before this. On my return, a few days since, I received yours of the 2nd. of January and take the earliest opportunity of communicating to you whatever I could collect that was material upon the subject connected with our Exchange.

The plans are all now put up at the Exhibition Room for public inspection. It is a most elegant and entertaining exhibition. Enclosed I send you a list of your competitors, no less than sixty-our, among whom, were I to determine, I should not hesitate, without any compliment, to give you the laurel. However, as I would altogether rely on my own judgment, or depend on it singly, I have consulted some friends, good judges of architecture, and have also taken the observations of some of the most eminent of the architects here (but not formally consulting the latter) these I also send you enclosed, which I would have you answer as soon as possible, in a distinct paper from your letter to me, and addressed to the gentlemen of the Committee. Something to this purpose:

'GENTLEMEN — Having received an account of some objections

to the plans I had the honour of submitting to you for a Royal Exchange, I hope you will pardon the liberty I take in endeavouring to obviate these objections, and in proposing some alterations, in which, should they meet your approbation, I shall deem myself very happy indeed, &c.,&c.,&c.'

I must mention to you that I acquainted some of the merchants that I received a letter from you complimenting them highly on the noble spirit and good judgment they have shown on the occasion, and hoping that the people of England will follow so laudable an example; at which they appeared much gratified, and requested to see the letter, which, unfortunately, I had lost: therefore I think if you were to write just such another, accompanied with your answers to the observations enclosed it might have a good effect; for even where real merit does exist, some little address is necessary; but this, of course, just as you think fit.

Amongst all the plans which are exhibited, six are generally allowed to be superior to the rest, which I have marked; but were I to say which one of the three, it should be Gandon, and the three best should be Gandon, Stephens, and J.W.L., which letters I am informed, is Wright or Wrighton, lately returned from Rome. This latter design really has great merit.

After some further remarks, he signs himself, 'Your obedient servant, Joseph Deane Bourke'.[50]

Altogether, it was a communication which must have occasioned in Gandon rather mixed feelings. Well-meaning, generous and friendly, the busy Rev Joseph must have seemed to Gandon to be dangerously out of control. However, he drafted a new letter, and setting out the heads of the various objections, he dealt with each. With the advice of his Reverend friend in mind, he prefaced it with some remarks complimentary to the merchants, but there is nothing obsequious about them. His conclusion, however, with its undertones of impatience, can have left the committee in no doubt as to his attitude towards them:

I believe it is pretty general that most architects would rather chuse to reserve some Trifles to themselves, regarding the execution of their Designs, till they have received some assurance of their conducting them. Upon the whole, I cannot conceive at present but that the Objections, etc., made to the intended Exchange may as easily be removed as they have been made; and submit, with all Due Deference and esteem, the Alterations to the Determination and Consideration of the worthy Committee, to whom I have the Honour to subscribe myself, their most Obedient and most Humble servant.[51]

Gandon's energetic friend, leaving nothing to chance, again tackled the committee. Indeed his enthusiasm is in odd contrast to Gandon's procrastination, for Gandon's letter did not reach Dublin until late in February, when the damage had already been done. If the Rev Joseph felt anything of this, no hint of it was allowed to appear in his next letter to Gandon, which, from his reference to the the Malton letter, must have been written a few days after 25th February. He relayed his activities to date, and then broke the bad news:

> But 'party', the predominant genius of the times, I fear, has crept into the councils, even of the Committee. Mr. Cooley is the person now talked of for the first premium; if so, it is hard to say how they mean to dispose of the rest, and it is now publicly reported that this was the point determined on before any plans were obtained.
>
> It is said that Mr. Cooley is a friend of Mr. Mylnes, whose interest with the citizens of London has great weight with some of the merchants here. How far this may be the case I do not take upon myself to say, nor do I wish to have my name mentioned, but this is the public report, which I thought might be of some satisfaction to you to be acquainted with, as, I imagine, you must be somewhat anxious about the determination of this affair.

He goes on to mention the Malton letter (about which more later) and the next committee meeting, and ends with: 'You may depend upon it, nothing shall be wanted on my part to promote and to do you all the service I can on the occasion. I am, Sir, Your very sincere Friend, Joseph Deane Bourke.'

There is some indirect evidence that Gandon took the news badly. He was probably acquainted with Mylne, and must have known Thomas Cooley, as they were of an age. (Cooley was born in 1740.) They had attended the meetings and the exhibitions of the Society of Arts, from which Cooley had obtained a premium in 1753, before Gandon became a student. He was the son of a William Cooley, who was in London in 1730, and who was thought to have been an Irishman. Thomas Cooley was first apprenticed to a carpenter, and after his studies at the Society of Arts, became a student of Robert Mylne. Robert Mylne, too, had spent some time in Rome, and on his return he found a competition in progress for a new Blackfriars bridge, and submitted the winning design. There was a public rumpus over the award in which Dr Johnson took part. The substance of the controversy seems to have been as to whether semi-circular arches were more stable than the elliptical arches of Mylne's design.

In this correspondence, Gandon's design received frequent, and on the whole, favourable mention. Citizens signing themselves by such pseudonyms as 'Exchange', 'Vitruvius', 'Civis', 'X.Y' and 'Tickletoby' held forth, primarily on the choice of the site at Cork Hill and when that subject was exhausted on the actual designs. Some were affronted by domes, others by plans derived from temples, and 'Exchange' was particularly annoyed by those circular plans 'like amphitheatres'. On 25th February, 'Scientifical's' letter appeared, and from then on, the references to Gandon's design were both more detailed and uniformly hostile. It is an interesting letter, for apart from the deep malice which it reveals, it is one of the few contemporary sources from which we can attempt to reconstruct the lost design.

> ... Having frequently visited the Exhibition, I saw heard and made Remarks in a cursory way as others but without descanting on this fine Drawing or that beautiful Shade, as most have done; for it did not appear to me that everything consisted in a fine Picture, without Disposition, Proportion, or Strength. However most Judgments seemed to Fluctuate until the London Designs should arrive.
>
> In this manner the Public continued above a Fortnight when some Particulars, and even some of the Committee from what Motive I know not, began to extol a certain Design; this raised my Curiosity considerably, as I had not seen any Thing so extraordinary so as to attract Notice in that more than others. (The Colouring only excepted) this I looked upon as a mistaken Notion and suspend my Judgment until the others should be exhibited; but to show how far Prepossession or Prejudice will take Place, a few days after (when most were satisfied with viewing the new Plans) some as formerly continued to point at the former coloured Design and lest I should have overlooked its Perfections, I took proper Opportunities to Examine it more minutely; and acknowledge the Ground Plan is much better laid out for the Purpose than most that were Exhibited (yet there are Plans much more to Advantage than this) but the Floor not being on a Level, and the Merchants obliged to go down Three steps to a small Area of 50 Foot square in confining that respectable Set of Men to too small a Space; had the Area been large, and raised one step, it would be much more eligible.
>
> The placing of Two massy and lumpish Peers on the Floor, at least 15 or 16 Foot square supposed to support a Dome, takes up too much Room and renders a disagreeable Contrast to all the Inside, and in such Peers to enclose small circular Stairs to convey to the greatest Room, is very injudicious and out of all Rule in such a Building, and would certainly be as dark as they are ill designed and misplaced, for such small Stairs can barely admit of any more than one Person up or down, and having no breathing Places (or Half-pace) by continually winding 40 or 50 steps high must both make the Head giddy, and prevent a free Respiration; and the greatest Room to which those Stairs lead is by no Means adequate for the

Purpose, being 53 Feet long and 21 Feet wide, besides its being injudiciously lighted, as all the Exchange by this Design would be; for no man of Experience would ever light by Lanthorns, Dalmations, or Egyptian Windows, when in his Power to light from the Sides, where Experience hath taught that all over lights confuse the Sight, and are hurtful to the Eyes, whereas Side lights have the contrary Effects; such Lights should never be introduced unless by absolute necessity; as is the Case of the Parliament house, which have been sufficiently explained by a late Critic.

An Attic Story over the inner Columns is altogether absurd, for such a story is never placed but on the Outside of very large Buildings, at a great Distance from the Eye, which at least looks heavy, but must be much more so on the inside where Delicacy should be one of the Principal Objects of View.

The Two Fronts consisting of one entire Order in Height, I much approve of: and that to Castle Street of Pairs of columns is the best Part of this whole Design could it be Seen at all in one and at any Proper distance as its Original (St Paul's West Portico) but the intermediate Spaces of the Ionic Order and Niches are out of all Character and the Front to Parliament Street, intended for the grandest is much degenerated from true Taste; the Number of Pilasters on each Side from Four middle Columns have too much of a Sameness and appear too flat, and the Two Heroes of Neptune and Liberty, are so improperly placed and monstrously loaded, that they more represent Slavery and Bondage than Liberty and Commerce, and viewing them reminds me of the Two Giants in Guildhall London.

The Spaces Between the Columns and Pilasters are very improperly filled with Niches: and the Medallions (like so many Platters) represent more the Inside of a Gallery than the Outside of a Public Building; for who can stand so near in so public a Street without Danger of Life and Limb, to know what is portraid on these Medals.

This Whole Design have no Windows from the Outside (the Ornament of all covered Buildings) is like a Man without Eyes, and in viewing it one must certainly entertain a very gloomy Idea of its Inside, especially of the Walk, or Ambulatory behind the Niches.

The Balustrade over the Entablature is proper, but take the whole Outside of this Design it only represents a high Wall decorated for the most part injudiciously ... the ill designed Crowd of Columns and Pediments on the T to surround a small Dome is as Heavy as that from which it is taken, at Bloomsbury Church in London, and no One till now ever attempted to Copy after its Designer, Mr. H(awksmo)re ... Nevertheless that its outward Appearance looks heavy, it might have passed with the Vulgar and Injudicious had this architect not drawn a Section; but here his Genius has betrayed his Want of Judgment, to see the Appearance of a Stone or Brick dome on the Outside, and that placed on Beams of Wood in the Clear or Inside of the Walls is absurd, injudicious and unprecedented, and the two little Arch vaults or Domes that crowns the whole (cannot in my Opinion) be executed in Wood, Brick or Stone.

To conclude it appears that this architect is more a Man of Fancy than of sound Judgment, and to adopt this Design will not only appear we are void of Knowledge of architecture, but will create a Notion that we are liable to be imposed upon by every Absurdity sent us, without being capable of examining into their Faults.

Thus so far I have essayed to give my Sentiments on this applauded Design, and as I have no other View in pointing out Errors than to be serviceable to the Public, that a just Taste among our young architects may as near as possible be established, and the worthy Gentlemen engaged in the Exchange Informed, and if received with any Degree of Approbation, shall give some Observations on others;
SCIENTIFICAL[52]

Within three days, this letter, with further letters of a similar tone, was published in the form of a pamphlet entitled 'An ESSAY on the several DESIGNS exhibited for the ROYAL EXCHANGE', and advertised in the newspapers. It seems to have been a characteristic of the Malton family to indulge in long letters, much at Gandon's expense, and to give them a certain permanence by collecting them and publishing them in book form.

Thomas Malton (the elder) first appears as the proprietor of an upholsterer's shop in the Strand, London. His work would naturally introduce him to the fitting out of the houses of the nobility and of public buildings, and being a man with an interest in matters of art, he would have been inclined to attach himself to that body of artists and architects, which, as purveyors of culture, enjoyed prestige and a certain degree of security. Perhaps the necessity to earn a living prevented him from entering into an apprenticeship in a regular way; but he educated himself, and forged the proof of his erudition in an abstruse and excessively complex work entitled *A Complete Treatise on Perspective in Theory and Practice on the Principles of Doctor Brook Taylor*, in 1775. He had three sons: Thomas, born in 1748, and William and James, born sometime about 1763.

Thomas Malton (the elder) was in Dublin in the early part of 1769, and apart from the conviction, both contemporary and subsequent that he was 'Scientifical', we know of no alternative candidate. It was a subtle piece of hatchet work, determined in its malice to prejudice both the committee and the public against Gandon's design. Maurice Craig points to the jealousy with which the less qualified regarded those regularly trained architects, and this is very true. Professional jealously has in its time produced surprising actions and reactions. There seems, however, to be something more here, some spleen directed solely towards Gandon. The only guess which is hazarded at this time is that Thomas Malton (the younger) is said to have been Gandon's apprentice, articled to him in 1765 when Gandon first set up in practice.[53] Thomas's five-year term would have been coming to an end in 1769 or 1770. If all had gone well, his father should have been the last person to attack his son's employer. In our ignorance of that relationship, we must conclude that it was sufficiently uncomfortable to engender in Malton (the elder) a deep resentment, a resentment which, either by chance or design in its manifestation, seems to have placed a serious check on the development of Gandon's professional career.

'Scientifical' must have been gratified when, a fortnight later, Thomas Cooley's design was chosen. Gandon received the second premium of sixty guineas, and his friend, Thomas Sandby, the third of forty guineas. But even the reduction of Gandon to second place did not suffice, for some days later, in part of a letter signed 'M', we find the following reference to Gandon, rather in Malton's style: 'At least the Committee determined right in favour of Mr. Cooley, but I am not quite so clear in regard to Mr. Gandon who appears to me no more than a fine Draughtsman without any idea of the execution.' It did not suffice either for Thomas Malton's youngest son, James, who, some thirty years later in his *Views of the City of Dublin*, falsifies the record by demoting Gandon's design to third place, and his premium to thirty guineas.

The building work pushed ahead without delay. In August, the viceroy laid the first stone in the presence of Church and State, and gave thirty pounds to the workmen on the site. During the following October, a strange skull was found on the site:

> A remarkably large skull was found in digging the foundations for the Royal Exchange on Cork Hill; and from the extraordinary size of the teeth, it is imagined it was that of a giant.
>
> An eminent goldsmith has got one of the teeth taken out of the large head, found in digging the foundation for the Royal Exchange, Cork Hill; it weighs eighteen pennyweights and a half troy, which is near an ounce avoirdupois; it is allowed to be the largest ever seen in this Kingdom.[54]

The whereabouts of this skull appears to be unknown. But what can we say? In two centuries time what will be said about us, for just down from Cork Hill we have buried the early history of Dublin beneath two large octagonal concrete cylinders.

ARCHITECTURAL NOTE

There has always been a certain amount of curiosity about Gandon's design for the Royal Exchange, for quite apart from the fact that it would now be Dublin's City Hall were it not for the intrusion of interested parties, it must, in its own right, form a significant link in his development as an architect.

The attempted reconstruction given here is merely a sketch which embodies the features suggested by our two main sources: firstly, Gandon's own reply to the committee, and secondly, the letter from 'Scientifical'. It may serve as a framework for further modification by others, or on the discovery of new evidence. Certainly, it is not as Gandon would have drafted it, with his sensitivity for proportion and significant detail. But if it is broadly, if crudely, representative of Gandon's submission, it may have some value.

Gandon's reply to the committee is detailed, and, at the same time, tantalisingly imprecise. Perhaps we may now summarise the information on Gandon's design contained in the letter from 'Scientifical' and in Gandon's draft.

The plan had an open central space, fifty feet square, lying three steps below the level of the ambulatory The ambulatory was vaulted, how deeply we do not know; and was screened from the central space by Ionic columns. These carried an attic storey, and here there were diocletian windows lighting the

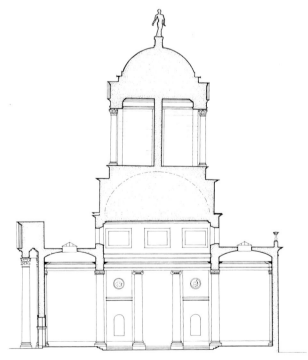

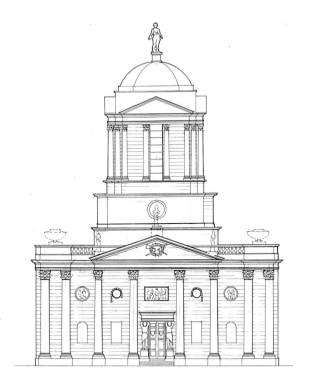

The Royal Exchange, 1768-69
above Façade   *below* Plan   *opposite* Cross-section

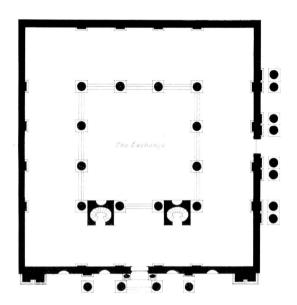

main space. There were two circular stairs enclosed within large piers, some fifteen or sixteen feet square, and we may infer that these were adjacent to the main entrance. These stairs led up to a room fifty-three-feet long and twenty-one-feet wide. This room was top-lit, and we may suppose the ambulatories were top-lit too.

The elevation to Castle Street consisted of one entire order, with the columns of the portico arranged in pairs, similar to those of the west portico of St Paul's Cathedral. The elevation to Parliament Street consisted of a portico of four Corinthian Columns, with flanking projections faced with ionic pilasters. There were niches and plaques on the front wall, but no windows. The absence of windows described by 'Scientifical' contradicts the mention of windows by Gandon. The main entrance was flanked by colossal figures. The balustrade on top runs behind the pediment. It is not clear where the Vitruvian scroll was situated, nor is it clear where the 'subordinate or Ionic Order' was introduced. The flat over the central break is also obscure.

The superimposed temple is similar to that on the Church of St George in Bloomsbury, and has been copied unchanged into the sketch. Gandon, of course, would have modified it in his own inimitable way. It represents a vertical projection of the central space, for we are told it rested directly above the columns surrounding this space. Perhaps they were double, as the single columns shown seem insufficient to support the superimposed mass. This temple is in the Corinthian Order with porticos. A twelve-foot-high bronze figure surmounts the dome. The form of 'the two little arch vaults or domes' mentioned by 'Scientifical' as crowning the whole is also unclear. There is mention of statuary, probably on the pediment, and in the spaces of the main elevations.

The sketches, though put together in broad conformity with the detail above, are clearly lacking Gandon's fine sense of proportion and sureness of touch. They should be considered only as an approximation of the main features of his design.

OUT AND ABOUT

In the Spring of 1769, with the disappointing affair of the Royal Exchange behind him, but with his plans for the Shire Hall in Nottingham going well, we find Gandon enjoying more pleasurable interests. His acquaintance with the painter Richard Wilson seems to have ripened into friendship. Perhaps Wilson's gruff and abrupt manner attracted Gandon, who appears to have needed the company of strong-minded people. They also shared a common interest in the convivial life of the taverns and coffee houses around Covent Garden. Gandon frequently visited the painter's studio, watching him at work and discussing matters of art. We are told by Farrington, the British diarist, that he had, at that time, made etchings of some of Wilson's paintings, and this work must have been a relief after the demanding labour of preparing the architectural plates for his *Vitruvius* It is likely that he carried out at least some of this work in Sandby's studio in Poland Street, in the house so familiar to him from the days of his apprenticeship with Chambers. Some of his evenings too may have been spent at the home of a Miss Eleanor Smullen whom he married the following year.

However, he did not spend all of his evenings with his future wife. The gregarious Gandon had never been content with a conventional way of life, and the bohemian style of the younger London artists seems to have held a continuing fascination for him, distant though it was from the cultivation of the nobility where his real ambition lay. He seems to have been confident that he could have the best of both worlds. (We have a glimpse of that in his relations with Sir Samuel Hillier.) But the description of a weekend in May 1769 by Thomas Jones, an artist, opens another window on the private life of James Gandon.

Thomas Jones was, like Wilson, a Welshman of good family. He had been educated for the Church, but became a pupil of Wilson in 1762, and first exhibited independently in 1765.

1769, Friday, May 5th. I embarked with my friend *Mortimer, J. Gandon* the architect, one *Ewen* mate of an Indiaman, and two others on board the *Seahorse* a pleasure boat of about eight ton burthen, belonging to three of the party – the same day we got a little below Gravesend – The next sailed round the Buoy of the Nore, and came to anchor in the harbour of Queensborough in the afternoon. Sunday, 7th. we all went to Church, where Mayor (an Oister Dredger) with a black cut-wig on his head and an Indian handkerchief about his neck, sat in great state having a large mace placed on a cushion before him – After the service was over, we returned on board, and dined on a boiled leg of lamb and spinage, hot lobsters etc. which our Seamen had contrived notwithstanding the inconveniences of our Little cabin to dress very suitable to our Appetites – The next day we landed with our Guns, leaving one man to look after the boat, and marched up the Country in search of wild fowl or anything that came our way – We had not gone far before we saw a number of people assembled at a cricket match – eager to partake of a favourite Diversion, Mortimer, our Captain, pushed forward with all his speed and the rest followed – to our great surprise when we arrived at the Ground we found the party dispersed excepting a few Old Men, women and children – Upon Enquiry we were told that the Cricketers had watched our landing and seeing a Set of Armed men in Jackets and Trousers advance in that formidable manner, had taken us for a Pressgang – but as we convinced them to the contrary they soon reassembled from their hiding places – We joined in the Sports, treated them plentifully with grog and in the Evening returned to our boat to sleep – the Day following we went on shore again and hearing that there was a fair *at Sittingburn* proceeded thither – on entering the town we caused the same alarm as we had the day before, but that soon subsided, and having engaged a front room in one of the Capital Inns, ordered an elegant dinner – while this was getting ready we sent for a Barber, and on Mortimer, (whose strong black beard he was first of all to encounter) remarking that his hand trembled very much the old man replied, 'Ah, Captain, I have been a barber above 30 years on board a man of war but I always took care to prime well before I fired – and please your honour, I would not like to foresake a good old Custom' – 'I understand you Old boy', replied Mortimer and ordered a bottle of brandy – After the old barber had finished about one third of it, he went through his manoeuvres with great dexterity – while we were at dinner, it appeared we had attracted the attention of both sexes of all ranks, who crowded about the windows and were as much at a loss what to make of us, as our landlord and his waiters were, I believe, – indeed having been huddled together for four days and four nights without taking off our Clothes – Our figures did not well correspond with our Style of living – To ingratiate ourselves we threw up the Sashes and handed out Wine and Punch to all who would accept of it – We then sailed forth in our dirty Jackets and Trousers, and met with many handsome well dressed Lasses who were not afraid or ashamed to parade with us up and down the Fair – and whom we presented with Gloves, Ribbands and such trifles – We then returned to the Inn, ordered Tea and Coffee, sent for a Couple of Fiddlers and mustering twelve or fourteen Couples including the Ladies with the Brothers and Cousins and commenced Country dances to the no small amusement of both the town and Country people who stood in Crowds about the Doors and Windows gazing at so ridiculous a Spectacle. This lasted until a genteel cold Collation was introduced which we all sat down to in the lightest Spirits and when our new Acquaintances thought it time to withdraw, retired completely exhausted to Rest – the next morning we paid the bill of the house which amounted to something more than two Guineas each and immediately set off for Queensborough where we found our boat determined to sail with the first of the Tide for London – the Wind was against us and the weather threatening and the Masters of the Fishing vessels who were waiting for the London market said everything to dissuade us from the Attempt – but we were Pot valiant and wanted to show what we dared to do Finding us fixeing in our resolution they described the Landmarks on the Essex Coast which were to be observed in steering through the Swach Way and wished us a safe voyage.

The Swach Way *as I think it was called is a narrow Channel or Cut across the Spit* of Sand that extends from the mainland to the Buoy at the Nore, which is placed at the point of outward extremity of the Sands as a guide to Ships entering the River Thames – Through this Swach Way small vessels at certain times of the Tide pass and repass to avoid the Circuitous navigation round the Buoy – The Buoy is a large Buoy strongly moored with Chains, with two lights burning at night. After we had taken in all the reefs in the Sails and well secured the Hatches – off we set – We had not been long clear of the harbour when the Wind, which from the first was unfavourable, began to freshen and the sea run high – we continued however, steering as we were directed, with an Obstinate perseverance even after it was too dark to distinguish the land marks – Brown the eldest and most steady Seaman was at the Helm, the Other, who was Younger, and more active, stood at the head and with the boat hook kept sounding every time the Vessel plunged. Mortimer and Ewen assisted the boy in managing the Sails – I sat with old Brown in the Stern while Gandon and the Others lay sick and insensible at the bottom of the Boat – it blew now a perfect storm – the whistleing of the Wind through the Shrouds – the bellowing waves dashing over the Deck and the Spray flying over the Mast head – the hissing of the distant breakers – and above all – the darkness of the night – produced a Scene the most Awful and tremendous! What a contrast between our Situation now and the preceding Evening! – The man at the head at length called out that we had but four feet of water and that he was afraid that we had lost the Channel – Old Brown likewise said he thought the rudder at one time touched the ground – and I could overhear him, in a low voice utter this short ejaculation, 'God provide for my poor wife and family' – We were all now dreadfully alarmed and the general Cry was About Ship – 'About she goes,' answered old Brown clapping the Helm hard alee – At that Instant I fully expected sh'd been upset, and all lost, but our little lively Bark soon recovered herself and we steered back to Queensborough guided by the lights in the Town, and flying as I may say, on the Wings of the Wind soon got into smooth water – we reentered the harbour after about three hours absence, amid the Cheers and Congratulations of our old friends, who gave us every assistance in bringing our little vessel to her former Station – The Master of one of the largest Smacks under whose leeside we were safely and snugly moored observing us to be in a very wet and drooping Condition very kindly asked us up into his Cabin where he said he had a good fire and where we might dry and refresh ourselves in a comfortable manner – Our seasick companions were by this time a little revived and we all accepted of his friendly Invitation, and staid to partake of a good hot Supper which he had prepared for some of his brother Captains, who all joined in praising not only our Courage and Address but the goodness of our Boat which they said must have done Wonders. Indeed I don't know which were most grateful, the Compliments to ourselves or those to our Vessel as we had all conceived such an Affection for her... but to return – Having sufficiently recruited our Spirits we took leave of our Hospitable Entertainer and his friends, and slipping down into our own little Cabin, slept soundly till the next morning, when we again weighed, and after a very pleasant Sail arrived at Blackfriars bridge in the Evening – [55]

It is disappointing that Jones has so little to say about his companions, apart from contrasting Mortimer on deck and in charge while Gandon lay in the bottom of the boat. His allusions to Gandon, both above and later, are neutral, and it is likely that Mortimer's friends and associates formed a sort of little court around him, some of the members of which might have little in common with each other. Their purpose was social, and they frequented the coffee houses and gin parlours in the vicinity of Covent Garden. Then as now, the good fellow was affable, bibulous and of a daring spirit. The London of their times was rough and noisy; street fighting was common, prostitutes paced the footpaths in the evenings, and in some places, if their approaches were ignored by a passer-by, he was likely to be attacked and beaten up. Hungry youths lurked in alleys awaiting the passing of the solitary reveller, whom they would rob and strip of his finery. Aggression was a common virtue, and anybody who was unfit to defend himself could only look forward to disaster at the hands of the desperate, the common thieves, the pressgang, the excise men, the prostitutes' protectors, and the bands of young blades who infested the streets after dark and even during the day. Another adventure described by Thomas Jones illustrates the hazards of life at that time:

1769, June 8th. Went on board the Duke of Glocester Indiaman with Mortimer, Marchi, Lawrenson, Farrington and Weston – in Coming ashore late at night we were attacked by a Custom House boat who wanted to board us supposing we had been on a smuggling party – Upon which a fray ensued and we beat them off – in the action Mortimer very nearly lost one of his hands, by a stroke that was aimed at him with a cutlass, which however fell short of him and I received a desperate blow from an

Oar which knocked me overboard, and gave me a dreadful Cut over the Eye – I was picked up immediately by my Companions and we all landed at Towerhill – What with loss of blood and darkness of the night I was so faint and confused that I could not keep up with the rest but with the assistance of a Watchman got to a night house in a narrow street called Darkness-Lane, and having tied up the wound which bled excessively, as well as Circumstances would admit of – Went to bed.

The next morning by frequent and repeated fomentation I unfolded by degrees the bandages, now become as one mass of clotted Gore and with the greatest Solicitude took off the last as I did not know whether I had not lost my Eye – When I found that safe, I was easy, and clapping a Plaster upon the Wound, and tying a black Barcelona Handkerchief over it, took a boat which landed me at the Temple Stairs, where I got into a chair with a bundle of Asparagus under each Arm as a present for the Worthy woman of the house where I lodged.

Passing by the new Church in the Strand on my way home I was met by Gandon the architect, who seeing a most grotesque figure came swaggering along, peeped in, and recognizing my person stopped the chair, in order to have his full indulgence of mirth at my Expense – He was going to dine with a party at the Devil Tavern in which I myself was engaged, but had not recollected it at the time. As soon as I had cleaned myself – I repaired to the Rondevous where I found Mortimer, Nat, Marchant, Gandon, Evan Lloyd, the Parson, &c. and after dinner my eye dressed by a young Surgeon who was of the Company – the next day I was confined to bed by a slight fever in which situation I was found by Fulke Greville, Esq...[56]

James Gandon,
drawing, after Clerisseau
(courtesy Irish Arts Review)

Marriage and Family

James Gandon was married on 26th July 1770 to Miss Eleanor Smullen of St Paul's parish, Covent Garden.[57] She was probably a friend of the Sandby family, for she was a witness at the marriage in the same year of Samuel Aubery to Arabella Venables, a relation of Thomas Sandby's wife, Elizabeth Venables.

It would appear that Gandon's marriage marked a turning point in his fortunes, because from this time on, his prospects clearly diminished. Certainly, the easy decline during the 1770s is apparent towards the end of the decade, when we find him associated with Athenian Stuart, a man whose work was already undermining the principles of Roman architecture to which Gandon was attached.

We are given no hint in *The Life* of the sources of Gandon's finances at that time We are told he bought a house in Broad Street, which, though nothing like the fashionable town houses of the city, would have been commodious enough. As his family grew, there would be increasing demands on his income, and it is here that the mystery lies, for his known work would scarcely have provided a sufficient income for his family and allow him to continue to indulge his fondness for the convivial company of his artist friends. Any attempt to explain his lifestyle must suppose some hidden source of income, such as ghosting for other architects. If his wife had come from a well-to-do family, we would have been told.

It was not, from any angle, a favourable decade for a young and comparatively unknown architect to develop his practice, for although the nobility and gentry continued to build, they relied on the older and better-known members of the profession. But Gandon was not completely idle. Indeed, by the end of the sixties he must have had sufficient work in hand to allow him to contemplate marriage. He had time, too, for other activities more to his taste, in connection with the arts and also of a social kind. However, they were not the kind of activities calculated to advance his prospects with the class that mattered, and a more prudent Gandon could have spent his days more profitably in the cultivation of the satellites of the great families. It was not that Gandon lacked connections: he had his apprenticeship with Chambers behind him, giving him a favoured entry to the world of patronage, and his friend Paul Sandby was brother to a favourite of the king. It would seem that his conviction of his own superiority in his art was the dominant factor in his failure during his time in England. He continued to expect professional success while pursuing the bohemian life of the younger

Eleanor Gandon (née Smullen) by Paul Sandby
(courtesy The Royal Collection, London)

London artists. We have had a glimpse of that in his relations with Sir Samuel Hillier at an early stage in his practice. A perceptive, professional man would have kept his dealings with his client on a more formal basis, realising that however affable his client might appear, his confidence in him would be eroded by any relaxation in his professional manner.

So, as the sixties came to an end, Gandon, if he took any interest in politics, must have viewed the future with mixed feelings. He had set up in practice under a new monarch who was not quite four years older than himself, and who, at the outset of his reign, had unseated the Rockingham Whigs. This had a certain significance for Gandon's future, as one of his patrons for the Nottingham Shire Hall was Sir George Savile, a member of that party. Here again, we have difficulty in translating the political ethos of the eighteenth century.

The English parliament of that time did not consist of political parties as we know them today. It was made up of a number of groups of people: there were the king's friends and the members of the Treasury who owed their position to the Court; the independents, who were landowners for the most part; members of the great English noble families; and the professional politicians who might have a connection with any of the previous classes or might not. All these groups combined or divided, as the issues which came before them appeared favourable to themselves or did not. The idea of a consistent opposition was regarded as unpatriotic, but during the sixties the Rockingham Whigs, a group of interconnected families who had, during the reign of George II, enjoyed power and patronage, only to be ousted by George III. In their resentment they came eventually to form a more or less organised opposition. This was due on the one hand to the belief of the young king that the Rockingham Whigs had, during their long and uninterrupted period of office, managed to erode the influence of the monarch for their own purposes and that he must reverse this tendency, and on the other, that George III was determined unreasonably and unconstitutionally to subvert the authority of Parliament by corrupt methods and so increase his own influence. Both parties clung to these beliefs with paranoid intensity.

In the vacuum left by the Whigs, George III was forced to make do with a series of incompetent ministers, for as soon as he became disappointed with each, he dismissed him and tried another. The uncertainty this produced rebounded on Parliament and on the country until the appointment of Lord North at the beginning of 1770.

* * * * *

At Christmas in 1770, Gandon again enjoyed a trip with Mortimer and Thomas Jones, leaving his wife, now pregnant, behind in London. Thomas Jones describes the occasion:

The Mill House, Eastbourne
(courtesy Eastbourne Library)

Heywood House, Ballinakill, Co Laois
(courtesy Courtaud Institute, London)

1770 December 21st. Mortimer, Gandon and myself into the Lewis Coach and arrived at that place about four in the Afternoon – the next day we proceeded on foot to Eastbourne, Mortimer's native town where his father and other relations resided. Mortimer's father had been in his time a great dealer in flour and owner of Three or Four Cornmills, but at present, as he was far advanced in years, he kept only One upon his hands and that chiefly for Amusement – This Mill was built of a circular form upon a rising ground above the Town – the vanes of which moved, not in a Vertical, but Horizontal direction, and the Current of wind was regulated by Valves which were opened and shut according to the point it came from – it was said to be one of his own inventions – the old Gentleman had built a similar one close upon the Beach, but having been dismantled of the wooden machinery shop by a violent Storm – the stone carcass was by the ingenuity of Our friend, Gandon the Summer before converted into very Commodious Apartments for two small families to reside in during the Bathing Season – One of the rooms of this building was made use of as a Study to paint Scenes after nature, as Cliffs, Waves, Shipping &c. Having spent the Holidays in the greatest festivity, on the 7th. January, 1771, we returned on foot to Lewis and the day following arrived in London by the Coach.[58]

Earlier in the year, Gandon had made designs for Frederick Trench of Ballinakill, Co Laois. Trench was greatly interested in the arts and was something of an amateur architect, as well as being a member of Sandby's circle. Gandon's design for his house at Heywood was exhibited at the Society of Arts by a Mr White.

* * * * *

On 24th March 1959, a sketch (lot 132) was sold at Christie's of London. It was described as being 'James Gandon and his Family playing soldiers in the Camp in Museum Gardens in 1780', by Paul Sandby, and was sold for 150 guineas. If the description is correct, this sketch features Gandon and his wife with three daughters and three sons. We need to be clear on the relationships between the ages of those children whose births are on record, to see if the extra children can be fitted in. Gandon was married on 26th July 1770, and his family grew, as follows:

Name	Born	Interval	Conception	Age (June 1780)
Mary Anne	17.7.1771	11m 22d	2m 22d	8y 10m
James	25.8.1772	13m 8d	4m 8d	7y 9m
(interval)				
Eleanor	21.3.1774	18m 26d	9m 26d	6y 3m
Anne	29.4.1775	13m 8d	4m 8d	died young
Elizabeth	6.7.1776	13m 7d	4m 7d	3y 11m

James Gandon and family by unknown artist
(courtesy National Portrait Gallery, London)

'Garden of the British Museum during the Encampment', 1780 by Paul Sandby
(courtesy The Royal Collection, London)

Except for the interval between James and Eleanor, the family grew in a notably regular manner. The elder unnamed boy could fit into this interval only if a premature birth is supposed. At that time, survival at full term was hazardous, and doubly so for an premature birth. There is no apparent difficulty about the younger boy who fits in after Elizabeth. But Gandon's collapse occurred in 1777 after the disaster of the St Luke's competition, and this seems to have put an end to the growth of his family. The baptism of Mary Anne is recorded at St Paul's Covent Garden. The baptisms of the other children we know are in the registers of St James's, Piccadilly, and Gandon's house in Broad Street lay in this parish. The other parish with which he might be connected is St Anne's Soho, an area where many of the Huguenots first settled. The baptisms of the two unnamed boys are not registered in any of these three parishes. These two boys are not mentioned in *The Life*, but neither is Elizabeth. In the sketch, they appear as naturally part of the family.

And when Sandby made his etching of the camp in the gardens in 1780, he reproduced the figures in this sketch, although differently distributed. However, here again, the description is definite; there is the note: 'Mr. Gandon, Architect, of Dublin and his Family' (although we must here take into account Oppe's reservations about this picture in his *Catalogue of British Portraits*). So, when Gandon came to Ireland, did he leave half of his family behind him in England?

THE LOST YEARS

On 17th July 1771 Gandon's first child was born. A daughter, she was baptised Mary Anne at St Paul's, Covent Garden. About this time, we are told, he bought a house in Broad Street. The new house was adjacent to Paul Sandby's house in Poland Street, and their warm friendship continued after his marriage. Sandby made a drawing of the young Mrs Gandon, and herself and her husband and their children also appear in sketches by Sandby. The convenient proximity of their houses did not last long, for during the following year (1772), Sandby moved to no. 4 George's Row, now 23 Hyde Park Place. The *Life* gives the date for this move as 1777. A surviving sketch of what appears to be the mews building of the new house suggests that Gandon had been at work on it: the urns, the single window and the string course are all compatible with Gandon's style.

There now occurred an incident in the rat race within the Royal Academy which must have been of great interest to Gandon. Sir Joshua Reynolds was the only knight in the Academy, a state of affairs repugnant to Chambers' conception of his own importance. Chambers was determined to level with Sir Joshua, and in 1771 he persuaded the King of Sweden to confer on him the Order of the Pole Star and then lost no time in obtaining the permission of George III to treat this title as if it was valid in England. From then on he assumed the rank of an English knight and the title of Sir William Chambers. The ploy was not without its drawbacks, for those hostile to Chambers referred to him derisively, and in public too, as the Knight of the Pole Star.

Before the end of 1771, the fifth volume, and Gandon's second, of *Vitruvius Britannicus* was published. Similar in size and content to the fourth, it was a wonderful addition to architectural literature. But despite Gandon's taste, energy and friends, the more important and more lucrative works eluded him.

From 1771 to 1777 there is little we can say about Gandon's progress, or lack of it. The *Life* is silent about these six years. We know that during the first half of 1771, Gandon gave lessons in architecture to Sir Watkin Williams-Wynn, having perhaps been recommended by Paul Sandby. He also provided designs for a small private theatre – as was then the fashion – for Sir Watkin at Wynnstay, as well as no less than five different plans for his proposed new town house. In January 1772 he was paid £50 for this work, but Sir Watkin went to Robert Adam for his plans when he came to build the house. It was another disheartening experience for Gandon, and one only of a number of others of a similar character. Gandon, throughout his life, seemed to be dogged by ill fortune, especially at times when he should reasonably be confident of success.

Later in 1772, on 25th August, his son James was born.[59] We know practically nothing of his architectural work during the early years of his marriage, but he cannot have been very busy, for he exhibited designs at the Royal Academy from 1774 to 1778, and again in 1780. In 1774, on 21st March, his second daughter, Eleanor, was born.[60]

In 1775 and 1776 he exhibited tinted drawings of Roman ruins in the style of Charles Louis Clerisseau, which seem to have attracted notice, for we find him again in 1775 engaged by Sir Watkin to enlarge one of Clerisseau's drawings. That year too saw the birth of a third daughter, on 22nd April, who was christened Anne,[61] but the little girl died the following November and was buried on the 19th of that month.[62] We have Sandby's sketches of Gandon and his children playing at soldiers together in the museum gardens. Subsequently, he turned his hand to printmaking, etching at least five plates after Richard Wilson. On 6th July 1776, a fourth daughter, Elizabeth, was born;[63] strangely enough we find no mention of her in *The Life*. By now, the war with the American colonies was imminent.

THE ACADEMY

Gandon, still pursuing his dream of a place in the world of art, was tempted to apply for Associateship of the Royal Academy. Two places were available, and on 4th November 1776, twenty-three applicants presented themselves for election. William Parry got fourteen votes, and Jn. Singleton Copley eleven, so the two painters were elected. Giuseppe Caracchi got seven, Sir George Chalmers got two, James Gandon got two, and most of the rest got no votes, with a few getting one only. We may suppose that Gandon's two votes came from the Sandby brothers. Chambers' interest was not in Gandon's favour, and it must be said that overt patronage by Chambers would have got him in. Certainly, 1776 brought no joy to Gandon apart, as we have seen, the birth of his daughter, Elizabeth

Chambers, however, although obviously he did not want Gandon in the Royal Academy, was nevertheless concerned for him. On 18th January 1777 he wrote to Lord Charlemont to put in a word for Gandon:

> It is a great while since I had the honour of hearing from your lordship, whence I conclude you have done little of late in the building way. For my part I have done nothing for these fifteen months past but labour at the works of Somerset House which are so extensive and complicated that they require all my attention, and have reduced me to the necessity of declining all private employment, at least for some time to come. I am therefore to return your Lordship many thanks for former favours, and if, while I am so much occupied, your lordship shall be in want of any designs, Mr. Gandon of Broad-street, an old pupil of mine, and very ingenious, will, I dare say, do them to your Lordship's satisfaction. He knows nothing of this recommendation, nor have I seen him these seven years but in the street. Yet, from various designs of his which have appeared in the exhibitions, I think he merits encouragement, and wonder he has been so little employed. Your Lordship's protection would probably make him more known than he now is, and more valued accordingly to his deserts.

It could be said that this letter marked a turning point in Gandon's career, although its effects, as far as he knew, lay dormant for nearly five years.

In 1777, Gandon found a client, a Captain Thomas Adams, who lived in Brentwood, Essex. Captain Adams asked for plans for a country house at Warley Place. These designs were exhibited at the Royal Academy in the same year, and the building work was put in hand shortly afterwards. The only photograph available gives very little idea of the design behind the obscuring ivy, but an earlier

Warley Place
(courtesy Essex County Council)

sketch is clearer and obviously a reasonably faithful rendering of Gandon's original design. The emphasis on the narrow end of the main part of the house and the horizontal string courses are typical of Gandon. Gandon's buildings have suffered greatly from fire, storm and high explosives: Warley Place was bombed during the last war and the ruins demolished about 1948.[64]

BETHLEHEM

Since his marriage, Gandon seems to have continued his disastrous social life, still clinging to the illusion that his merit alone was sufficient to attract clients. Then, in 1777, he entered an architectural competition, as *The Life* incorrectly tells us, for a New Bethlehem Hospital. He was thirty-five years old at that time, and should he be successful, his future would largely be secured. The

Life conceals Gandon's plight in a masterly manner:

> Why he should have been induced at this period, established as he then was, to enter into any public competition for any work, which, in the ardour of more youthful days might have been praise-worthy, we cannot well imagine, except we refer to that consciousness of his own powers, which rendered it a difficult task to restrain his habitual energies and industry.
>
> The arrangements contemplated for this building were on a very extended scale, and demanded, on the part of the architect, not only a concentration of all his skill, but nearly the undivided attention of his whole time, which, just at this time, was of great value, occupied as he then was, most extensively...

As was his habit, Gandon went to the best authorities for advice. John Howard, the philanthropist, was an expert on prison design, and Gandon's plans for the lunatic asylum engaged his interest. Together they produced what was obviously a superior scheme, for the committee awarded it first prize. Gandon, by then in low water, must have been greatly elated by his success. Now he could look forward to several years of reputable work and freedom from financial worries. Then he suffered a severe shock. The work was given to George Dance, who already had some connection with the hospital. He had laid out Finsbury Square; his assistant James Peacock had designed the houses on the west side of the square, most of which were burned in 1941. At first, the terrace was alone, in the fields between St Luke's Hospital and Bedlam, the city's two large asylums. Dr Johnson had to have his say: 'I think a very moral use may be made of these new buildings. I would those who have heated imaginations live there, and take warning.' The *Life* dismisses Dance as a 'man of straw'.

Dr McParland has identified the hospital as St Luke's and not Bethlehem, as mentioned in *The Life*.[65] Gandon himself has this to say:

> I am now much advanced in years and it has pleased the Almighty God to spare me, and to have enabled me to complete all the public buildings committed to my superintendence; but the design I made for that Hospital very nearly terminated my existence. It was necessary that I should visit every apartment in the original structure, and more particularly those to which the public had not access, in order to learn the improvements required. In those visits I encountered the most deplorable cases of the wreck of the human mind. To this appaling part of my duty I submitted for several days; but at last I experienced sleepless nights, and when I did procure my rest I was troubled with horrible dreams of the miserable and afflicting scenes of its wretched inmates. I was at last attacked with brain

fever and neither my family nor my medical attendants had any hope of my recovery. But I was mercifully spared, and, through the affectionate care of my wife, and the skillful attentions of my medical friend, aided by a strong and vigorous constitution, I gradually recovered.[66]

This account was shown to a few medical practitioners who very kindly commented on it. The conclusions of one of these, at that time a consultant in a Boston hospital, are as follows:

> From the details provided I would surmise that James Gandon, having been severely shocked by the sights he witnessed in the old Bethlehem hospital, developed a severe anxiety state (as evidenced by the Insomnia and recurrent dreams); this anxiety state apparently progressed until he developed a severe hysterical reaction (as evidenced by the development of brain fever). The term 'Brain Fever' as used in this context may mean that the appeared to his observers to be in a state of coma, or that he became Psychotic and was illogical and having illusions, hallucinations and delusions. It would be interesting to know if at any other time in his life he portraid any evidence of Psychiatric Disturbances, such as unusual anxiety, Depression or Psychoses.
>
> However, the experience he had in the hospital may have been so foreign to his normal environment that it was sufficient to produce a severe mental Disturbance in a man who was otherwise quite stable.

We do know of two other periods of severe disturbance in his life, and there are hints of more. One followed his father's bankruptcy, and the other after the death of his closest friend, Paul Sandby. This trouble we are considering seems to be divisible into two parts: one of sleeplessness and unpleasant dreams, and secondly, a complete nervous collapse. We are tempted to wonder if here again, as with his father and Brooks, that Gandon is not running two distinct occurrences together. We can understand the first part and its causes, although the streets of London of that time were thronged with people suffering from every sort of disability, both physical and mental, and Gandon must have been familiar with much we nowadays would find shocking. Indeed, it was a Sunday's amusement for the fashionable to visit Bedlam to be diverted by the antics of the insane.

It is clear that such a severe illness did not occur during the competition, for Gandon would not have been able to prepare and submit his designs in time. But the illusion of success, suddenly swept away, would have been a severe shock to his system, and we must concede that his illness followed.

It is curious that the winning design has not survived. Perhaps Gandon in his disappointment tore it up. Nothing survives either of his design for the Royal

Exchange, which may have met with a similar fate. Dr McParland mentions the odd circumstance that two of the designs for the Exchange, by Cooley and Gandon, were retained and framed, and hung up in the Exchange, but these too have disappeared.

ATHENIAN STUART

The *Life* devotes several pages to Athenian Stuart and to his progress, although Gandon remarks that 'on the early life of Stuart I could never obtain any satisfactory information.' But *The Life* is silent on Gandon's association with him, so we may indulge in a little speculation.

We know that Lord Charlemont and the Marquis of Rockingham, confirmed Whigs both, subsidised Stuart on his visit to Greece and the eastern Mediterranean; and it is not outside the bounds of possibility that Lord Charlemont, seeing the inactivity to which Gandon had been reduced, prevailed on Stuart to give him employment. It would have been a bitter day for Gandon, now no longer independent, and especially as Stuart, a man about twenty-years years older than himself, was responsible for popularising the architecture of Greece by his drawings of the Greek temples. The character of this new and ancient architecture fascinated many at that time, and displaced Gandon's Roman architecture in popularity. It was a coming together of opposites and could not have lasted for long, although both, as we shall see later, incurred the displeasure of no less a person than Mrs Montague when they were working on her new house. She had this to say:

> I avoid letting Mr. Stuart or Mr. Gandon interfere in ye affairs as from partiality to their glazier they wd find fault with the glass, besides they are so dilatory that they retarded everything instead of forwarding ye business of the House, and the trouble they give me by that means is intolerable.[67]

This was Gandon's last known commission in London. Mrs Montague was building her new house at no. 20 Portman Square, to which she moved in 1781 from 11 Hill Street. In 1780 we hear from her again when she writes from Bath to Leonard Smelts, who was superintending the work for her:

> I have found out that in dealing with Mr. Stuart great caution is necessary. I choose him for my Architect on account of his disinterestedness and

Elizabeth Montague by Lowry
(*courtesy National Portrait Gallery, London*)

Stuart by W.C. Edwards after Proven
(*courtesy National Portrait Gallery, London*)

contempt of money; I did not see how ... what workmen did by bribery of guineas to many architects, could be effected on him by pipes of tobacco and pots of porter in ale houses and night cellars. I speak it not on suspicion but certain information that since he began my house he has been for a fortnight together in the most drunken condition with those fellows ... it is impossible to rely on anything he says. Mr. Gandon writes me by this day's post that Mr. Stuart has put the designs for the Chimney pieces in hand: I wish this may be so, but as he told you he should send the designs to me and has not done it, I fear he may not have delivered it to the artists. In business the strait line is the line of beauty, but Stuart is apt to choose the waving line.[68]

This was probably the house for which Gandon designed a Classical screen, and not the house in Hill Street. Mulvany, who gives the date as 1767, may be in error.

Here we have firm evidence for what was so far merely an inference: that Gandon neglected his clients. If Gandon had applied himself seriously to the work for Mrs Montague, he could easily have found a place in her regard and gained an influential patron who would have had his interests at heart. But she comes at the end of a series of clients who seem to have avoided any continuation of their dealings with him. It was to be his last chance in London, but he seemed to be unaware of this.

Gandon often repeated details and larger features from his earlier work. Dr McParland points out the similarity between the design for the altar end of the chapel in Greenwich hospital, upon which Stuart and, it seems likely, Gandon were working in 1779, and the end feature of the Benchers' dining room in the King's Inns in Dublin – two buildings with which Gandon was associated and which have not so far been destroyed or vandalised.

Sketching and engraving gave Gandon much pleasure, and were, no doubt, a consolation during hard times. In 1778 he published a sheet of twelve engravings illustrating 'antique and modern ornaments', as well as twelve sheets of engravings, being a 'Collection of Friezes, Capitals and Grotesque Ornaments'.

Towards the end of 1780, on 15th November, his sister Mary, now thirty-seven years old, was married to Captain James Handyside.[69]

PRINCESS AND PEER

In 1779 a new face was added to the little gatherings which took place on Sundays at Sandby's house in St George's Row. This was Ekaterina Romanova, the Princess Dashkova. Gandon has this to say about her:

> Shortly after I had made my designs for the new Bethlehem Hospital, I was introduced by Sandby to a pupil of his, a Russian Lady, known by the title of Princess Dashkof. Why she chose to reside in London I never learned. She was highly accomplished, and had a great knowledge of the Arts; she was also perfectly conversant with the French Language. I saw many of her drawings in water and body colours. She also undertook what few ladies ever attempted, etching on copper. I have two of her etchings of Windsor Castle, with her name signed, 'Princess Dashkof, printed at Sandby's private press'.[70]

No doubt, Gandon's friends, and Sandby in particular, urged on her the many architectural merits he possessed, for soon she made him a proposition. It was that he should settle in St Petersburg and conduct the erection of some public buildings there, which were being contemplated. She further offered to procure for him a commission in the Russian Army. This offer placed Gandon in some-

'The Dublin Volunteers in College Green' by Francis Wheatley RA
(courtesy National Gallery of Ireland)

thing of a quandary, for at that time, as we shall see, there was the promise of work for him in Ireland. He temporised by 'acknowledging the high honour of the Princess's offer', and asked for time to make up his mind. In the event, another architect, Charles Cameron, went to Russia in 1779 to build palaces for Catherine the Great. Perhaps Gandon was as well off, for we have a picture of the Princes Dashkova from the pen of Bishop Hever who met her in Russia in 1806. Writing to his mother he says:

> I am not sure whether in my last letter I mentioned the Princess Dashkof, the friend and fellow conspirator of Catherine II. We often visited her, and found her conversation, when she was disengaged from afar, very lively and interesting. She of course has lost her ancient beauty but still retains her eccentricities: her usual dress is a man's greatcoat and a nightcap with a star.

Princess Dashkova visited Ireland the same year, and appears in Wheatley's painting of the Dublin Volunteers in College Green on 4th November. She is at the tenth window from the left, under a parasol.

The offer of work in Ireland was somewhat vague, less attractive, but probably more welcome. Gandon already knew some of those associated with Lord Carlow, whose enthusiasm for Classical architecture was well known. Lord Carlow wrote to him later in the year:

Dear Sir, – Since my arrival here, having often thought of 'the ways and means' of making it worth your attention to come over to us, I imagined that if I could raise, which I think I could, a subscription among a few friends to give you an adequate salary for two years, as in the course of that time you would be well established here. I shall therefore be obliged to you to let me know if you approve the plan; and if you do, how much a year, for two years, would answer.[71]

We do not know how Gandon replied. Malton, with his usual omniscience, tells us that the scheme was for twelve gentlemen to contribute £50 each to give Gandon £600 a year. Lord Carlow's next letter is rather more non-committal:

February 1780.
    Dear Sir, – Since I received your letter I have not had the opportunity of seeing the gentlemen here to be able to let you know if we can make an offer worth your acceptance; I shall soon write to you on the subject.[72]

Again we do not know how far Lord Carlow's scheme was successful. As Gandon did nothing further that year about it, it is likely that the proposal fell through. But this is not certain, for Gandon, although faced with circumstances which cannot have seemed hopeful, was not the sort either to loose his native optimism or to do anything drastic in a hurry.

    Then two things happened which made their own impressions on Gandon's mind. Each would seem to have impelled him in an opposing direction, and although they may have cancelled each other out, they could not but have added to his indecision. The first was the sudden disappearance of Sir William Chambers, and his disgrace which followed it. In May 1780, at a time when his portrait by Sir Joshua Reynolds was on view at the first showing of the Academy in Somerset House, Sir William was found to be missing. The rumour spread that he had embezzled the funds at his disposal for the building, and had fled the country. The affair was puzzling, and on 24th May, we find Horace Walpole writing to William Mason: 'The story of Sir William Chambers is odd. He is certainly in Flanders, but there is no embezzlement; he has money in his bankers' hands, writes to his family and sends orders to his workmen at Somerset House.' On 28th he wrote again: 'sir William Chambers has re-appeared and been to the Royal Academy. His absence is now said to have been an equipe of gallantry.' No explanation of the incident has ever been discovered. At an enquiry in the House of Commons into charges of 'jobbery', Chambers was absolved. However, he lost standing with the king and Court, although he continued to dominate the Academy as before.

    Perhaps Gandon felt himself in some way touched by Chambers' disgrace;

Lord Carlow by unknown artist
(private collection)

more likely it was an object lesson to him on the power of rumour, and on the damage which a professional man can do to his reputation by imprudent conduct. He now felt reluctant to leave London, perceiving it to be an irreversible step. The second occurrence which disturbed Gandon, and may have made up his mind for him, followed almost immediately on the first. It was the Gordon riots.

THE GORDON RIOTS

In 1780 Lord George Gordon was twenty-nine, having been born in 1751 into a family noted for its instability. Many of the Gordons were distinctly odd, and not a few of them more than eccentric, but George was to surprise them all, for he had the faculty, beneath his affable and gentle manner, of communicating his madness to large numbers of people.

After a childhood running wild on their estates in Scotland, he was sent to Eton, and then to sea as a midshipman in the British navy while still a boy. Here he made a name for himself by siding with the crew in all their disputes, so that the Admiralty Board soon decided he was a 'damned nuisance, wholly unsuitable for promotion'. At the end of ten years in the navy, he was still a lieutenant. At last, recognising that his naval career was unfruitful, he turned to politics, choosing to stand for Inverness against a General Frazer. It was the General's seat, and a safe one, but Frazer became alarmed by Gordon's energy and winning ways, and so bought him into the pocket borough of Luggershall. Thus, Gordon entered Parliament in 1774 at the age of twenty-two.

Over the years, his influence in Parliament grew. Typically, he became a thorn in the side of Lord North's government, and equally so of the opposition. His often-repeated declaration that 'The voice of the People was the voice of God' made them all uneasy, but he remained harmless until it was realised that Catholics could be recruited for the American war. They had been barred from the services by the requirement to swear that they were Protestants. To get over this, it was proposed to pass a Relief Bill to abolish some of the Penal Laws. This proposal angered the Protestants and infuriated the Dissenters. The bill was pushed through, but its passing gave rise to the most exaggerated rumours: the king was a Catholic and heard Mass in his private chapel; twenty thousand Jesuits were hidden in tunnels in the banks of the Thames, ready to blow them up and flood London; a gang of Benedictine Monks, disguised as Irishmen, had poisoned all the flour in Southwark, so that for days the people there were afraid to eat bread. Throughout the country, similar tales grew and spread. To counteract the menace, Protestant associations were rapidly formed everywhere and they aggravated the fear and hatred of Popery by a continuous stream of alarming pamphlets.

Lord George was invited to Edinburgh to lead the Protestant cause. In January 1779, rioting became serious, and Mass houses and the homes of Catholics were attacked and burned. The government quickly announced that the bill did not apply to Scotland, and Lord George returned to London, the sole and victorious champion of the Protestant cause. Here he became president of the London Protestant Association, but his motives were at odds with the popular view. He was not afraid of Popery, but was indignant that Catholics could be recruited to fight those whom he regarded as the noble people of America. So he threw himself into the organisation of the Protestant cause with energy and vigour.

A petition was drawn up, and some one hundred thousand Protestants signed it. Now the government attempted to bribe Lord George to drop the business, but this only reinforced his self-esteem and determination. He called for the whole body of the Protestant Association to meet in St George's Fields and march on Parliament.

Friday, 2nd June 1780 was a warm, sunny day. As the great crowds made their way to St George's Fields, they were already sweating in the heat. They were orderly and well behaved, and appeared to be composed mostly of respectable tradesmen and artisans. While waiting for Lord George they sang Protestant hymns, but when he arrived at eleven and started to make a speech, their impatience would not allow him to go on for long. Having suffered his first frustration of the day, he got into his coach, and the long procession moved off behind him in good order. However, as they approached the river, they were joined by thousands of the less reputable sort, and it was a very mixed crowd which eventually gathered outside Parliament House

Now an extraordinary violent excitement seized the petitioners. As the Lords drove up to the House they were set upon, dragged from their coaches, pelted with filth and beaten. Their coaches were attacked and some of them were smashed to pieces. The members of the Commons escaped more lightly, but when Parliament eventually gathered, they found themselves to be a pitifully dishevelled gathering. With the mob shouting outside and also in the public gallery, they debated the day's events for the next six hours. During this time, Lord George behaved like a madman, now addressing the mob outside, now joining in the debate, now lobbying with his supporters; he 'seemed to be everywhere at once'. In the end, the petition was rejected by a large majority, and this news provoked the mob to a greater expression of violence. The Foot Guards were called out to charge the crowd, and did so, but without causing any serious injury. It was owing to the courage and tact of Justice Addington that the mob was eventually persuaded to disperse, and the members of the House were at last free to go home.

That night, a body of men armed with pickaxes and crowbars, and carrying lighted torches, marched towards Lincoln's Inn Fields. Here they broke into the Catholic chapel of the Sardinian Ambassador, and, aided by a large crowd which they had gathered during their march, they wrecked the building, dragged out the furniture and vestments, and piling them up in the roadway, set them on fire. They then burned down the chapel. No justices appeared to stop the riot, and when the guards from Somerset House barracks arrived, everything was over.

On the Saturday night, a mob attacked the Irish colony in Moorfield. On the Sunday night, they wrecked the Catholic chapel in Ropemaker's Alley, and went on to burn out the Catholics living in the vicinity. The Lord Mayor of London and his magistrates were there, and when Lord Beauchamp told him it was his duty to act, he replied that 'the mob had got hold of some people and some furniture they did not like and were burning them, and what is the harm in that?'. On Monday night, the mob came together again, but now it was seen to be organised and directed. It enlarged its target to include Members of Parliament who had voted for the Relief Bill, and turned its attention to the more select parts of the town, wrecking any house which did not display lights in its windows and a 'No Popery' sign on the door. Many houses were burned that night, while the troops stood idly by.

Wednesday was another hot, sunny day. The sightseers were out in their thousands, viewing the appalling destruction of the previous night. Troops began to come into the city, for it was no longer a matter of the burning out of Catholics and Catholic chapels. Members of the government and of the House of Lords had suffered grievous loss, and measures must now be taken to put an end to the trouble before worse occurred, for the mob's main objective had become the property of the members of the government. At a meeting of the Privy Council, the king himself threatened to take a hand unless the powers of the military were greatly strengthened. It was now discovered that there was little or no legal basis for the belief that the military could not fire on the mob unless ordered to do so by a magistrate, and a royal proclamation was then issued giving officers full discretion to order their men to fire on the rioters. By evening, the city was full of troops, garrisoned in various public buildings, the palaces, the bank and the exchange, and also in the grounds of the British Museum. Here, Gandon came with his family to see the Troops' billets and to play at soldiers with his children, Accepting his abhorrence of civil commotion, he probably came to satisfy himself that matters were at last under control. But in this he was mistaken.

It was Wednesday night. At dusk the town had grown ominously quiet, and the sightseers left the empty streets as a curious silence fell. The soldiers drew themselves up around the bank where an attack was threatened, and at other strategic centres. Then, as dusk fell, the rioters began to muster. Just as the sun set, the rioters began to gather at the corner of Old Jewery and Poultry, and charged on the bank, but were frustrated by ropes which had been stretched across the streets by the soldiers. They were thus broken up, but advanced in small groups to be met by a volley of fire. Some twenty were killed, and the bodies were dragged away by their comrades. At the same time, two other groups attacking the bank were driven off also by the soldiers' fire. Here, at least, for a short time, there was no further trouble.

But in other parts of town, the attacks on the prisons were renewed. Soon the King's Bench and Fleet prisons were blazing and empty of prisoners. The Borough Clink and Surrey Bridewell were also set on fire, and all around were burning buildings, for where the rioters were blocked in their attacks on the prisons, they wrecked and burned the houses in their way. The horse and foot soldiers arrived too late to protect the prisons, but here again they did not hesitate to fire on and charge the mob, and many were killed.

Perhaps the most horrible scenes of the week were enacted in the burning of Langdale's distillery. Langdale was a Catholic, and had already been threatened. Now, when most of the available troops were at the bank, his house was wrecked and set alight, and the mob broke into the distillery and continued their work of destruction. Those inside were too drunk to realise their danger, and many were burned to death. Spirits and gin flowed into the street and down the gutter. Here crowds of men and women gorged themselves on the raw and poisonous spirits, and soon the street was littered with the bodies of the unconscious and the dead. A fire engine commandeered by the rioters added fuel to the flames by pumping streams of gin into the blazing buildings, and now, for the first time in that hot and still week, a breeze began to blow, fanning the flames and spreading the fires from house to house. When, at last, the soldiers arrived, the streets were empty, save for the hundreds of drunk and dead rioters lying on the ground, and the only targets for their fire were a few pickpockets moving among the inert masses.

These troops now moved back to repel another attack on the bank. Wave after wave of rioters were driven back by heavy fire, and although they were kept at bay, nevertheless the troops here were hard-pressed. When the battle was at its height, Lord George appeared – frantic, disordered and apparently out of his mind – shouting to the mob to disperse. The soldiers pushed him out of the way and the battle continued. When it was over, a number of well-dressed men were found among the dead in the streets, but the rioters had been careful to recover many of them and carry them off to throw them in the river. Throughout the night, they showed anxiety to conceal the identity of these men whenever they were killed. Inns of Court were also attacked and partly damaged by fire, but by this time, one fire more or less made little difference to the terrible scene the city of London now presented, with great fires raging in all directions, interspersed with the smaller fires of individual houses and many streets strewn with the bodies of the dead and injured. Bodies were floating down the Thames, to be washed up on the lower reaches of the river or out to sea. At about four in the morning, the bank was attacked for the third time. The rioters had some firearms, and the attack was pressed with great determination, but in the end they were driven off. By this time the troops had entrenched themselves on the bridges over the river, and this was decisive. The mob melted away, and by dawn the streets were empty and the city quiet. The riots were over. On Friday, Lord George Gordon was arrested and taken to the Tower.

EMIGRATION

The wreckage left behind by the riots provided plenty of work for London architects. That Gandon did not share much, if any, of this work may have reconciled him to change. Still he lingered on, unable to decide to accept the encouraging offer of Lord Carlow. Perhaps he knew too well the quirks of the financial habits of the aristocracy in England, and wondered if the Irish offer might owe more to the optimism of Lord Carlow than to a genuine desire on the part of his Irish friends to dig into their pockets to subsidise an architectural practice. The offer by the Princess Dashkova may not have seemed to him to be any better, and considering the remoteness of Russia in that age, must have appeared the more uncertain of the two. Thus, the summer passed, leaving Gandon face-to-face with the ruins of that high promise of fifteen years before. It was a prospect which must, at times, have greatly depressed his sanguine temperament, but he seems to have shown no outward signs noticeable to his friends. Then, in November 1780, he received a letter from the Right Hon John Beresford, Chief Commissioner of the Irish Revenue, King's Street, St James's.

> Sir, – I should be glad to have the pleasure of seeing you for half an hour, as soon as convenient to you, at this hotel. Lord Carlow requested of me to see you and to give you an opportunity of considering a new plan for a building of a public nature in Ireland. I have some materials on the subject, and as I am at present confined by an indisposition, I should have the more time to explain to you what may be wanted.
>   I am sir, your obedient servant, John Beresford.[73]

The cautious Gandon, however, went first to see Lord Carlow, no doubt to find out who Beresford might be, and to get some idea of the degree of reliance which might be placed on his promises. As he puts it in his diary:

> Lord Carlow, afterwards Earl of Portarlington, was then in London: I waited upon his Lordship in Harley-street, the next day, to make my acknowledgement for his kind recommendation to Mr. Beresford, and to state to him the communications made to me by that gentleman; on which his Lordship said: 'You may place every reliance on Mr. Beresford, but great secrecy must be observed: as yet nothing must meet the public ear'.

It is to be regretted we have no report from Gandon of his interview with Beresford. Beresford was a man of great power in Ireland, and in his conversation, took no pains to hide the extent either of his influence or of his desires. Possibly because of Lord Carlow's reassurances, Gandon's distrust of Beresford seems to have ben allayed, for he immediately set to work on what was to be his first masterpiece. Gandon's diary mentions their next meeting:

> Early in the following December, Mr. Beresford called at my house in Broad-street and we had a long conversation. He informed me that his business in London was finished, and it was absolutely necessary for him to bring over with him to Dublin the hasty ideas I had been enabled to compose for some parts of the intended building. I regretted much the necessity of parting with my sketches, as my mind was so occupied with the subject, having, for several days, laid aside all other professional concerns, and as I had not sufficient time afforded me to take copies of my sketches for either the north or south fronts, they being all required over in Dublin, However, on parting he said that I should shortly receive further instructions from him probably in a very few days; which was the case, for in the month of January I received the following letter:

Dublin, 15th January, 1781

Sir, – I have the pleasure to inform you that I have at length obtained an order from the Government for the building of a new Custom House, with all possible expedition, and I have proceeded so far as to send to take possession of a large lot in the lower situation I expect to accomplish this in the course of this week, and the sooner afterwards we can settle our plans the better. This business must be kept a profound secret, as long as we can, to prevent clamour, until we have everything secured.

Our first step will be to wall in the ground as soon as we shall get possession of it. This will discover us and the clamour will then be made that there will not be sufficient room for shipping: to answer which it will

John Beresford by G.C. Stuart
(*courtesy National Gallery of Ireland*)

be right to have our plans for the new docks ready, to show the people how well they will be accommodated.

I therefore request you will turn your thoughts immediately to that subject, and, as I hope we may hereafter claim you as our own, that you attend to us in the first instance, as the business is of a delicate nature, and must be managed still with dexterity, having the city (Corporation) of Dublin, and a great number of merchants, together with what is considered as the most desperate of the mob, to contend with, on this side of the water: and also some persons of high interest and weight on your side, who will make use of every exertion to prevent us.

However, a Custom House must now be built, so we shall now expect you; and I must beg to know when you think you can come over?'

We shall wall in and carry on the dock as soon as we can, and the plans for the building may be adjusted during this period. I would recommend it to you to come by Liverpool by all means, as you will then see their docks, and procure every information about them: let me hear from you immediately.

I am sir, your humble servant, John Beresford [74]

Beresford's letter puts Gandon's appointment on a formal basis, and now his mind has been made up for him. He is also left in no doubt about the expectations of his brisk client, and perhaps, at last, he sees that he must exert himself, for he turns his energies to the task of designing the docks and stores which will be needed for the new Custom House. Beresford's next letter gives him a little more time before he has to leave London, and perhaps also a hint of some of the frustrations he was to endure in Ireland.

Dublin, 11th February, 1781

Dear Sir, – Since I received your last letter in due time, covering your plans for the docks, &c.,&c., I have been obliged to delay thus long to answer you, because I have been in daily expectation of being enabled to agree for the ground we require. But I find great difficulty in accomplishing this matter, as the proprietors endeavour to impose greatly on us. I am, therefore, obliged to lie by for a little time, but hope soon to conclude.

I am, Sir, your obedient servant, John Beresford [75]

The move he was about to make was a grave one. Only direct necessity or a deep dissatisfaction with a way of life grown distasteful can prompt a middle aged married man to leave the city in which he grew up and settle in a foreign land, especially in Ireland, which was, at that time, the natural refuge for those wishing to evade their creditors or the hazards of the criminal law. Even now, Gandon temporised. He decided to leave his family in London and go over alone. His experience, and the sobering experience of many architects, was that no matter how promising a new project might seem at first, there is little certainty about it until the actual building work has started. Wisely he decided not to risk being stranded abroad with his family. Even then he was disturbed by the journey he was facing. He says

> I found myself in a very unpleasant state of suspense, apprehending that the abruptness of my departure from my family and my establishment in London might injure my character, and, should my visit to Ireland prove unsuccessful, endanger my professional pursuits at home.[76]

We notice how he always puts a good face on his professional position. But there were other considerations which must have added to his unease. There was the memory of the Chamber's scandal. The crossing of the Irish Sea, with its sudden storms, was at that time a serious risk for all who sailed between the two islands. And now there were other perils to menace the traveller. The American war had crossed the Atlantic. Froude tells us that in the summer of 1777, there appeared on the Irish Sea three fast sailing and heavily armed privateers carrying the American colours. They were two eighteen-gun sloops, the *Reprisal* and the *Lexington*, with a ten-gun brig, the *Dolphin*. These were supported by further armed sloops, fitted out in the estuaries of Kerry and Cork, and the force was manned by a mixture of French and Americans with a strong Irish contingent. They preyed on the traffic between Ireland and England, putting prize crews on board the ships they captured to take them to French ports for sale. The English navy sent four ships of the line to hunt them down, but without success, and these returned each summer to their profitable hunting ground.

The war in America was now going badly for the English. During October 1780, there was the rout of their army at King's Mountain, and in January 1781 came the defeat of Cornwallis. All these considerations may have come together in Gandon's mind and reinforced the helplessness of his situation, and we must remember the effect on him of the Gordon riots, which must have shaken his sense of security in the city and country in which he lived. His people were Huguenots, and he had seen at first hand the suffering of the various classes of immigrants in London. So, early in April, we are told, he left for Liverpool, where he inspected the docks and then committed himself to the sea and to the future in Ireland.

———

'James Gandon, the architect, against the Custom House' by Horace Hone, c.1807
(courtesy National Gallery of Ireland)

PART II – GANDON IN IRELAND

ARRIVAL (1781)

On the morning of Thursday, 26th April 1781, the packet boat from Liverpool passed the Poolbeg light and came to anchor near the Pigeon House fort. Among the passengers in their three-cornered hats and skirted coats was a man who limped slightly and leaned on a stout cane as he crossed the deck. He was in his thirty-ninth year, and the signs of middle age, apart from the gout which slowed his progress, were already upon him. Now, with nearly half of his life behind him, for the first time he could see, about two miles to the west, the outskirts of Dublin where the real work of his life was waiting for him.

In those days, the approach to the city was leisurely. His carriage rolled along the top of the South Wall for a mile or so, with the sea on either side, before it turned in through the fishing village of Ringsend and on to the old road north of Merrion Square. Across the river lay the tidal flats of the North Lotts, and beyond, on the far side of the bay, rose the green slopes of Clontarf where Lord Charlemont's new Casino gleamed white between the trees. Perhaps from his carriage window he caught a glimpse of it, and recognised it for what it was with the consolation a familiar object gives in a strange land. Soon his carriage reached the city, and he was brought to the home of the Hon John Beresford, where he was welcomed and held in polite imprisonment for many weeks.

Thus, James Gandon came to Dublin, the time, the place and the patron coinciding to the greatest advantage for him. He was providentially fitted for the work before him. Since his time with Sir William Chambers, his genius had

Poolbeg lighthouse, Dublin

matured during the years of seeming stagnation in London, where, because of his misdirected efforts, even moderate success had eluded him. Now the frustrations of his long apprenticeship were over, and it was in the midst of a conflict moving towards great tragedy and in the wreckage it left behind that his major works would be carried out.

The Ireland in which he found himself was inhabited by three distinct classes of people. In one class, comprising the majority of the people, were the native Irish. Still speaking their ancient language, they were variously called the Celts or the Natives, or – since they had held fast to their Catholic faith – they were called Papists, depending on the context from which they were viewed. Their condition was that of slavery. The various assaults which they had endured through the centuries from the time of the Normans, increasing in savagery under the Elizabethans, the Cromwellians and the Williamites, and culminating in the Penal Laws under Queen Anne, had left them without property and without rights. They lived in cabins on strips of the poorer parts of their former lands, now let to them at a rack rent by the new owners, or served the middle classes in the towns in a menial capacity. Their lives, and the lives and bodies of their wives and children, were at the disposal of their masters. They had little significance in the course of events until the last decade of the century.

In another class were the Presbyterians of northern Ulster. Their ancestors had been planted on the good lands which had been confiscated by James in the previous century, and they were descendants of a mixed English and Scottish stock, with the Scots predominant. Earnest, industrious and perhaps a little dour, they had prospered. As Dissenters, they were second-class citizens, and suffered a number of disadvantages – for example, their marriages were not legally valid, which implied all sorts of difficulties. They lorded it over the Papists whenever they could do so safely, but were, in turn, treated with disdain by the established church in Ireland. They suffered because of their industry, due to the rapacity of their English landlords, who, after the year 1793, put many of their holdings up for auction. The Papists were prepared to offer a higher rent, so in effect, many Presbyterians were dispossessed. They were forced to copy the methods of the Whiteboys in the south, and banded themselves together under such names as the Hearts of Steel and the Oak Boys, and harassed the Papists who had taken over their holdings. Their distress was such that about thirty thousand disaffected Presbyterians left Ulster to join their co-religionists in the American colonies.

James Froude, an English historian, writing a century later, had this to say:

> ...the working members of the community and the worthiest part of it, flying from a soil where some fatal enchantment condemned to failure every effort made for its redemption – such was the fair condition of the Protestant colony planted in better days to show the Irish the fruits of a

117

nobler belief than their own, and the industrial virtues of a nobler race: who can wonder that English rule in Ireland has become a byword? Who can wonder that the Celts fail to recognize a superiority which has no better result to show for itself?

The governing classes, the smallest numerically, were, for the time being, in possession of the land. Wealthy and powerful, secure in their inheritance of confiscated property, they farmed large holdings, their sons filled the professions, and the hundred or so titled families among them drew rents from their great estates and governed the country to their own advantage. It should be remembered that at the time the only professions were the law, the Church and the army, and those who practised other skills were generally regarded as tradesmen. English by descent, they were looked upon by the English as Irish, and by the Irish as English. Generally known as the Anglo-Irish, their ruling families were by now referred to as the Ascendancy. They called themselves Irishmen, and believed themselves to be of the Irish nation, a belief which has been the cause of much confusion and suffering. They also called themselves British, a happy adjective invented by the English for those things inferior to the English, but which they felt were in some way to their credit. Nominally Protestant, the Anglo-Irish were brilliant, drunken, witty, promiscuous, eloquent and venal to the end.

Although all three classes were admitted Christians, we must deal with them on the basis of the religious categories to which each adhered, because they themselves spoke and acted on this basis. But behind it all, the ownership of the land was the significant source of conflict, as it had been in England and throughout Europe since the Reformation. The confiscation and plantation of the land in Ireland was for the descendants of the newcomers of too recent a date for complacency, and the ever-present consciousness of the dispossessed on the borders of their estates still represented for them an alien and slightly menacing presence. But as the years passed, this became discounted. This body of aristocrats and their dependents had its headquarters in Dublin, in the parliament buildings on College Green and in the political clubs of the city. It was a close-knit body, many of its members related to each other by marriage, and their main policy was to defend and enlarge their already almost unbounded privileges and possessions. It is with this compact and circumscribed body we are concerned while following James Gandon's progress in his new country.

Although these three classes were quite distinct, there were naturally exceptions where, for one reason or another, they merged at the boundaries between them, as mainly in the north there was some intermarriage between the Presbyterians and the native Irish. On the other hand, the Presbyterians and the Anglo-Irish shared a common language as well as an abhorrence of the Catholic Church. While the native Irish remained quiescent, this community of interest

'A Caricature – Irish peers: Sir Thomas Kennedy, Lord Charlemont,
Mr Ward and Mr Phelps' by Joshua Reynolds
(courtesy National Gallery of Ireland)

119

was little regarded, but when their joint security was shaken, all differences between them were dropped.

There was also what might be termed a fourth group in the country. This was the corps of agents of the Westminster parliament in Dublin Castle and in the residence of the viceroy in the Phoenix Park. The influence of this small body was powerful, since they held the favours of honours and places.

In 1781 the Anglo-Irish were greatly excited. As the eighteenth century progressed, they had come to realise that in spite of the 'Glorious Revolution' against James the Catholic, they were no more to the English than a colony and a garrison in Ireland. Dean Swift and the incident of Wood's halfpence had merely underlined their subordinate position, and the arbitrary way in which the English government restricted their trade and ruined any Irish industries which might compete with those in England was a constant irritant. They welcomed the English army in Ireland: it was necessary to keep down the native Irish. At the same time, it ensured their obedience to the decrees of the English government. While the army was there, they were helpless, but when, in 1775, the English got into trouble with the American colonists, and most of the English troops in Ireland were withdrawn, the Anglo-Irish were given their opportunity.

At first, nothing exceptional was done. The landlords in those areas from which the troops had been withdrawn organised their Protestant tenants, with perhaps a few of the tradesmen from the town, into small corps. They patrolled the countryside and kept order at fairs. That the English were getting the worst of it in America worried nobody in Ireland, least of all the Anglo-Irish, who felt themselves to be in a similar position relative to the English government as that of the American colonists. They were naturally upset when it was rumoured that George III had decided to train his Catholic subjects in Ireland for the American war. Such a scheme would undo all that had been achieved by the Penal Laws, which, for a century, had kept the native Irish untrained in every way, and the Protestants were determined that so they should remain. From the time of this rumour, the recruiting, the arming and the training of the local corps was intensified, and soon these bodies merged into an army and came to be known to history as the Volunteers.

The Irish parliament, some three-hundred strong, was always willing to obey the dictates of the English parliament. This satisfactory state of affairs, from the point of view of the English, had its source in the methods by which the members of the Irish parliament were chosen. The lords were the owners of boroughs or districts, which were represented in the Commons and which returned their nominees. These nominees formed the majority in the Commons and supported the government, provided the owners of the boroughs were sufficiently rewarded for their allegiance. Even so, they had much to tolerate. Among other humiliations, they had to watch, impotently, year after year, a significant part of the Irish revenue diverted to provide pensions and other rewards for the royal bastards, the retired mistresses, and Court favourites, along with others who were deemed unfitting to be included in the English honours list.

Thus, the Irish parliament had, so far, been completely docile to English influence. But soon, many of the members realised that they now had a weapon capable of forcing the English parliament to reverse many of its restrictions on Irish prosperity, which had accumulated over a long period. A number of the lords now became known as Patriots; that is, they decided their interest lay in better trading conditions for Ireland. Their nominees in the Commons followed their new policy, and in a short time it was carried to its logical conclusion: that the English parliament had no right to legislate for Ireland. The balance of the Commons was such that a minority of the tied boroughs voting with the independent members could defeat the government. At the time of Gandon's arrival in Ireland, Henry Grattan, an independent member of the Commons, a forceful orator, and unique in that he was incorruptible, led the Patriots. In the Lords, Lord Charlemont was the leader if this new body. He became Commander-in-Chief of the Volunteers, and Flood and Grattan were senior officers under him.

As was usual, a threat of force in Ireland at a time when the English were thin on the ground alarmed the English authorities. The Volunteers had some startling successes, but a deplorable tolerance now took hold of their leaders. It was suggested that the time had come to relieve the burdens on the native Irish. There was an immediate reaction from the castle. 1781 was a year of intense political activity, and in the year that followed, numerous titles and honours were offered to and accepted by many of the Patriots. The viceroy and the government stood for English influence, and their position of authority was reinforced. Gandon's patron, the Hon John Beresford, was one of those whose views on the English connection, and the dangers to it inherent in any leniency towards the Catholics, were extremely rigid.

The most influential families at that time were, firstly, the Fitzgeralds, and the first in rank in the kingdom was the Duke of Leinster. He had married a daughter of the Duke of Richmond, and was the father of seventeen children, one of whom, born in 1763, later became known as Lord Edward Fitzgerald. Next came the family of Lord Shannon, the son of Henry Boyle, Speaker of the House of Commons. He married Speaker Ponsonby's daughter, had enormous wealth and influence, and aimed steadily at controlling the castle. The Ponsonby family came next. The Speaker, the Right Hon John Ponsonby, was second brother to the Earl of Bessborough.

And so we come to the Beresfords. The Hon John Beresford was, after Fitzgibbon, whom we shall meet later as Lord Clare, perhaps the most formidable character in Ireland. He was unscrupulous and coldly calculating. Although he could not be described as a man of intellect, he was intelligent enough, in an age of privilege and precedent, to recognise the basis of political power and possess himself of it. In 1768 he became a Privy Councillor; in 1770, a Commissioner of the Revenue, and in 1771, he intrigued for the speakership. The Viceroy, Lord Townshend, was agreeable, but as Beresford wished to retain his Revenue commission, the viceroy felt that the duality in Beresford's hands would deprive him of a valuable exercise of patronage; he wanted Beresford to give it up. Beresford was unwilling to drop the substance for the shadow, and withdrew his application. He had no doubt he was on the right road, and after some twenty years busily spent packing his relatives into the public service, he had attained a position of such influence that the appointing of a speaker and the dismissal of a viceroy were now both within his power.

This stubborn man was secretly intrigued by his ability to overcome apparently insuperable difficulties. In him, this characteristic was reinforced by an asset of incalculable value: he was possessed of a quality of perseverance beyond the ordinary. It was a lively perseverance, subtle and burrowing, which, when frustrated, would disappear underground and emerge successful in some unexpected place. In November 1760,[77] he married Constancia Ligondes of Auvergne. She had intended to become a nun, but her aunt, the Countess Moira, persuaded her to come to Ireland, and once there, to marry Beresford, no doubt with Beresford's help. What affection he had for her we do not know, but to have perverted the intentions of a young girl, and to have carried her off in the face of the deep displeasure of her Catholic superiors was perhaps for him reward enough. She bore him at least nine children, two of whom became notorious blackguards. She died in November 1772. Eighteen months later he was preparing for his second marriage.

On 4th June 1774,[78] he married Barbara Montgomery, daughter of Sir William Montgomery. She was one of three sisters, another of whom married Luke Gardiner, Lord Mountjoy, and the third had become the Marchioness

John Beresford
by G.C. Stuart
(courtesy National Gallery of Ireland)

Townshend. The three sisters can be seen as the graces in the painting of that name by Sir Joshua Reynolds. Thus, Beresford allied himself to a rich Irish family and to a rich and powerful English one. From the start of this second marriage, Beresford moved closer to the English governing classes, both in heart and mind.

The Irish Ascendancy had always looked back to their spiritual home in England. Whenever possible, their children married back into the English nobility, and thus they might have gradually withdrawn to the place from which they came. Some of them did so withdraw, but retained their Irish estates, farming them out to agents, and, indifferent to the atrocities of these creatures, lived the carefree lives of absentees on the tribute of the original owners of their lands.

Beresford's second marriage seems to have been a reasonably happy one. They had at least eight children, five daughters and three sons. Barbara was referred to jokingly as the 'Barb', which may imply a freedom of speech on her part which caused Beresford to respect her. A rather different impression is given by the Duchess of Leinster, who wrote: 'Castletown is besieged, I think. Poor mad Mrs. Beresford comes flying down there every two or three days, with three sisters, no better, and a thousand other people for various reasons.' [79]

In Dublin (1781)

In 1780 Beresford became First Commissioner of the Revenue. Without delay, he put in motion two schemes he had had in mind for some time. The first was an improvement in the methods of revenue collection. Up until then, a significant part of the revenue had managed to find its way into the pockets of certain privileged individuals. These were people of influence and of high standing within the Ascendancy. While Lord Townshend was Viceroy, we are told 'that a large cargo of tobacco had been seen at a spot where it was deliberately overlooked, and that the cargo of an East Indiaman on which the duties would have been £13,000, had been landed surreptitiously at Cork, and that no inquiry was made'. Beresford would have none of this. He attacked one individual of importance and influence, and cut off the source of his perquisites. There were strong protests, but Beresford stood his ground and revealed a little of his power. The protests died down, and Beresford, his prestige greatly enhanced and his fitness for this position declared, stood well with the government and the English authorities.

He now moved on to his second scheme. This was for a new custom house nearer the mouth of the Liffey. His brother-in-law, Luke Gardiner, owned a con-

siderable area of land to the north-west of the city which he was anxious to
develop. While the shipping had to go up the river to the old custom house at
Capel Street Bridge, it was not possible to connect this land to the city by a
bridge. A new custom house to the east would solve this problem, and this
Beresford was determined would be built. It was a perilous affair. There had been
suggestions made from time to time for such a building, but they never got very
far against the powerful vested interests which had grown up for over a century
around the old custom house. That Beresford was extremely active at this time
we need not doubt, but his moves were hidden, and none of the parties against
whom he plotted was aware of what was going on until he had most of the site
acquired. That he failed in this business was to a certain extent due to over-confi-
dence. He was careless in the negotiations for some of the land required, and in
the end had to pay through the nose for it. During the three months when the
deal hung in the balance, Gandon had plenty of opportunity to get acquainted
with his new patron, for he was virtually Beresford's prisoner. Gandon now found
evidence that his first impressions of Beresford were well founded. The ground
had not been fully secured; indeed an essential area of it was not yet purchased.
The secret was out, and the old city merchants and traders, backed by a mob of
dependents, were in an ugly mood. But more serious still from his point of view,
was when he visited the site of the new custom house early one morning, he
found it covered with tidal water. Easily depressed by adversity, these various considerations must have tortured him during the long nights in the gloom of can-
dle-lit rooms during the interminable weeks of waiting. From time to time, he
seems to have been able to escape from Beresford's vigilance, and walk the streets
of this strange city, probably armed against possible violence with his sword stick,
which he carried, as he tells us, during the construction of the new custom house.
What he saw of Dublin did not impress him, and much of his early impressions of
this Anglo-Irish city have a familiar ring. He was quick, too, in understanding the
significant preoccupations of this strange society.

> In traversing a city of such large extent, the capital of a kingdom, I was
> greatly surprised to find but one print shop. There were two others in
> which prints were sold, but their trade was that of glaziers. The few houses
> to which I had access scarcely possessed a picture or print, and those
> which they had were but indifferent, mostly suspended from the wall,
> without either frame or glass. Hence I concluded that the Fine Arts were
> little attended to, and the profession not much respected. I afterwards
> found this to be the case: there were few painters of eminence, and but
> two architects, properly so called. The painters were Home, Wheatley and
> Hone in portrait; Ashford and Fisher in landscape, but these last two gen-
> tlemen depended more for their income on places which they held, than

on the results of their professional labours. But it was no wonder that the polite arts should not prosper in a country continually in political ferment, and where most of the families of distinction seemed wholly employed in converting their political influence into source of family or personal aggrandizement. The polite arts, or their professors can obtain little notice and less encouragement amidst such conflicting selfishness. A stranger, indeed, on a visit to Ireland, if his stay be short, will find every possible attention to render his reception agreeable, but should he become a resident he will perceive a cold indifference and neglect, and, like many of its highly gifted natives must seek for personal encouragement and celebrity in England.

The Architects of repute were Cooley and Ivory. Amongst the public buildings, particularly the churches, few showed anything like an attempt at style, and only two of them had steeples, viz., St. Patrick's and Werburgh's. The House of Commons was the chief amongst the public buildings. The Royal Exchange next, which was then but recently finished. The Blue Coat Hospital was then nearly completed. The Lying-in Hospital had been erected several years previously. There were no halls belonging to public companies, and with the exception of the Duke of Leinster's, the Marquis of Waterford's, the Earl of Charlemont's and Viscount Powerscourt's, there were scarcely any other houses which bore marks of the residence of the nobility. There were but four collections of pictures of consequence: these were the Duke of Leinster's, the Earl of Farnham's, the Earl of Charlemont's, and Lord Londonderry's. The houses of the gentry were generally inconvenient in their plans, having in most cases but two rooms on a floor, and these adapted for large parties, and as to architectural style, in embellishment, or finish, they were very imperfect. But such must ever be the case where professional architects are not employed, and that was the practice here. The propensity for building was so general that all professions embarked on it; even the gentry were almost always their own architects; therefore, skill in arrangement or good work was not to be expected. The parties whom they got to contract for the building were generally poor journeymen who, when left to themselves, were totally ignorant of the true value of what they undertook to execute, and in the scramble for employment the prices were so low, that they were in many instances more impoverished than benefited by the job; in addition to all which, when the works were completed, instead of receiving cash according to promise, they were constrained to take bills at six or twelve months as a settlement of their accounts. This led to endless petty differences for debts contracted during the work, by those very incompetent contractors, and the poor wretches they employed to assist them.[80]

THE CUSTOM HOUSE (I) (1781)

The weeks ran into months, but still Beresford kept Gandon a virtual prisoner. He was not allowed to present his letters of introduction or to visit friends he had made in London. His suspicions of the whole project must have been heightened when he realised the opposition was so violent as to keep Beresford in a state of anxiety lest it became known that the architect had arrived. In his account he tells us:

> I found myself in a very unpleasant state of suspense, apprehending that the abruptness of my departure from my family and establishment in London might injure my character, and, should my visit to Ireland prove unsuccessful, endanger my professional pursuits at home.[81]

Here he seems to hint at the scandal of the previous year when Chambers disappeared so mysteriously. He goes on to say:

> I had already remained in Dublin more than three weeks, in a kind of imprisonment when I ascertained that my presence was not yet necessary, the greater part of the grounds on which the new docks and stores were to be erected, not having finally been agreed upon. This delay was caused by the exorbitant demands made by the owners of the various lots of ground necessary for the great work, and with which demands, Mr. Beresford, as Chief Commissioner, did not feel himself justified in complying. Hence the unavoidable interruption of the works.
>
> Some time after my arrival in Dublin I was introduced by Mr. Beresford to the Right Honourable Burton Conyngham, at that time a strenuous advocate for the removal of the old Custom House to a more advantageous situation, and anxious also for many other improvements in the city. This gentleman had very large possessions in different parts of Ireland, and had a princely residence at Slane, on the banks of the river Boyne; he also was a great patron of the Fine Arts.
>
> Mr. Conyngham, being perfectly aware of the very awkward position in which I was just then placed, requested me, in the kindest manner, to accompany him to Slane, a distance of about twenty-two miles from Dublin. I accepted his invitation and remained in privacy there for several days, enjoying the hospitable courtesies of his noble establishment. While there, he consulted me on many alterations which he desired, and for which I made several slight sketch designs.

'View of the Corn Exchange, Burgh Quay and Custom House' by S.F. Brocas (detail)
(courtesy National Library of Ireland)

It is consoling to find that then, as now, professional guests were regarded as fair game by their hosts. Gandon continues:

> Just after I arrived at Slane, a note came to me by Mr. Beresford's order, by which I learned that he particularly wished me to come there.
>
> Friday
>   Mr. Meara presents his compliments to Mr. Gandon; he received the enclosed letter from Mr. Beresford, who thinks it would be advisable for him to go to Slane directly, as by the time he shall return, matters will be accommodated with certain parties Mr. Beresford will be in town this night or tomorrow.

Gandon continues:

> On my return to town I was again constrained to submit to my seclusion, and what greatly increased my annoyance was, that I was thereby deprived of obtaining any knowledge of the localities of the grounds, or acquiring any information from the various artificers; added to this, my sketches for the north and south fronts were in Mr. Beresford's possession, in order to be submitted to the Government and to other influential persons.
>   At last I ventured, but at very early hours in the morning, to walk over the grounds particularly those parts which had been procured for the site of the new Custom House, and the more I reflected on the situation and localities of the place, the more I became alarmed at the difficulties with which I had to contend in having the foundations laid; a vast body of river water overflowing near a square mile of surface, which portion became always inundated at spring tides.
>   These considerations, added to the uncertainty of the pending negotiations for additional grounds, rendered my situation by no means agreeable.
>   At length, after a period of three months, the negotiations for the purchase of the grounds were completed, and I received my sketches, with orders to commence forthwith by opening the grounds, as nothing but uncommon activity in the commencement would prevent the violent opposition of a most formidable party who were making every possible effort to stimulate the mob, and to procure petitions against the removal of the old Custom House.
>   I proceeded, of course, but, however elated I might have felt of having the opportunity of conducting a work of such magnitude, yet I could not avoid feeling great regret indeed, in being compelled to hurry into the

execution of such a structure, without having sufficient opportunity of considering, with proper attention, a plan of such immense extent, embracing such a variety of official departments, on the regulation and adjustment of which, and on all details of the plans, so much of both the beauty and the fitness of the structure would depend.[82]

Once again, we find that then, as now, clients who have large projects in mind are imprudently impatient with the practical difficulties. Gandon goes on:

> With my orders to commence immediate operations, I also received instructions to send to London for assistants and clerks. I was likewise directed to submit my drawings to Mr. Secretary Hamilton, and to consult with him on the necessary official departments, and the general accommodations required.
>
> To Mr. Hamilton's kind communications I was much indebted. He possessed an enlightened taste for every branch of the Fine Arts, and was eminently skilled in the science of architecture. In the arrangements of my designs for the Custom House, his suggestions were of the greatest importance.

At that time, the system of carrying out building works did not necessarily depend on a general contractor, and the architect, under certain conditions, might have to act as the general contractor and, at times, as the quantity surveyor, and carry on the works as if he were dealing with a series of subcontractors. Present-day practice demands that the architect, the quantity surveyor and the contractor act more as a committee than as separate entities. Gandon's wise stipulations have lost none of their force.

> I requested the artificers might be persons of some property, of known integrity and knowledge in their professions, and not given to litigation. Mr. Henry Darley was appointed stone-cutter, Mr. John Semple, bricklayer and rough mason, and Mr. Hugh Henry, carpenter; persons whose abilities were equal to any other of their respective trades.
>
> The obstacles which opposed themselves to the commencement of our operations, and the sudden orders which I received to proceed with the works, placed me in the unenviable position of a general who is forced to take the field without a staff, or even non-commissioned officers; for the assistants whom I was ordered to procure from London, I could not hope to have for several weeks. I, therefore held a meeting of the principal artificers on 10th July, 1781, and had the general plan marked out, and gave directions for opening the ground on those parts of the plan which were

the site of the east stores. This was, in great measure, a detached building, yet so arranged, that should afterwards connect itself and form an eastern front to the remaining building yet to follow.

As soon as this was known it became the absorbing subject of city conversation. Meetings were held to defeat it. The Pimlico Parliament were assembled in the Liberty, so termed. They were a restless, turbulent set of persons, accustomed to harangue the rabble, even to tumult and outrage. On the following Sunday, many hundreds of the populace met on the grounds. Whiskey and gingerbread were in great demand. It was apprehended that a riot would ensue, and that the trenches would be filled up: such was not the result; on the contrary, they amused themselves by swimming in them.[83]

Gandon was soon in trouble from several directions at once. The press was hostile, as we can see from the *Dublin Evening Post* of 21st July:

A correspondent informs us that the front of the new Custom House will be three hundred and seventy five feet, but adds that from the opinion which the public in general seem to entertain of the many injurious consequences likely to be experienced by the city from its situation, that he would venture to lay three hundred and seventy five pounds the plan is not carried into execution during the remainder of this century at least.

Or this on 24th July:

The workmen employed for sinking the ground for the foundations of the new Custom House are so few and their business seems to proceed so slowly that it is imagined the Commissioners are apprehensive of what may be the result of the City of Dublin's address to his Majesty, and therefore wish to make as little progress as possible before a final answer is received by the Committee of Merchants.

And again on 31st July:

The water flows so fast on the workmen who are sinking the ground for the new Custom House that they are obliged to pump continually night and day. It is imagined therefore the expense of laying the foundation will be the greatest expense of the building.

The omens too were not propitious. A comet appeared in the sky over Dublin, visible at night for about a fortnight; there were violent thunderstorms and heavy rain. Nevertheless on Friday, 27th July 1781, Mr Semple declared that a good foundation had been reached, and the actual work of building started. During this time, the petition against the erection of the custom house was hawked through the coffee houses, and a great number of signatures obtained. On Thursday, 4th August, it was carried in state to the viceroy, the Earl of Carlisle, who appears not to have been at his best that day, according to the *Evening Post*.

> When the Lord Mayor and Corporation waited on his Excellency, the Lord Lieutenant on Thursday last, with the address, they were most graciously received. After the first was read by the Town Clerk, which was an address to his Excellency himself, he said: 'the City of Dublin may depend that I will without delay, transmit this Address to his Majesty.' The address to his Majesty against the removal of the Custom House was then presented, to which the same answer, verbatim, was given. By which it appears his Excellency had unfortunately got off but one answer, which he would have given to forty different addresses had they been presented on that day.

From this time the work proceeded rapidly, and soon Gandon was able to write:

> On Wednesday, the 8th. August, 1781, about sixty feet in length, and fifty feet in breadth was cleared out and levelled, and the first stone was laid by the Right Hon. John Beresford, without any formality, as we were apprehensive that a riot might be got up by the assemblage of a number of interested persons. This part of the foundations proceeded with rapidity, and was enclosed with a wooden paling, which prevented the works from being interrupted.[84]

The *Dublin Evening Post* carried a somewhat different story:

> Yesterday, at one o'clock in the afternoon the first stone of the new Custom House was laid by Mr. Semple's and Mr. Darley's two foremen, who had thus the honour of immortalizing themselves on the occasion. Let not the public, however, imagine that these two workmen are to carry off the more blooming part of the fame: they were godfathers only to the stone by proxy, representing the personages of Luke Gardiner, Esq., and the Right Hon. John Beresford. To the everlasting credit of his Excellency the Lord Lieutenant it is reported he absolutely refused to be concerned in the dirty business.

There were now 150 cars drawing stone for the building, and the Corporation became alarmed. Gandon tells us:

The Corporation of Dublin of that day, feeling a perfect conviction in the utter impossibility in erecting such a structure as the new Custom House on such a swamp of ground as the North Lots then were, desisted from any violence, or opposition; but when it was found that the foundations were going on with activity and vigour and that success would be the necessary result, and by which their movements, and their anticipations, were being frustrated, they called a post assembly, and determined to do all in their power to prevent any further progress of the works.

Having passed their resolutions, without any intimations to, or communications with, the Commissioners of Revenue or Excise, by whose orders the works were progressing, or without any instruction, or sanction of Government authority, but solely of their own free will and motion, as entered in their books of September 1781, the High Sheriff, accompanied by an influential member of the Corporation, who subsequently became a conspicuous personage as a military general [this was Napper Tandy], followed by a numerous rabble with adzes, saws, shovels, etc.,etc., came in a body on the grounds, and levelled that portion of the fence, which had been thrown up, adjoining the North Wall and River Liffey.

This outrage was committed under the pretence that the grounds so enclosed were a portion of the Corporation property, which claim was soon found to be utterly false and illegal. The evening after this violent outrage I received, from Mr. Beresford the following note:

'Greenwood, Saturday, 3 o'clock

Dear Sir, – I find that the jury have prevented the enclosure on the North Strand. The Sheriff will come down of course: if it can be, let the enclosure be replaced instantly. You can have the holes made tomorrow, and set your posts to put it up, as fast as it is pulled down. Prevent all opposition, and laugh at the extreme folly of the people.

Yours sincerely, John Beresford' [85]

The tone of the press changed after this attack, and we can now detect a certain grudging admiration for the resolute action taken by Gandon, as in the *Dublin Evening Post* of 13th September:

After all the row that has been made of marching and counter-marching, bombarding and battering – undermining and blowing up the fortifications and Chevaux de Frieze erected by their High Mightinesses to conceal their advances upon the North Wall, and which was attacked in so irresistible a manner by the Pipe Water Pioneers on Tuesday last, that scarce a trace of their former position could be found, we are positively assured that such excellent dispositions were formed by the vanquished foe, so great an additional body of men were at that same night employed that they instantly repaired the breaches, sunk their intended shore, perforated the wall, and fixed their floodgates so that the water is now carried off with ease at the ebb of tide and will not in future in the least incommode the workmen – We will now see whether the Common Council have spirit sufficient to take any further step to remove works effected upon this ground in direct and avowed opposition to their resolution and interest.

The works of the New Custom House seem to be carrying on with so much spirit and such indefatigable industry excited in prosecuting the undertaking, that by the time Parliament meets next month – they will be able to show the people at least something for their money.

So confident are the Commissioners of overcoming every obstacle and every opposition that the inhabitants of the Capital can possibly use to oppose the erection of this new edifice that no less than seven large vessels, entirely freighted with Portland Stone are expected every tide by Mr. Darley, in Abbey Street, who has a contract for the freestone of that building, the foundation for which is now digging.[86]

An official apology has been made to our Chief Magistrate for the unwarrantable conduct of the architect of the New Custom House in having without permission taken upon him to enclose a part of the North Wall.

Gandon does not mention the matter of the apology, but says:

This was the last opposition given by the Dublin Corporation of that day. But there were interruptions given on other occasions, and at subsequent periods, to which I may, perhaps, feel myself constrained to allude.

On 22nd September, the press reported:

The City is in high spirits upon having discovered, as they imagine, a mode of totally blowing up all the works at the new Custom House and preventing the least possibility of their ever being reinstated – the committee for setting leases after rummaging all the old city parchments they could meet with in the Town Clerk's office cannot find the least trace of any grant whatever being made of the ground which was lately taken by the Commissioners for their present site; they further allege that the person who let the ground up on the North Wall could convey no right which rests absolutely with the City, and for which reason they have given to the recorder to file a bill soon as possible to restore that part of their estate and to give every obstruction to the works.

ARCHITECTURAL NOTE

By every standard, the Dublin Custom House excels as a work of architecture, and any attempt at criticism is therefore hazardous, particularly so at the present time when the accepted attitudes of the eighteenth century are, to a large extent, alien to our contemporary society. It was, like all public buildings then, designed to enhance the prestige of those who commissioned it, and this is still apparent to modern eyes, even though its scale is domestic and its dignity has been diluted by adjacent structures. It is not one of those overscaled buildings which look as if they had been designed for giants, and with which we of this century are familiar. Those are the fantasies of Hollywood and of the fascist states, whose object was to emphasise the personal helplessness of the citizen.

Albert Speer, when asked what effect the gigantic structures of the Third Reich would have on the average man, replied that they were designed on such a scale as to make his presence negligible. In other words, the public buildings of that state expressed exactly the principles on which it was founded. And when we look at the enormous beehives of glass and metal erected by the multinationals and by modern states to house their servants, the meaning is clear too: there are those who belong to the hive and those who do not. It was no different in the eighteenth century, although then the emphasis was on more personal and more human aspects of power.

The eighteenth-century ascendancy class belonged to a relatively settled and continuing world in which they had a legitimate part, acknowledged by all and confirmed by long centuries of tradition. Their place was assured by the universal belief in hereditary rights and duties, and the idea of a corporate society, even then entertained by the odd individual here and there, was as offensive to their philosophy of life as the idea of socialised industry is to the North American company director. Thus, the basically feudal society of that time was an affair of individuals who held their places by hereditary right, by the blood which flowed in their veins, and they had no need to resort to exhibitions of power, as such, to reinforce their security, for they were strangers to the insecurity of tenure in the modern sense. But they greatly desired to proclaim their status, and this they did by the opulence of their entourage and the grandeur of their residences. Thus the Custom House must not be judged by its fitness for trade and commerce, but by its qualities of a palace: the public expression of the status and influence of the Hon John Beresford.

And it was to another palace that James Gandon turned his mind when he was casting about for that basic idea which is essential for the inspiration of all art. Gandon seems never to have been greatly influenced by the French architects whose designs he must have seen during his time with Chambers. Rather surprisingly. he became interested in the work of the seventeenth-century English architects, and now the palace of the Churchills engaged his attention. He discounted the theatrical excesses of the architect and dramatist Vanburgh, by which the main approach to Blenheim is enhanced, but found in the composition of the rear elevation a sober and correct expression of the elements of the building which appealed to his idea of architectural order. From this he developed the basic features of his design, transmuting them into something new and possessed of a character totally distinct from the baroque of Vanburgh.

The central element in the plan of the Custom House was the Long Room, with its ancillary accommodation. Here the public business of the shipowners and captains was transacted, and it ran from just behind the dome and peristyle of the river front to the Beresford Suite at the rear, facing Beresford Place. This element was expressed in the front elevation with emphasis, and also, but to a lesser extent, in the rear elevation. So it can be said that Gandon's preference for the entry into a building on the long axis is seen here too, for the significant body of the Custom House ran from front to back.

But this formal emphasis on the central block is only apparent if one has the plan in mind. Gandon is, as was his habit, equivocal here, and presents the main façades of the building as if their main direction is from side to side. In fact, the attic story which binds the three central units, reinforces this directional feeling, for it is cut off sharply at the rear of the façade, and gives no clue as to what is behind it. And when we observe how the Portland-stone finish of the river front is terminated at the corners at each end of this front, we get a mild sense of staginess. Perhaps later theories of architecture are behind this feeling, for such treatment was common in the eighteenth century and accepted as legitimate. In fact, Gandon seems to have been a little ahead of his time, for he took the trouble to continue the cornice, the frieze and the plinth in Portland stone so that our sense of continuity is largely satisfied, and the combination of Portland stone and granite at the west façade of the building gives a far more pleasing effect than if the whole of the structure were faced to match the river front.

Many architects, having achieved success on one façade, would have been content to let the rest of the design work itself out, but not Gandon. Few comparable buildings come to mind, where, on turning the corner at either end, we are faced with the same lively variety of imagination.

At the west end he has placed one of the link units from the river front, but has completely reversed its subordinate character. He has both isolated it from the end pavilions by arched entrances, and linked it to them on the first floor, while at the same time thrusting it forward to dominate them, and so form with them an original composition. We notice too how he has dispensed with the void in these end pavilions by bringing forward the central bay, so that they now present a solid mass in contrast to the originally arcaded void of the now dominant west block. In the same way, he has closed the east end of the complex with

The Custom House by James Malton
(*courtesy National Gallery of Ireland*)

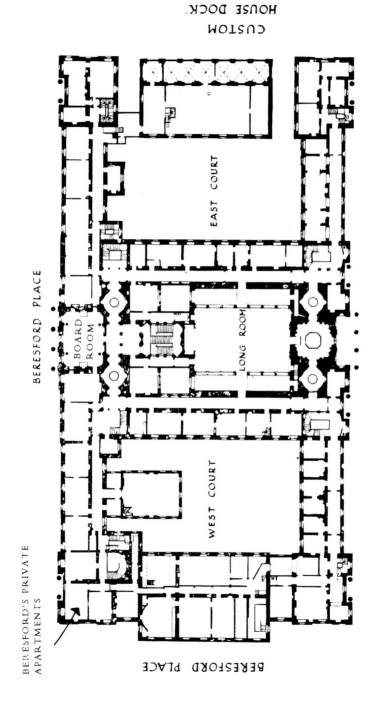

The Custom House, 1781-1800
First-floor plan (prior to the 1921 fire) and cross-section
(courtesy Irish Architectural Archive)

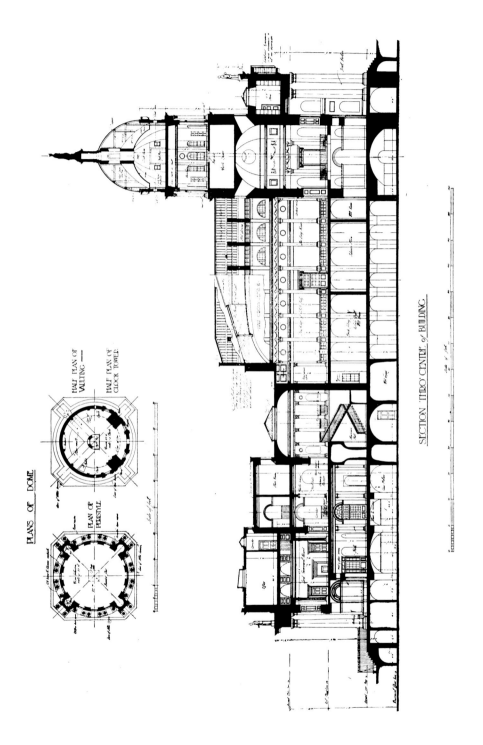

PLANS OF DOME

HALF PLAN OF WAITING

HALF PLAN OF CLOCK TOWER

PLAN OF PERISTYLE

SECTION THRO CENTRE of BUILDING

The Custom House – Long Room, cross section and plan
(*courtesy Irish Architectural Archive*)

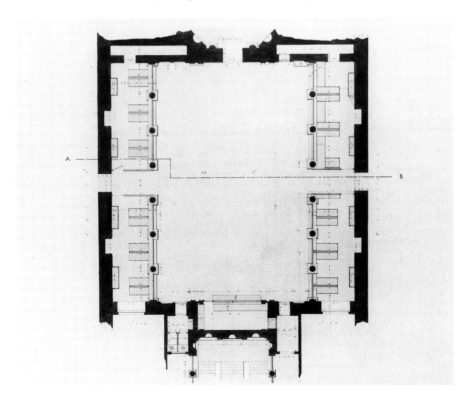

a charming single-storey arcaded unit, which at that time faced the quiet waters of the new dock.

The northern façade is plain. Here too the Long Room is expressed by the slight advance of the central portion and by the strong attic storey, with a simple portico below. Gandon disdained to cap the portico with a pediment in the accepted manner, but turned it into a delightful feature by placing a statue above the cornice over each column and against a background provided by the attic storey. Note the entrance which echoes a triumphal arch. This façade is quite different in character from the formal gaiety of the river front. It is restrained and severe in every way; even the frieze of Portland stone is omitted.

It is fanciful to suggest that Gandon had so quickly summed up the Hon John Beresford that he strove to express his philosophy of life in architectural terms, but looking at this part of the building, we suspect he has unconsciously done so. It is a palace façade, but not a palace like that suggested by the river front. Here is no ornate face, but an approximation of an early Renaissance Roman palace. There is no nonsense about it. It was perhaps the first efficiently organised taxing office in these islands, and it has about it something of the modern faceless bureaucratic machine, and with this, a hint of the austere dignity of its occupant, for the central first-floor rooms constituted Beresford's office. Here, hidden as always, the shadowy power of the Hon John Beresford had its life centre, and all around, totally at his command, the servants of the palace laboured to ensure that his government – and we must remember that he did not think of it as of the state, but rather as a family concern – got its full share of the plunder.

On a summer's evening, when the sun shines obliquely across the granite ashlar of its walls, casting shadows beneath the cornice and darkening the space behind the central portico, it evokes a charm and softness which belies what has been written above, but look at it in winter under grey skies and the effect is very different, almost sombre. Beresford choose to look inland across the then tidal grasslands towards the higher ground of Summerhill, part of the estate of his brother-in-law, Luke Gardiner. He was able to watch the development of that area, following the initiation of the new custom house, as the trading centre of Dublin, and over the years, with Gardiner Street laid out to line with his suite, and with the decorous London façades of the houses of Beresford Place enclosing the gardens below his windows, he had every reason to be content with his achievements.

On 25th May 1921, the IRA, under the command of Brigadier Oscar Traynor, took over the Custom House. There was a sharp encounter in which five of their number were killed. The staff was hurried from the building which was then fired. It burned for five days, and at the end of that time, 130 years of British records had disappeared. A major work of art had also been irremediably scarred. The heat calcined much of the Portland stone, and the walls, which had for so

The Custom House
Façade to river

The Custom House – façade to river

The Custom House – north elevation

*The Custom House
– west end*

*Riverine head by Edward Smyth
– Liffey*

long stood unflawed as a monument to Gandon's skill, developed cracks. During the reconstruction work, the internal planning was much altered, and the great Long Room was omitted. Two crossing blocks of offices, one on each side of the space in which it had stood, were constructed. In spite of this wholesale replanning, the Custom House still presents broadly an unchanged appearance, apart from the absence of its many chimneys. Probably the chief loss, apart from the Long Room, is the white stone of the peristyle beneath the dome, which must have been quite a striking feature. It was rebuilt in Ardbraccan limestone, which darkens with weathering to an unpleasant muddy colour. Elsewhere throughout the building, there are many features which have been lost: the fine arched flying staircase to the Long Room; the well in the first floor which gave a vista up into the cupola; and there are many other modifications, generally for the worse. These have been catalogued by Maurice Craig and make sad reading. But the building was so rich in detail that even such seemingly extreme destruction was unable to rob it of its essential character. In the year 1630, Inigo Jones designed the Covent Garden arcades. They too have vanished, but it is not unreasonable to suggest that their memory haunts the arcades of the Custom House, for much of Gandon's early life was spent beneath their shade, and he did not forget them. The tower, too, of the Greenwich buildings – features of the London horizon of his youth – are reproduced, but modified, in the dome and peristyle, and the bands of Portland stone are from the London streets and perhaps from Hampton Court. The end pavilions remind us of features on Gibbs' St Martin in the Fields, with the square pilasters broadened into wide stone panels. In this building on an alien shore he seems to have stored the memories of his early life.

The Custom House is adorned with a surprising number of remarkably fine sculptures: Edward Smyth's heads of the river gods, the great coats of arms, the urns and swags, the rich pediment, and the many skyline statues. Successive visits always reveal new aspects of Gandon's design. Some obvious features deserve comment.

Although apparently a two-storey building, there is a third storey hidden behind the balustrade above the cornice, a typical Gandon ploy to avoid windows. Gandon's original river front had only thirty-nine visible windows, perhaps only twice as many as would be found in a pair of contemporary semi-detached houses. There are more today, for niches have been opened up and some doors are now windows. But Gandon's predilection for the pure contrast of solid and void without the unwelcome intrusion of windows can be detected even here in a building which seems to be liberally fretted with openings.

The Custom House became the centre of a complex of docks and

The Custom House
– east end

Riverine head by Edward Smyth
– Barrow

warehouses. It dominated the eastern expansion of the city, and became the terminal feature of a new river scape until the construction of the Loop Line railway bridge in the nineteenth century. Thereafter, it stood alone, cut off from and largely unnoticed by the citizens who thronged the new Sackville Street, and who owed their environment there to its construction. Today, the nearby contemporary office blocks force upon it a mildly surrealistic presence, and have sadly diminished the dominant character it once possessed.

COOLBANAGHER (1781-85)

September of 1781 merged into October. The candles were lit earlier now as the dark days approached, but the coming of winter brought no relief from the storms of the summer. In December, Gandon was invited to spend Christmas at Dawson Court, near Portarlington, with Lord Carlow and his family.

John Dawson, Lord Carlow, of Dawson Court, Queen's County (Co Laois) was born on 23rd August 1744, two and a half years after Gandon. He succeeded in 1779 to the title of Viscount Carlow and Baron Dawson on the death of his father, and he became Earl of Portarlington in 1785.[87] He was also Colonel of the Queen's County Militia. He represented Portarlington, and later, in two successive parliaments, Queen's County, of which he had been appointed governor on his father's death. He married, on 1st January 1778,[88] Lady Caroline Stuart, fifth daughter of John, Earl of Bute, who was Prime Minister of England at the start of the American War of Independence. They had five sons and four daughters.

Lord Carlow, one of Paul Sandby's circle, took a keen interest in architecture and in the arts, and now, with Gandon in Ireland, he felt the time had come to put in hand his plans for developing his estate. He decided to make a start with the construction of a new parish church for Coolbanagher, a village on his lands and near his house which was in the care of the Rev William Dawson.

Gandon arrived in good time for the festivities to find the household discussing the news that a Miss Cripps, a much sought-after young lady, had gone mad. Lady Carlow summed up the incident with, 'I think all the people who have wanted to marry her may hug themselves upon not succeeding.'[89]

The stormy weather continued, and to add to the unease of the household, a baby was cutting teeth. Lady Carlow writes:

> I really have been quite uncomfortable for some time past from the violence of the storms. The night before last I believe there was not a soul

could shut their eyes, and I thought of nothing but the house coming down every instant.

And again

> We have had another storm tonight, which is not yet abated and you must not wonder if I appear out of spirits, for nothing worries me so much as a high wind, besides that it hinders my sleeping ... I was uneasy last night about the boy. His teeth hurt him so much he could not help groaning and crying, and nothing would divert him. He seems better today, though he had a very bad night, but he does not grind his teeth and work his mouth about so much. I can hardly find a place to sit today, being turned out of the drawing room by smoke, and there is a whirlwind in the library. All our brilliant Xmas set are almost collected. Miss Dawson we expect today, little Damer came yesterday, and William Dawson and Mr. Gandon the architect have been here some time.[90]

They were confined to the house over Christmas, and got on each other's nerves. Lord Carlow was full of his schemes for a church for the Rev W. Dawson – a lake and a cascade, as well as the great scheme for a new house. No doubt he and Gandon discussed these matters ad nauseam, much to the disgust of the ladies of the party, which was not a success. On New Year's Eve, Lady Carlow wrote: '... some of our party was broken up already, Mr. Dawson and Mr. Gandon being gone. I cannot say I regret them very much.' A Miss Herbert, who was staying with Lady Carlow, was more outspoken: 'A merry Xmas party, we all wish you a happy New Year. If Lady Carlow has not told you the Xmas party, I will. A Methodist parson, a painter, a builder. Two fine beaus were expected, but never arrived, alas!'[91]

It was shortly after Christmas when Gandon returned to Dublin, having escaped the violent storm which descended on the city on Christmas Day, and which took down the chimney stacks around St Stephen's Green and in other parts of the town. There would have been several sessions with Lord Carlow to discuss the design for the church, with, perhaps, hints of his scheme for building himself a new country house to replace Dawson Court, which was old and inconvenient. There was also a move afoot to extend the House of Lords in Dublin, and if Gandon did not find there the conviviality to which he was accustomed, nevertheless he returned to Dublin with at least the prospect of a couple of respectable projects to enlarge his practice.

Soon Lord Carlow put the work of building his church in hand. The site is a field near the village of Coolbanagher, which commands a surprisingly wide prospect. Work started in the spring of 1782, and the site had to be cleared and

*Church at Coolbanagher
Co Laois, 1781-85*

Church at Coolbanagher
above View attributed to James Malton
below Plan

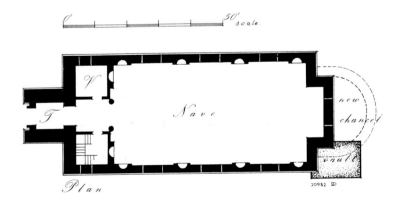

the foundations excavated. The lime had to be burned and slaked, and a start made in quarrying the stone and drawing it to the site. Lord Carlow was a careful man, distrustful, and with reason, of the progress made during his frequent visits to Dublin and to the House of Lords. Therefore he would have kept his labour force small, and as a consequence, the progress of building would have been slow. This conjecture is supported by the few letters which have survived. He wrote to Lady Carlow, then in London, on 18th November 1783: 'The church has been neglected but now gets on apace, and I believe I shall have the whole body of it fit for roofing before the winter sets in. I shall not, however, put on the roof till spring.' [92] In this he was over optimistic, for he writes to her again on 10th December: 'I have concluded my work at the church for this season. It will make a very conspicuous object to the new house and to the whole province of Leinster.' [93] It was fortunate that he finished the work so early in December. The mortar should have set sufficiently by the end of the month to resist damage, for a severe frost set in on Christmas Day and lasted until 21st February 1784.[94]

No further reference to the church appears to be extant, either from Lord Carlow or from Gandon, until we come to a letter written from Dawson Court by Lady Carlow, and dated simply 'saturday, March 1785'. She says:

> We are going to have great doings here next week. The new church is to be consecrated on Tuesday; the Bishop and all the clergy in the neighbour-hood are to attend, besides all the country, I suppose, and Lord Carlow will ask them all to dinner both on that day and on the next, as there are races within three miles of us. I own I am sorry to begin all this sort of work so soon, but there is no help for it.

At some time, Gandon designed a tomb for Lord Carlow which was built beside the sanctuary, and the church remained at peace and undisturbed for more than eighty years. Then the church was Ruskenised by the addition of an apse. The work was designed by Thomas Drew FRIAI of 60 Upper Sackville Street (now O'Connell Street), and the contract for the work was signed on 22nd August 1868. The drawings include a Hiberno-Venetian facelift for the tomb. Fortunately, this was never carried out. The existing roof trusses appear on his drawings, so it would appear that Gandon's vaulted ceiling was replaced by a flat one, which was at some time taken down.[95]

In 1972, the Rev Cecil M. Wilson and his committee initiated a careful programme of restoration work, which has secured the building for at least a generation. Then, in 1981, urns, similar to those originally planned, were placed in the niches; the generous gift of Mr Cholmeley-Harison of Emo. Now, except for the open trussed roof, the main body of the church approximates closely Gandon's original design.

ARCHITECTURAL NOTE

In 1779, the old parish church at Coolbanagher was maliciously burned down. It had been a poor building of rough stone and roofed with thatch. Lord Carlow was anxious that the new structure should reflect his good taste and the classical culture of his time.

Gandon had produced a number of curious sketches, which seem to link themselves to Coolbanagher. They are exercises on the theme of a drawing by Clerisseau for a sepulchral chamber, and suggest that Gandon's first thoughts envisaged the proposed building as having the character of a mausoleum. However, these, if they had any connection with the church, were abandoned, and, as Dr McParland has pointed out, Gandon reverted to his original ideas for a public space related to his concourse for the Nottingham courthouse.

This theme is developed and refined at Coolbanagher. Niches in vertical panels give rhythm to the walls, and are carried across the segmental ceiling, while recessed panels between take the place of the columnar screens and central coved entrance. It is basic Gandon refined to a classic simplicity. Externally, too, the near-Diocletian windows, set in shallow panels, and the predominant areas of wall are features echoed in the older part of Naas courthouse and at New Inn. The incorporation of a vestibule and hallway, a vestry and staircase, a gallery and the nave and chancel in one building, with, in the original design, only four noticeable windows is a typical Gandon achievement. The nave proper is thirty-feet wide and sixty-feet long. Is it merely coincidence that the church at Covent Garden, one of Gandon's favourite haunts, is in the same proportion, being fifty-two-feet wide and 104 feet long, or a proportion of 1:2? Also, there is the Gandon niche: the curved envelope enters the wall directly, without the confusing emphasis of a moulding or architrave. The internal strings, swags and medallions are pure Gandon.

When we contemplate this unique building today, we must remember that in Gandon's time it was then just as difficult to travel around Ireland as it is to move around Africa today. His visits to the building cannot have been frequent, and client and master mason were apt to introduce their own variations; the client for the sake of economy, and the mason from custom. Gandon would scarcely have left the external walls unrelieved and unpunctuated by ornament. His absence, too, may explain the one shocking anomaly of the building: the Gothic spire. The proportions of the building – the broad section, the short nave, the low pitched roof – are all alien to the gothic tradition. Some of Gandon's drawings which have survived show an obelisk above the tower. Why Lord Carlow accepted the spire is hard to understand; perhaps the masons talked him into it. An identical spire tops the tower at Ballinakill in the south of the county, so the same masons may have been involved. The Coolbanagher spire is topped by a metal rod carrying a copper ball, which, for over two centuries, has proved Gandon's conviction that this was the correct method to protect his buildings against lightning. Oddly enough, a similar ball tops the spire at Ballinakill.

Like all Gandon's buildings, Coolbanagher suffered from neglect, but not as badly as most. His art still shines through. The unity of the main building and the tower is harmonious; but it is in the nave that Gandon's genius can be appreciated. Here is the skill of the professional at work. The interior is large, indeed larger than the average assembly hall, but it has been unified, embellished, and, by a fastidious choice of relative proportions, brought down to a comfortable domestic scale. The casual visitor leaves with the impression that he has been in a large room, for the true size is not apparent. This is in conformity with eighteenth-century ideas of scale. At present, this can only be appreciated to any extent by viewing the interior with one's back to the added chancel arch and apse, which have destroyed much of the effect. We can only be thankful that the improvers left us with what we have today.

MRS GANDON (1782)

The editors of *The Life* now tell us

> ...he received a letter informing him that his children were well, but that Mrs. Gandon's health was in a declining state. He therefore made arrangements for progressing with the east wing of the Custom House, and, having obtained leave of absence he went to London, intending, amongst other arrangements, to dispose of his house, and then to return to Dublin.
>
> But he soon perceived that the alarming indisposition of Mrs. Gandon wholly unfitted her for the fatigues of so long a journey. He therefore was constrained to stop much longer in London than he had intended. Her illness increased, the sad result was her death, and thus he had to follow to the tomb, the beloved object of all his affections.
>
> He remained in London until the following March, and then, accompanied by his children, one son and two daughters, and also his clerk of works, a Mr. Harman, he returned to Dublin.[96]

At first sight there is nothing remarkable about these three paragraphs. There is the simple statement that he went to London, a difficult journey at that time, including a hazardous sea-crossing as well as four or five days in an unheated coach during the worst part of the winter. The death of his wife is mentioned briefly and without detail. Is this an example of unusual Victorian reticence? For they seem to have liked medical detail, and became expansive about death and funerals. We are told he returned to Dublin with his children. These were his son James, aged eight (later a collaborator with Thomas Mulvany in producing *The Life*), and his two daughters, Mary Anne, aged ten, and Elizabeth, aged six. It is only when we look for confirmation of Mrs Gandon's death that some curious factors emerge. No record of her death at about that time has so far been found,

Paul Sandby's accounts
(*courtesy Irish Architectural Archive*)

nor is there any record so far found of the death of his third daughter, Eleanor Margaret, who would have been seven.

Dr McParland has called attention to the payments made by Paul Sandby in London on Gandon's behalf. Sandby's bill to Gandon for his disbursements from November 1787 to May 1789 has survived, and in it there are payments for a 'Mrs. G.' There is also a payment for 'Miss Gandon and sisters for stays', which implies the presence of the third sister, Eleanor Margaret. The last 's' in sisters is quite clear, although it only escapes by a fraction from being blotted out by a fold in the paper. In the bill, there are various payments, some to Gandon's sister, Mrs Handyside, one to a Mrs Mortimer, and a few now obscure, but most of the payments are to or on behalf of Miss Gandon, and some for 'Miss Eliz.', two of his daughters, apparently at that time living in London, aged about seventeen and thirteen respectively. The payments for the daughters are all for expenses such as frocks, gloves, laundry and so forth, and they are irregular. But there are four quarterly payments shown for July and November of 1788, and for January and April of 1789, and these vary from '£12.14.0.' to '£13.6.6.' They are entered as 'Payne's quarter, etc.'. One entry, 'Mrs. Payne coming to London for Mrs. G. etc.£-.10.-.', links Mrs Payne with Mrs G., and we might suppose Mrs Payne to be perhaps a housekeeper or companion to Mrs G. Each of the quarterly entries is immediately followed by a payment for Miss Gandon. There are other payments for Mrs G. for 'necessaries', for 'dying an old gown for Mrs. G.', for 'quilting, etc.', and for 'mending, etc. her gowns'.

One is tempted to identify Mrs G. with Mrs Gandon, especially as Miss Gandon is equally entered as Miss G. in a number of places. If this is true and Mrs Gandon was living near London, then we might assume that Gandon's daughters were staying with her. It is hard to imagine where else they could be safe to their father's satisfaction in the London of that day. Then there is Mrs Payne's visit to town for Mrs G. Only one visit to town in a year-and-a-half would probably indicate that Mrs G. was not well at that time or she would have come herself. The refund to Mrs Payne of ten shillings does not tell us anything of the distance travelled, as the 'etc.' is not known.

It is hard to know what to make of all this. Sandby's accounts evoke a strong and compelling temptation to believe that Gandon's wife did not die during his visit to London in the early half of 1782, but there is no firm evidence of this. On the other hand, why should her son and Thomas Mulvany, although adept at misdirection, as we have seen, propagate such a curious story? We may suppose that Mrs Gandon refused to go to Ireland with her husband, and kept one of her daughters with her in London. But, if this is true and there was some shameful element in the matter for the family, why mention it at all? The problem will only be solved when records of the deaths of Mrs Gandon and of her daughter, Eleanor Margaret have been found.

THE CUSTOM HOUSE (II) (1782-83)

O n his return from London, we are told that Gandon brought with him a Mr Harman, who would be his clerk of works, for the rising walls of the east wing of the Custom House were coming up rapidly, and it was now time to tackle the main building. The north and south fronts were marked out, as well as the new docks and stores, and the excavations commenced. Gandon's description of the work is most interesting:

The labourers had scarce got down two feet below surface when they came to water, which four men emptied with scoops as they continued to extend the line of the trenches, which were carried on in short lengths, and, for convenience, of different depths. It became necessary to make dams across parts of them with sods, and to empty the water from the lower to the higher dam, until it was at last sent off in a drain prepared for that purpose, our pumps not being then ready. The ground was opened first at the north and continued round to the east front; then to the south end, where a boiling spring with sand appeared at about four feet below the surface, which filled up as fast as it was cast out. It extended for a considerable distance. Inch and a half sheet piles, about seven feet long were driven down with a maul to keep up the bank, and sods were fitted in layers between it and the piles, which prevented the sand from being washed out, thereby enabling the men to clear out the trenches to the depth required. The general texture of the ground was gravel, mixed in some places with a layer of blue clay and sand, under which was a hard stone gravel. When the trenches were thus prepared and cleared out, the rough masons then proceeded to carry on the first bench or course with all possible expedition with the black stone, and immediately filled in with earth, in order to give less water to pump. In the meantime, another length, and of the same depth, was got ready, and an additional number of masons set to work. In this manner the whole was continued until all was brought up to the level of the ground.

The sort of pumps required could not be obtained; those now procured were only for temporary service: they were one foot square and vertical, worked by two or more men day and night. We afterwards used inclined pumps, which were very convenient being easily removed when required. They were such as I had seen used in making excavations in England. They seldom exceeded twelve or thirteen feet in length, but I had occasion to try some larger, and with great success.

The excavations and pumping out of the water of this portion stood at 10 1/2 d. per yard; the labourers were employed by the day, and from their indolence required close watching. It was deemed advisable to set the remaining portion by contract, and a person offering to undertake it for 6 d. per yard, an agreement was made with him accordingly; but at the end of the work he was the loser, and upon my representation of his loss to the Revenue Board, they allowed what they deemed sufficient compensation.

The quay wall or road on the south front was an old embankment, made about the year 1725; it was sixty feet wide at top, and badly constructed; the walls of black stone; its foundations laid on the surface of the strand; on the side next the river it was twelve feet high, but on the inside only eight; the filling between the walls was a sand used ballast; the base of the foundations stood at least six feet above the bed of the river; the tide not only soaked under them but filtered in several places through the joints of the masonry. It was therefore deemed most prudent to commence with the north east wing, after the portion of the store room, it being less liable to be incommoded with water from the river.

Directions were now given for excavating that part of the centre of the south front for the cupola and portico, and as this advanced so near the river we were certain of much obstruction from the flowing of the tide, which was the only water which now gave us any trouble, for the springs were now pretty well dried and kept under. The pumps hitherto were but thirteen or fourteen feet, we now used two of eighteen feet in length. The ground altered in its texture towards the river, becoming less loose, with small sandy gravel, like that of the south west angle. We deemed it prudent to bore it in several places which were near the angles of the front of the portico, but particularly where the walls of the cupola were to be erected, to the depth of eight feet below the then surface, and it appeared to be much of the same substance as that already described. A pile ten feet long and one foot square was driven down in the centre to nine feet depth; but after twenty strokes of the ram it could be driven no further, which assured us that we had got down to firm ground.

Upon consulting with the principal artificers on the spot, it was then thought advisable to desist from sinking any more, but to make an artificial foundation, in order to sustain the great weight of the cupola; but whether by piling or otherwise was submitted wholly for my consideration. This part of the work had long occupied my thoughts, and to it I had given every attention, my conjectures having led me to expect great difficulties on this subject. I had nearly made up my mind as to the means I should adopt, and was the more strongly confirmed in my intentions, having remarked a circumstance which had escaped the notice of those around me. Immediately after the pile had been driven, I perceived a small stream of water arising up close all round it, as if it had pierced a spring, and recollecting an observation in Labelye's account of Westminster Bridge, 'that piles sometimes loosen and open fresh springs which often make it very difficult to get rid of the water', I was now apprehensive of just such an impediment. The great expense of preparing the piles, and the very long time it would take to drive so great a number as would be required, presented a strong objection to the use of them. I therefore gave directions to have a grating of Memel timber prepared, the timber to be one foot square, to have the upper ones notched down three inches in the ground pieces, which were to be bedded on a layer of cut heath, the whole ground being first correctly levelled; the interstices of the grating to be filled in with hard sound stock bricks, up to the level of the timbers, swimming in mortar well mixed, which answered nearly as well as tarras, over which was laid four inch fir planks fastened down on the grating with oak trennels, which was all completed. The foundation walls were then set out on 17th, September. The part directly under the cupola was laid out with rough blocks of mountain granite in regular courses; in the first course was sunk an iron chain of flat bars, four inches wide and two and a half inches thick, into collars which were run with lead, but the bars were only covered with a cement of wax, resin and stone dust. The rest of the foundation was done with the usual black stone, and was carried up to the plinth by 16th. October, 1782, thereby completing the whole of the foundations in one year and four months from the opening of the ground.

The novelty of this operation drew many visitors to the works, and a very whimsical opinion, delivered with suitable gravity, was very nearly giving some interruption to the progress of the works. Amongst the visitors were several of the 'faculty', and one of these gentlemen, who had increased his fortune, more by speculating in building than in gallipots,assumed vast knowledge and consequence on the occasion, and, of course, was by many attended to. He gave his opinions freely and without fee! He surveyed the grating, and inquired of the master bricklayer for what purpose such large baulks of timber were laying down? On being informed, he observed with great sagacity, 'that it would answer no durable purpose, as fir was an improper timber to lay in salt water, an immediate decay being brought on by its destruction of the turpentine!'. This he averred, from his own knowledge, to be the fact. To this it was observed fir trees are frequently taken out of bogs, after centuries of immersion, in a perfectly sound state; but the Doctor's reply was that bogs contained a sort of tan which preserved timber. He added that he would give the architect his opinion, if required, and would convince by experiment as to the action of marine acid on fir timber.

When I was informed of this, I requested my informant, when next he should meet the Doctor, to present my compliments, and to say that Doctors differed, and that, as I was under no apprehension of the consequence which he had predicted, I would therefore take leave to follow the old Building Dispensatory.[97]

What we have of Gandon's narrative of the work on the Custom House ends here on this familiar note, for there is scarcely a building in the country which has not suffered from interfering busybodies. But the work on the Custom House continued, and, no doubt, was carefully described by Gandon as it grew. To the layman, building work always appears to be slow; in Gandon's time, the construction of a large building of the complexity of the Custom House was a work of decades. Even when the work apparently came to an end in the seventeen nineties, we find mention of additional and concluding work as late as the end of the century. It was a work with which he lived for the rest of his life in Ireland.

WATERFORD (1784)

Late in 1783 or early in 1784, another commission was forced on a reluctant Gandon. For some time, Beresford's brother, Lord Tyrone, had in mind to build a new courthouse and jail in Waterford. He wrote to the philanthropist John Howard for advice on the planning of prisons, but Howard had too much work on his hands to be bothered with amateur architects, and passed him on to Gandon in Dublin.[98] Lord Tyrone must have felt himself unfairly frustrated in his attempts to get this project under way, for when he applied to Gandon, he found Gandon had little enthusiasm for it. Gandon says:

I expressed many objections to undertake this building. The distance from Dublin being more than seventy miles (these are Irish miles) rendered it very inconvenient: besides my whole time was occupied in attending to the works I was then superintending, and my heavy professional engagements left me no time whatsoever, to undertake any new engagements; but at the urgent request of Mr. Beresford to whom I could not appear ungrateful, I promised to furnish the necessary designs, from documents furnished to me.[99]

Apart from his now busy life, the prospect of frequent trips to Waterford would be

Waterford Court House by James Malton
(*courtesy National Gallery of Ireland*)

no temptation to Gandon. The Waterford coach left Falconer's at six in the morning, usually on one day of the week, and returned some three days later. The narrow, stony tracks, thick with mud in winter and with dust in summer, promised no ease for the continuously jolted passengers, while the cold and the heat penetrated the thin walls and the windows of the coaches without respite. It was too much for Gandon. He continues:

> I found the old courts of the city and county of Waterford separate buildings situated at some distance from each other, and in a very ruinous condition. At a meeting of the Grand Juries, it was resolved to erect a united court house for the accommodation of the city and county, and also to erect new gaols adjoining to the court house, thereby to form one general design, to be placed on an elevated piece of ground, where the barracks had formerly stood. The ground for this building was opened in the spring of 1784.[100]

Here too, he was soon in trouble: the authorities in Waterford, as well as quarrelling among themselves, misunderstood Gandon's profession, and the tradesmen went unpaid. He continues:

I experienced more vexation and trouble with the Court House at Waterford, than from any of the public works submitted to my superintendence. This principally originated in conflict between the Grand Juries and the Corporation, relative to raising the necessary supplies of money to pay the various artificers, whose just demands were for a considerable time withheld from them. The consequence was they became dissatisfied, and declined any further proceedings with the works. I was therefore constrained to go to Waterford to remonstrate with the Grand Jury, on the payment of the various parties.

In my interview with these gentlemen I found they had a very erroneous idea of the profession of an 'architect', as it stood in England. Some of them considered me as a contractor, or, as they termed me: 'A projector and undertaker', not one of those sable personages whose occupation it is to bury the dead, but to bury stones and mortar. Having explained to them what my profession really was, and that I only conducted Works, not contracted for them, the artificers were promised a settlement.[101]

Worry always meant for Gandon an attack of gout, and the journey back to Dublin would have been most unpleasant. He wrote immediately to Beresford in London, telling him of his troubles and stating 'his anxiety to relinquish any further superintendence of the Court House and Gaol at Waterford'. The reply was in the soothing and optimistic style cultivated by Beresford for trouble at a distance:

> My Dear Sir, – I had great pleasure on finding, by a letter from Lord Tyrone, that you have been down to Waterford, and that everything is satisfactory to him. I told you all along that it was a mistake of each other which occasioned the jumble, and you see I was right. I hope you have seen Winder and that all accounts are brought up to your satisfaction. You must not distract or fret yourself: all will be right, depend upon it.
> I am, dear Sir, Very sincerely yours, John Beresford.[102]

* * * * *

ARCHITECTURAL NOTE

The public concourse, shown in Malton's drawing is similar to that in Gandon's first scheme for Nottingham. Here we see the end wall in detail, and also the position of the gallery in the courtroom. The floor of the courtroom is raised by three steps. Here too, we note Gandon's favourite arrangement of overlapping openings, as featured on the courtroom façade, which is essentially a Classical screen.

NEW GENEVA (1784)

The prosperous middle classes of Geneva, mostly disciples of Rousseau, had been suppressed by the intrusion of troops from France and Savoy when those in authority became alarmed by their liberal beliefs. They decided that the only expedient left to them was to emigrate en masse, taking with them their craftsmen, particularly the watchmakers, on whom the prosperity of the city was dependent. Invitations from other countries to settle and increase the local prosperity were not wanting. One such invitation came from George III, but the Geneva rebels were not too keen to settle in England, preferring Ireland, to which they were attracted by what they had heard of the Volunteers, and where they felt themselves to be akin to the people who were in bondage. The Irish Ascendancy were keen to have them, for they thought that a vigorous Protestant settlement would in some way persuade the Papists, by its example, to abandon their superstitions and admit to and recognise the superiority of their English masters.

John Beresford was a member of the commission which was set up to deal with the Geneva settlement, and it appears that Gandon supplied a plan for the proposed Geneva New Town in Co Waterford, which would be built to accommodate the settlers. There were great hopes for the scheme. There was talk of setting up a university – capable of competing with the Academy of the Sciences of Geneva – as well as houses, a bakery, a cotton factory and a laundry.[103]

Some of the refugees came over from Geneva, and then the scheme went sour. The Genevans discovered the autocratic character of their hosts, something very different from what they had been led to expect by the reported sentiments of the Irish Volunteers, and the Irish landlords were affronted by the dangerous liberal philosophy of the Genevans. The plan was quietly abandoned, although various quarrels about it continued for some time. The site was left in a semi-developed state, and later a barracks was set up there, which has become infamous in Irish history – its memory lives in the ballad, 'The Croppy Boy'.

THE WIDE STREETS COMMISSIONERS (1780s)

On 1st May 1758, the Wide Streets Commissioners held their first meeting. They were brought together and supported by an Act of Parliament to open a 'new ... street from Essex-bridge to the Castle of Dublin'. They were all prominent men, mostly Members of Parliament, and having dealt with their first task successfully, their powers were extended, enabling them to lay down rules for the widening of existing streets and the laying out of new ones. Until the 1780s, their work continued on these lines.

In the 1780s the Commissioners included John Beresford, of course, as well as Luke Gardiner, Lord Carlow, Frederick Trench and Andrew Caldwell, all friendly towards Gandon. There was also William Burton Conyngham, John Foster, the Speaker, and Samuel Hayes, who were somewhat hostile towards Gandon, and who had their own favourite architects. These rivals of Gandon were Robert Parke (or Parks), who had served as clerk of the works for Thomas Cooley; James Cavendish Murphy, who engraved scenes of Moorish Spain, and was a favourite of Burton Conyngham, and also Thomas Penrose, who was Clerk and Inspector of Civil Buildings as well as acting as agent for the English architect, James Wyatt.

In 1790 they engaged Gandon to design Carlisle Bridge, and on 26th November of that year he received approval from the Commissioners for his designs for Beresford Place – the crescent to the north of the Custom House. He had already worked for the Commissioners on the Rotunda and the Lying-in Hospital, of which three of the Commissioners, Luke Gardiner, David la Touche and Frederick Trench, were governors.

The Wide Streets Commissioners, all men of taste and culture, shaped the city of Dublin during the last twenty years of the eighteenth century. It was extremely fortunate that they were an enlightened body of men, who, in spite of political differences, were prepared to work together for a cultural ideal. The Act of Union blunted their efforts; support for their vision was not forthcoming from the London Parliament, and during the nineteenth century they were left to wither and disappear.

———

THE ROTUNDA (1784-86)

The Rotunda, a circular building at the north end of O'Connell (Sackville) Street has given its name to the adjacent lying-in hospital. This hospital, the first in these islands, was founded by Bartholemew Mosse and opened in 1757. The hospital relied for much of its support on the moneys raised by functions in the Rotunda Gardens, but, Irish weather being what it is, the architect Ensor was commissioned to design a building in which the social activities of the gardens could be continued when conditions outside were unsuitable. It was an undistinguished brick building with an awkward conical 'pie-crust' roof, as it was described at that time.

The popularity of the gardens and of the Rotunda continued to grow, and in the 1780s Gandon had become a consultant to the Wide Streets Commissioners. An elaborate block of assembly rooms was proposed. It was conceived and put in hand by Richard Johnston (a brother of Francis Johnston, the architect), planned by Frederick Trench, and modified by Gandon. The foundation stone was laid on 17th July 1785. The building committee included Lord Charlemont, David la Touche, Frederick Trench and Luke Gardiner, all Wide Streets Commissioners and all friends of Gandon. They appear to have asked Gandon to do something to improve the appearance of the Rotunda itself, and to give some attention to the approaches to the hospital.[104] He raised the parapet of the Rotunda with a frieze of Coade stone and a cornice. He reconstructed the roof, skilfully introducing a flat about half way up the slope. This original feature had the effect of blunting a discordant vertical tendency, and harmonised with the strong horizontal character of the new parapet. Then he added the flanking pavilions to the curved colonnades. A curious feature of the building is that the floor is some five or six feet below the external ground level. It is difficult to suppose a reason for this, unless Ensor's building was constructed around an existing cockpit or bear-pit. So far, no reference to any such pit in that locality has been found. It was a remarkable piece of work on Gandon's part, both in its simplicity and in its effect. There was then, in the city, an architectural complex which was the focus of social activity, while the lying-in hospital continued to serve the poor and save lives.

Dublin has quite a number of statues to its sons and some to its daughters, a few perhaps of dubious character. With their backs to Trinity College, Oliver Goldsmith and Edmund Burke survey College Green, the same Edmund, who, in 1790 is reported to have said: 'A woman is an animal, and not an animal of the highest order.' There is no statue to Bartholemew Mosse, who, in his life and after it saved so many women and children.

'The Lying-in Hospital' by James Malton
(The Rotunda Hospital and New Assembly Rooms)

The Rotunda was to play an ever-recurring part in Irish history. A great number of the significant meetings of two centuries took place there. This charitable and social centre eventually fell into the hands of people who did not appreciate it. An extraordinarily attractive composition, as Malton's view confirms, was destroyed when the medical people built the new hospital – an unsightly mass against the central block – and in so doing, removed the west pavilion and colonnade. Even though this part is largely hidden from O'Connell Street, it is an example of architectural vandalism of the first order. A nurses' home was built in the centre of the gardens, and the Rotunda itself, which had served Dublin so well for so long, is now a cinema. The east pavilion was altered unnecessarily, and only the colonnade to the east, and the east front of the east pavilion remain untouched. The shelters for the sedan-chair carriers – two small Gandon-like buildings at the north-east and north-west corners – disappeared without protest while the self-styled guardians of the city slumbered.

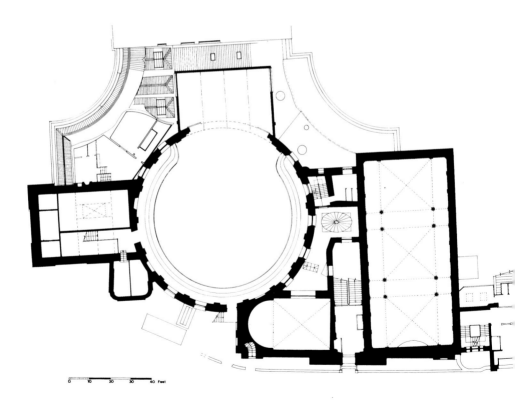

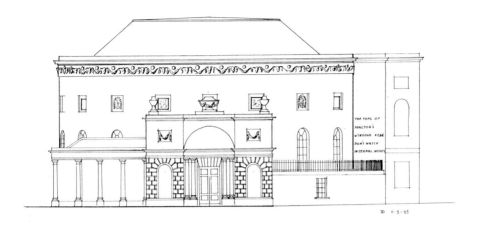

The Rotunda and New Assembly Rooms, 1784-91
above Façade (reconstructed from a survey by W.M. O'Dwyer, 1953)
below Section (do.)

opposite 'Plan of the Rotunda (Ambassador Cinema), Tea Room and Ballroom
as it appeared in the 1950s' (survey by F.M. O'Dwyer for Irish Georgian Society)

(courtesy Irish Architectural Archive)

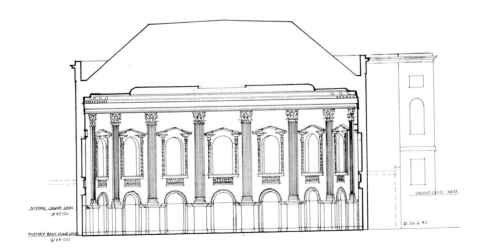

The Rotunda and New Assembly Rooms

The Rotunda and New Assembly Rooms

JAMES MALTON (1782-1785)

D
uring his first two or three years in Ireland, Gandon became remarkably busy. The Custom House was well under way, and he was at work on Coolbanagher church and on the courthouse and gaol at Waterford. There was also New Geneva, and his work for the Wide Streets Commissioners at the Rotunda and elsewhere. He would have been unable to attend to the office work for all these, and carry on proper supervision at the same time. He had Winder, an English clerk, but now he was in need of a draughtsman to draw up details for these works. Curiously enough, it was, we are told, Thomas Malton senior who now approached him to take on his son, James, as a draughtsman, and surprisingly Gandon did so. There are some other incidents in his life of a similar nature which would lead one to suspect that he had, in his character, a certain admirable innocence which seemed to carry him over moments of grave imprudence.

The origin of the connection between Gandon and the Malton family is obscure, but may date from his time in Shipley's or from his attendance at the Royal Academy School. A footnote in *The Life* has this to say:

> We have already alluded to the pamphlet which Mr. Malton Sen., anonymously published, in which he reviewed with so little of either taste, judgment, or honesty, the designs for the Royal Exchange, censuring with much unmerited severity those by Mr. Gandon. Notwithstanding, immediately on the commencement of the Custom House works, he solicited Mr. Gandon to employ his son as a drawing clerk in his office, urging at the same time his own extreme poverty. Mr. Gandon was too benevolent to permit any recollection of his former unjustifiable conduct to prevent him from employing the son, who then appeared quite a promising person. He took him into his office, and kept him employed for nearly three years; but he so frequently betrayed all official confidence, and was guilty of so many irregularities, that it became quite necessary to dismiss him from the employment. He subsequently published views of the public buildings in Dublin, which, so far as delineation went, were certainly accurate, but his letter-press descriptions were envenomed with the most malignant misrepresentations.[105]

It is surprising that Gandon was not aware of the awkward nature of the son, and that he did not ask himself why he would be willing to come to Ireland when he could obtain ready employment in London. The Maltons were superb draughtsmen, and this would have been a factor. They also impinged on the circle about

Paul Sandby. Gandon would, at that stage, have instinctively distrusted an Irish draughtsman, and so perhaps felt himself fortunate in having James Malton. No mention is made in *The Life* of any contact with Thomas junior. In the outcome, the association with James Malton was to be disastrous for Gandon, as we shall see later when we discuss the Four Courts.

THE HOUSE OF LORDS (1783-84)

The lords had long been anxious to improve their accommodation in Parliament House, and as early as 1778 had asked Thomas Cooley to prepare plans for the new extension. When, in 1782, the repeal of Poyning's Law appeared certain, they decided to proceed with the work under the direction of Cooley. Almost immediately they changed their minds, and abandoned Cooley and his plans. Other architects were consulted, but these too were abandoned in favour of Gandon.

It was an unlucky year for Cooley. His patron, the Protestant primate, had in the same year employed Cooley to erect a new tower on his cathedral in Armagh. It was to be similar to that at Magdalene College, Oxford, and when Cooley had raised the tower to about sixty feet, trouble started. Some elderly ladies in the congregation, who had viewed the new scheme with mixed feelings, now allowed themselves to become alarmed for the safety of the structure. Their panic proved infectious, and soon the primate had to choose between his tower and his congregation. He had the tower pulled down, and parted with Cooley. Francis Johnston was called in to construct a new tower, and there was no further trouble.

Gandon's preliminary plans for the House of Lords were approved by the new building committee as early as 11th June 1782. Some old friends from his London days were on the building committee. As well as the Duke of Leinster, there were the earls of Charlemont, Portarlington and Tyrone, the latter a brother of John Beresford. They were assisted by Frederick Trench and Sackville Hamilton. The earls of Charlemont and Portarlington, with Frederick Trench, were of that group of gentlemen which had offered to subsidise Gandon if he would come to Ireland, and they felt they had a stake in his success. Sackville Hamilton was Under-Secretary to the Administration, a position which he held for twenty-five years. Gandon remarks on his enlightened taste: '...in every branch of the fine arts ... and a violinist and a diligent picture collector...' In the event, the discussions of the plans were pleasant and cordial, and the work was

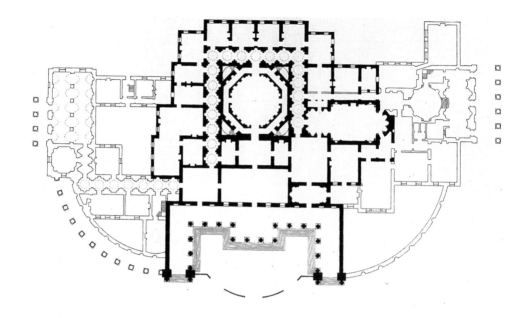

The House of Lords
above Ground-floor plan, c.1790
(drawing by Maurice Craig – Pearce's original Parliament House in bold;
Gandon's Lords extensions on the right, the Commons extensions on the left)
below Plan superimposed on previous street pattern

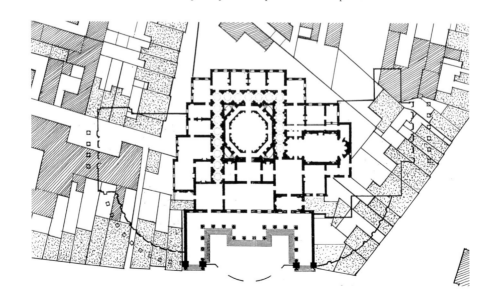

The House of Lords

The House of Lords
– portico on Westmoreland Street

to proceed smoothly. Of the public works carried out by Gandon in Ireland, this one was unique in that no suggestion was made to pull it down while under construction.

Another fortunate coincidence favoured Gandon's progress. From February 1784 until October 1787, Charles Manners, Duke of Rutland, was Viceroy. He had a passion for the arts and for architecture, as well as the traditionally concomitant tastes for women and wine. It is told that, one evening, the Duke visited a well-known actress in the town, and his carriage was, as was usual, escorted by a mounted troop. On leaving early in the morning, he found the troops still drawn up in the street where they had spent the night, for he had forgotten to dismiss them the night before. In the theatre that evening, the actress was subjected to some heckling on account of the incident, but she delighted her audience with the remark: 'manners, gentlemen, please', while shaking her finger at the hecklers.

There had been no viceroy of culture since Chesterfield, and Rutland encouraged and supported the mood of the day to embellish the city with fine public buildings, and during his time, Gandon was largely protected from the efforts of his enemies to frustrate his work. The extension to the House of Lords provides us with a good example of Gandon's resource and originality. Here he had two problems: firstly, to link the new building with the existing Parliament House while preserving its dominance. This he did by a curved Classical wall. He meant it to be plain so that it would not compete with the main building, but three-quarter columns were added when the building was converted for banking purposes after the Act of Union. His second problem, and this had defeated the other architects consulted, was the very large difference between the floor-level of the main building and the ground at the side. Gandon dropped the floor level of the new portico by using the more slender Corinthian columns, while keeping the same level for the cornice, and preserving the apparent unity of the whole. He added weight to the new portico by bringing forward the rear wall. This unique feature is generally unnoticed, although it contravenes the accepted canons of the time by placing a solid mass where a void would naturally be expected.

He located this portico so as to respond to the dome of the parliament chamber, but this did not please Colonel Burton Conyngham. *The Life* tells us:

> The situation of this portico [Gandon's new portico] was opposite the centre of the House of Commons, a circumstance supposed by some critics as very unimportant; it was felt to be so by the late Colonel Conyngham, who was thought to possess great knowledge of the arts; he regarded it as a useless restraint on the arrangements of the architect, in consequence of the great recession of the dome from this front, and which, therefore,

according to his calculations, could not be seen over this portico. However, a diagram being drawn from the station at which a spectator should stand in order to view this front with advantage, it demonstrated to their Lordships' perfect conviction the fallacy of the Colonel's opinion, as even the old dome, depressed as it was, became quite a feature, and, had the proposed improvements surmounted it, it would have been an object both conspicuous and commanding.[106]

It was typical of Gandon's insensitivity towards others to humiliate the colonel with his friends. A more prudent architect would have discussed it privately with him and avoided the creation of another enemy and a powerful one. Burton Conyngham did not forget. From then on, the building progressed without incident. The dwellings on the site were acquired at a cost of £7,761, and cleared away. The work started in May 1785, and the building was completed by 29th April 1789, at a cost of just over twenty thousand pounds.

INTERMEZZO (1784)

Within a year or so, Gandon attempted to dismiss Malton, who then applied to Paul Sandby for his support. Sandby wrote to Gandon in February 1783 saying:

> Young Malton has sent me a letter for you which I now enclose. I have not been able to bring him to an account for you yet, but probably his letter may in some measure remove your indignation at his breach of the confidence reposed in him. I will in no way interfere with your displeasure caused by his misconduct.

Gandon subsequently took him back. In the same letter we are told of a sobered Gandon:

> I am sorry to hear that you will not be able to visit us this season, and begin to fear that I shall never have the pleasure of a hearty until you once more visit St. George's-row. You say that you are almost dead to risibility, which curls up the mouth of all who hear it, even mine and my wife's gravity vanish at the thought of you being grave, and our worthy Paton smiles even in mourning.[107]

With Beresford in the background to ensure Gandon's gravity, the work on the Custom House progressed. It would seem that an impatient Beresford was not satisfied that work was progressing fast enough. Indeed, on a project so large, a numerous workforce was needed to bring all of the parts together, so tradesmen from England were brought on to the works. The results were interesting, as an example of the evolution of trade unionism, and in some aspects have a familiar flavour. Gandon tells us:

> Hitherto none but Dublin masons were employed in the city, but for the expedition of this great work it was found necessary to employ all who would offer. This was opposed by the Dublin fraternity, unless the aliens would take an oath of secrecy, subscribe one guinea each and submit to their laws and combination. This, in some cases, was at first resisted, but gradually, and of necessity afterwards complied with, and generally these reluctant converts subsequently exhibited a zeal more turbulent and refractory than the others. It was just the same with English carpenters and stone cutters who were invited over; they were very orderly at first, but in the end, more refractory than the natives, more exorbitant in their demands for increase of wages, and worse by far as to drunkenness.
>
> The fund collected by these combinators was not applied, as in England, to relieve in time of sickness, or in case of death, to meet the expenses of a decent funeral. It was given to a few idle vagabonds as a stipend, enabling them to live without daily labour. These fellows were called orators, and were attached to each of the fraternities, attended the clubs of the various artificers in order to keep up a perpetual ferment, rendering the men dissatisfied with their employers. Whenever an order for any great work was given, particularly if much expedition and exertion were required, then there was a 'strike' or 'turn out' for more wages; as long as this lasted they were supported in idleness, and if any were sent to prison they fared best of all, being deemed martyrs.[108]

But during 1783 it was not only among the artisans of the Custom House that turbulence existed. The parliament, now free and independent of England, found itself in the position of a Frankenstein which had breathed life into a monster. The Volunteers, feeling their stand to have been crucial in setting up the new constitution of 1782, saw themselves as the superior force in Ireland, and, in a sense, superior to the parliament. Although any external threat to the country had vanished after the conclusion of the American War of Independence, they had no intention of disbanding. Throughout that spring and summer they were active, marching to and fro in the streets, and holding manoeuvres in the Phoenix Park within sight of the Viceregal Lodge, their contempt for Parliament encouraged by the many areas of indecision left by the new constitution.

About this time there appeared on the scene one Frederick Augustus Harvey, Earl of Bristol, and at the same time, Lord Bishop of Derry. He was supported by his nephew, George Robert Fitzgerald of Turlow. George Robert was also a character. He indulged in duelling to excess, and wore a chain shirt under his clothes, which from time to time frustrated opponents who were better shots. Thinking that his father, who had also been a considerable blackguard in his day, had lived too long, he shut him up, we are told, in a cave with a muzzled bear as a companion, where he kept him for three years, and this at the time of the Convention of 1783. George Robert was hanged for murder shortly afterwards.

The bishop was active in calling the Convention, which took place in the Rotunda on 29th November 1783. When the great day arrived, Dublin became saturated with armed men. What Gandon thought of it we do not know, but we can guess at the anxiety induced in him by any public show of armed force. His recent opponent, James Napper Tandy, was prominent, leading the Dublin artillery, but the scene was stolen by the bishop in an open landau drawn by six horses. He was magnificently apparelled in purple, his white gloves fringed with gold and with golden tassels attached to them. He wore buckles of diamonds on his knees and shoes. George Robert rode in front leading a squadron of dragoons in gold and scarlet uniforms. They passed through College Green, pausing for effect outside Parliament House, and continued on, as Froude tells us, '...past King William's statue, over the river, and up the broad line of Sackville Street ... to the Rotunda'. Froude is relying on his imagination here, for at that time there was no bridge between College Green and Sackville Street.

The Convention had a liberal agenda, with proposals it wished to have carried in the House of Commons. The Members of Parliament were intimidated by the show of force and by the strength of public feeling which supported the Convention. However, one man, John Fitzgibbon, later Earl of Clare, was not intimidated. In a short speech, he brought the members to their senses, and the proposals from the Convention were rejected. There was no confrontation. For a while, and quietly, Crown forces had been filtering back into the country, and General Burgoyne had his troops in barracks in Dublin. In the circumstances, the Volunteers were not anxious for a conflict. The Convention petered out, and the Lord Bishop of Derry returned to the North to await another day.

After the collapse of the Convention, the winter of 1783-84 appeared relatively quiet, but under the surface there was much unemployment, poverty and misery in Dublin. Gandon's time was at last fully taken up with his various projects, and by now he had the commission for the new Four Courts under consideration. But with the coming of spring, the stirrings of discontent began to grow. The Reform Bill was still on minds of the disenfranchised – the Dissenters, who were suffering from long-standing injustices, and the Catholics for whom certain

John Fitzgibbon, 1st Earl of Clare by G.C. Stuart
(*courtesy National Gallery of Ireland*)

Penal Laws were still in force. In April, a mob took over the parliament building. In May, a tarring and feathering committee was set up. Prominent citizens who were known to have opposed the bill were taken out at night, stripped, tarred, rolled on goose down, and turned loose in the streets. The efforts of the Administration to obtain a conviction for these crimes were unsuccessful until the end of August, when a Garret Dignam was found guilty and sentenced to be flogged through the streets behind a cart. Before the punishment was half over, there was a riot. The troops fired on the people and killed one man and wounded several. The Crown forces at that time patrolled the streets of the city at night. As is usual when troops are used for police duties, there was confrontation and violence. The authorities became gravely concerned, so much so that the Duke of Rutland sent to England for spies to infiltrate the deliberations of Napper Tandy, who had Dublin Corporation in his pocket, while others were sent to the North to keep an eye on the turbulent Lord Bishop of Derry, armed with warrants for his arrest should his conduct deserve it.

It was proposed to send petitions to George III, and, later, moves were made to call a congress of the representatives of the Irish people – that is, Irish noblemen and gentlemen. The authorities feared that if the congress was allowed to meet, there could be an armed conflict between the Volunteers and the Crown forces. Napper Tandy had instructed the sheriffs of each county to secure representatives. The Duke of Rutland then told the sheriffs that this would be illegal. Most of them took the hint, but Stephen Reilly, the High Sheriff of Dublin, persisted, and summoned the freeholders of Dublin to a meeting. While this was in progress, Fitzgibbon walked into the room, and solely by the force of his personality, dispersed it. On 25th October, the day of the congress, a handful attended at a house in William Street, but finding themselves powerless, they went off again. Thus, the congress went the way of the Convention, and Gandon enjoyed a peaceful winter until December 1785, when new and unexpected troubles assailed him.

THE FOUR COURTS (I) (1784-86)

In 1776, Thomas Cooley started the work of building the new Dublin records office. The Public Monies Receipts Book in the King's Inns shows that on 11th October he received £100 to start the work. During the following years, the payments continued at fairly regular intervals, but in irregular amounts. Cooley died in 1784, and no payments are recorded during the year until 17th December when £1,672 is noted 'to pay bills due for the work on the law offices at the death of Mr. Cooley'. This payment was signed by Gandon, so he appears on the scene rather earlier than is usually supposed. By this time, Gandon was considering his scheme for the Four Courts, and in the meantime very little work was done there. On 26th August 1785, Gandon signed a further £1,000, most of which was probably used to start the work on the new scheme.[109]

As we have seen, the viceroy was the popular and dissolute Duke of Rutland, who had taken up office on 24th February 1784. He was a man of wide cultural interests, and under his patronage, the arts in Dublin were given a new life. He interested himself particularly in the scheme to replace the ruinous law courts. It is in the main due to his appreciation of Gandon's designs that we owe the support of the chancellor and the chief justices, as well as the continuous help which Gandon received in the face of strong and influential opposition. Gandon tells us this himself:

> The designs being made and submitted to the Chancellor and Chief Judges, they expressed their perfect approbation of them, and I then had the honour of attending on His Grace, the Duke of Rutland with them, who was pleased to approve of them in terms quite too flattering for me to repeat. They were left with His Excellency for some time and became the subject of frequent conversation and criticism. Mr. Secretary Hamilton, who's knowledge and taste in architecture was well known, was directed to communicate to me the various remarks which had from time to time been made upon them, but being perfectly satisfied with my explanations, he stated in his report that every matter connected with the subject had been most maturely considered, and the objections that might occur as effectively guarded against as the very circumscribed extent of the ground would admit. I was thereupon ordered to make the necessary preparations for proceeding with the works'.

Characteristically, Gandon had not forgotten his difficulties:

> In making my designs I found myself restricted by the limits of the ground, and the previous arrangement of the offices. The whole extent being but 432 feet, 294 of which were occupied by offices, leaving only 140 feet square for the plan of the courts.
> When consulting with Lord Chancellor Lifford, and the Chief Judges, they expressed their desire to have their rooms on each side of the Courts, and to have private entrances leading to them, without passing through the great hall. They also desired that the courts should be lofty and spacious for air, yet sufficiently contracted to ensure hearing distinctly. To combine such conflicting attainments was a matter of no common dif-

'View of the Law Courts looking up the Liffey'
by James Malton

ficulty; I therefore requested their Lordships' opinions as to the precise dimensions which they deemed most likely to secure these results, or to refer me to any Court which approached nearest to their desires. But I found they knew of none which quite met their wishes. It was therefore left to be tried by several experiments.

I hope, however, I may with truth assert, that in my arrangements I approached as nearly to that which was required as the difficulties I had to contend with would permit, and I trust it will be allowed, when the plans shall have been carefully inspected, that none of the ground which could be usefully occupied has been lost, and that, therefore blame should not attach to the architect for not having provided offices for departments which did not then exist, although, since that period, succeeding Judges have required them.[110]

On 6th October 1785, the *Dublin Evening Post* mentions, in rather flippant terms, the start of the work:

The new Four-Courts, for which the ground is clearing on the Inns Quay will extend from the Law-Offices to Charles-street where the grand entrance is to be. This temple of Themis will not only be built with a grandeur consonant to that of all the other public edifices now erecting in Dublin, but contain within its circumference everything for the ease and convenience of the Courts, and all who have occasion to resort to them.

Generally the Dublin papers had not been kind to Gandon, but soon he was to suffer a series of extremely malicious attacks by them. His assistant, James Malton, who had been apprenticed to him three years before, was an uneasy spirit who was convinced of his own natural superiority. Impatient of all restrictions, he had already been dismissed once by Gandon. Now, towards the end of November 1785, he seriously offended Gandon and was dismissed again, this time finally.

THE MALTON LETTERS (1785)

Soon after Malton's dismissal, a series of long, fluent and embittered letters appeared in the *Dublin Journal*, deploring the incompetence of Gandon and lauding the unremarked excellence of Malton. With characteristic modesty, he mentions one of his suggestions for Dame Street: '...the very idea of it is ravishing to the Mind that is susceptible to it; an Idea which cannot be surpassed, perhaps not equalled in the World.' The author of these letters has traditionally been identified as James Malton, but it must be said here that there is no proof of this, and an examination of the text has, for some, suggested others as authors. However, they are generally attributed to Malton, and for convenience we shall refer to them as the Malton letters. They were published as *Letters to Parliament by an Admirer of Useful and Necessary Improvements*.

These letters are long, involved, and eloquent of deep injury; indeed he must have been writing them continuously during December of 1785. The second letter appeared on the 8th, the third on the 13th, the fourth on the 15th, the fifth on the 17th, and the sixth on the 20th December. They are a bewildering and confusing series, and no summary could give an adequate idea of their cease-less flow of words nor of their inimitable style. Everything Gandon does or has in hand is attacked and disparaged. The Four Courts is attacked from many angles, but always he returns to Dame Street and the treatment of his own designs for this scheme.

After the fifth letter, Malton tells us he felt, as some writers do, that as the year was coming to an end, a supplement was called for. His sixth letter is by far the most damaging of the series. In this letter he plays on the fears of the clients, and certainly must have made them uneasy. He harries them over the projected cost of the Four Courts, and is openly scornful that it is possible to make an accu-rate estimate of expenditure. He frightens them by hinting at the size of the dome and the difficulties of construction:

> Now as neither Mr. Gandon nor any of the Builders or Directors at the Custom-house were ever concerned in such a Building before, with such an immense Dome and the whole so superbly elegant, and withal so whim-sical in its Form as this is in the Design, I query if Mr. Gandon, or all of them together can give an estimate of it; they may employ a Month or two in the attempt, and then give a guess at it, and when done they will not be within 25 or £30,000 of the real Expense, which will be known only when it is completed. Quere, have not the Public a right to see the Design, by exhibiting it for their Inspection publicly, and to know how much will be expended on the Building according to the Design? I should imagine they have, it is but reasonable.

It was a vindictive performance. How Gandon felt we can only imagine, for here he has been silent. One letter would have been serious enough, but to have his name and reputation publicly assaulted twice every week during that December must have scarred his sensitive mind and tried his self-control. The knowledge that the letters would have been read with amusement, and in many quarters, sat-

185

isfaction, throughout the city had to be faced as a daily torture. Any professional man, and especially one who takes himself as seriously as Gandon, gets very little sympathy from the public when held up to ridicule, for not only is the public jealous of the apparent ease with which he can enrich himself, but most people resent the unconscious superiority of his treatment of them. For Gandon, the letters were destructive of his relationship with his titled clients who would feel vicariously associated with his embarrassment, and also erosive of his authority over the works he managed. He was helpless. To take Malton to court would only provide him with a pulpit; violence would be farcical. The tormented Gandon endured. Wisely he had kept silent so far, but, probably urged by his clients and his family, a reply appeared in the *Dublin Journal* on Christmas Eve, signed Philopolis. He may have hoped by this tardy insertion to catch Malton on holidays. Malton immediately identified the letter as from Gandon, and on the 29th, in his seventh letter, he replied to it with surprising brevity. After this short letter, Gandon heard no more from him during January 1786, for he was occupied in writing to the trustees of the Royal Exchange, complaining of their treatment of him in taking down the drawings he had put up there himself. He left for London on 2nd February, but before he went he wrote another letter attacking Gandon. The letter was not published, but Malton discovered this only on his return to Ireland in the following May. In the meantime, Gandon had other and more serious troubles on his hands.

Before the New Year arrived, Gandon suffered another attack. Possibly as a result of Malton's letters, the *Dublin Evening Post* of 29th December had this to say on the extensions to the House of Lords. It runs very much on the lines Malton had already laid down:

> According to estimate, the new building in addition to the House of Lords will cost this country twenty-five thousand pounds, besides the usual douceur of five percent to the architect. The building will be superfluous, and the number of rooms double to those which are annexed to the House of Lords in England.

It went on to suggest adding the Courts of Justice to the building to use up so much waste space and so save '...a vast sum for building the new Courts of Justice...' It concludes: 'The whole House of Parliament cost but £31,000 as appears from the architect, Sir William Pier's report. The addition to the House of Lords only, will cost £25,000.'

———

186

THE FOUR COURTS (II) (1786-88)

I n 1786, the winter was severe. Cold northerly winds blew through the city streets, bringing showers of sleet and snow. After Christmas there were heavy falls, but the labourers worked on, clearing the site and digging the foundation·trenches of the Four Courts. Half-starved and clad in ragged clothes, many in bare feet, they laboured to feed their families at all costs. During the first week in March, the streets were deep in slush and half-frozen snow, and in this bitter weather, the foundation stone for the Four Courts was laid. Gandon tells us:

> The ground being nearly covered with houses, occupied by tenants, retard-ed the commencement of the work until 1st October, 1785, when the excavations were begun, but, owing to various obstructions it was not ready for the foundation till 3rd March 1786, on which day, His Grace, the Duke of Rutland, accompanied by the Lord Chancellor and Chief Judges, in state, laid the first stone, under which was deposited a copper plate, with the following inscription: The first stone – of – This edifice – erected for the more convenient administration – of the Laws of the Realm – was laid – on the third day of March – M.DCCLXXXVI – In the twenty-sixth year of the reign – Of His Most Sacred Majesty – King George III – By His Grace Charles Manners – Duke of Rutland – Lord Lieutenant – And General Governor – of Ireland – James Viscount Lifford – being – Lord Chancellor – James Gandon, Architect.
>
> After His Excellency the Duke of Rutland had retired from laying the first stone of the Four Courts, a gentleman of considerable fortune and influence, a privy councillor and a member of the Irish Parliament, from whom, on my first arrival in Ireland, I had experienced considerable atten-tion and hospitality, and with whom I had no previous difference of opin-ion upon any occasion, stopped his travelling carriage, to enquire the cause of the enclosures being made on the quay, as also the assemblage of so many persons; being informed that the ceremony of laying the first stone of the New Courts of Law was the cause, this gentleman left his car-riage, and addressed me in a manner not very courteous. 'What is all this going on here? Who ordered the quay to be enclosed? &c.,&c.,', I informed him of the reason for enclosing the ground, and stated that, as the architect, I was in no way responsible for the situation of any public building, but merely acting as a professional man, employed by govern-ment, had been requested to make designs for the new Courts of Law, adjoining the Law-offices, which had been previously erected. I stated I

William Burton Conyngham by G.C. Stuart
(courtesy National Gallery of Ireland)

had submitted my designs to the Lord Lieutenant, who, with the Lord Chancellor and Chief Judges, had on consideration, approved of the design, and had given directions for the building to commence, and that His Grace, the Duke of Rutland had further sanctioned it by the honour of his presence at the laying of the first stone.[111]

This gentleman was Colonel the Hon Burton Conyngham, and Gandon should not have had far to look for the cause of his unfriendly manner. Members of the Ascendancy were unused to having their opinions challenged by an architect, and no doubt the incident rankled. Gandon lacked sensitivity when dealing with his titled clients, and on this occasion, his rather ponderous reply, if indeed it had been given in this form, could hardly have been soothing. Colonel Conyngham took his leave of Gandon with the parting remark 'that if the building proceeded, it should be pulled down'. Gandon seemed fated to find his successes almost immediately followed by some kind of disaster. He continues:

> Knowing the gentleman's influence, and thinking to prevent clamour, I was induced at the particular suggestion of a noble peer, the Earl of Portarlington, for whom I had a great respect, to set back the portico, originally designed to cover the footway. This I considered a great sacrifice to the beauty of the front, but even this sacrifice of my design was not sufficient, for as the gentleman had not been consulted about the building, he disapproved of the designs, which he condemned in every particular, stating the most singular objections, which shall be noticed in their proper place.[112]

Colonel Conyngham gathered around him numerous persons sympathetic to his opinions. They formed a compact body opposed to the works being carried on by Gandon. No doubt, he was joined by those already affronted by Gandon during the designing of the additions to the House of Lords and the alterations to the Rotunda. There may well have been a political slant to the opposition to Gandon, for by now he was firmly identified with the Beresford faction, although there is no mention of this factor in *The Life*. This opposition were shortly to receive voluble and valuable support for their views from James Malton, who now returned to Dublin.

He came back from London in May 1786 to find that his last letter had not been published, and immediately rushed into print. He had a letter in the *Dublin Evening Post* on 10th June and another on the 17th. It must have been a severe shock to Gandon to find his tormentor at work again, and as vociferous as ever.

Perhaps Beresford, and maybe Higgins, felt it had gone too far to suit their own books. The newspaper proprietors, too, may also have become tired of devoting comparatively large areas of their papers to Malton's vendetta. In the event, no further letters were published. Letters of complaint followed and were ignored. But if they thought these methods would muzzle Malton and leave him voiceless, they were mistaken. Malton came from a family which had a taste for printers' ink, and was not to be denied. He conceived the idea of publishing all of his letters in pamphlet form, which he hawked about Dublin and later had bound into a book. There should have been a good market for these, and as Gandon had 'picked the plums' of the previous four years from under the noses of the Dublin architects, they must have read Maltons diatribes with relish. Then, again, the public generally had no use for the Beresfords, nor for those connected with them, and in an era when vigorous journalism was appreciated, Malton's style should have been popular.

The book was produced in 1787.[113] It ran to 334 octavo pages, and consisted of his letters in the order of writing, with various footnotes and, in some cases, further thoughts as long as the letters themselves. It is completely anti-Gandon, and is probably the only instance of a book solely against an architect. There seems to be only one copy extant, and that is in the National Library. Dr McParland is of the opinion that it was perhaps the sole copy produced.

As already mentioned, there are certain difficulties in ascribing parts of the text to Malton. Perhaps the most curious factor is the apparent ignorance of the Maltons to the fact that Gandon's father was a bankrupt. If they had known, they would scarcely have hesitated to use such a damning circumstance. But some instinct urged him to harp on Gandon's origins. His most damaging shaft is to remind people, especially the aristocracy, that Gandon was of humble birth. This is why he repeats the question over and over again: 'Who is Gandon?' It is a common refrain.

> Who is Mr. Gandon, Sir, that a few men in power should give all public business to him? nay contrive business for him, unnecessarily, but to enrich him, and he is all the while laughing at their egregious folly.

On 15th July, a short paragraph appeared in the *Freeman's Journal*, commenting favourably on the sculpture on the Custom House, and praising the building itself. Malton scornfully alludes to this paragraph as Gandon's 'puff', and goes on:

> The paragraph in the Freeman's alluded to is manufactured by Mr. Gandon himself; artfully intended as if coming from the Committee (who are THEY?) of that Partial Paper, being supposed dis-interested Men, to take off the Edge of the Accusations laid against HIM by PUBLIUS, whose Pen he dreads more than ever Child dreaded Rod; because he knows, is conscious that Publius knows HIM, and that his letter are replete with

TRUTH, with FACTS, which are Gall and Wormwood to him and which he cannot digest.

Later he says:

Oh for the Spear of Ithuriel who's heavenly temper made the hellish squat TOAD resume his real, though more diabolical, Shape and Character; that this wondrous Phoenominon might, by a touch of it be seen in his true colours.

It would be possible to go on quoting paragraph after paragraph of similar inspired abuse, but perhaps we may conclude with the following, extremely damaging extract:

QUERIES for Mr. GANDON'S Consideration.
Imprimis. Did he not assert in confidence to a Mr. Low (his trusty and most sincere friend) long before the Building was begun, or the Design drawn, that (as no Estimate was required) The Custom House should cost them two hundred thousand Pounds, which would put ten thousand into his Pocket for Commission? Can he say, that the said Mr. Low would ever have betray'd his Confidence? would he not have risqu'd his life to serve him rather, had he not treated him most vilely, from the Quarrels of two infamous W****s Sisters?

Malton's writings must have had an effect on Gandon's contemporaries and eroded their respect for him, on the general principle that there is no smoke without fire. Particularly damaging was the suggestion that he was laughing at them. To them he was an Englishman, perhaps even worse if there was, in his speech, a hint of the continental, for he was a second-generation Huguenot. In addition, there was the implication that he was incompetent and was acting the confidence man. Overall, the reaction, perhaps muted but still there, was to distance oneself from a dubious character, and something of the kind possibly took place. However, such an effect cannot be separated from the general envy which grows naturally towards a favourite. But Lord Clare and John Beresford were unaffected by such adverse publicity. Beresford would 'laugh at the extreme folly of the people', while Lord Clare held the opinion of the people in open contempt. From the few hints we are offered here and there, it would appear that Gandon himself was not very sensitive to the feelings of others, being sensitive to slights to himself. His origins would have left him insecure in a society secure in its own origins, and in compensation he relied on the conviction of his own excellence. This he paraded, rather pompously, if we are to believe his own accounts of his pronouncements. He did not seem to realise that nobody likes to be lectured, and not least his noble clients, who were accustomed to being in full control of their schemes.

From this point on, Gandon's progress was impeded by various difficulties, some of his own making, some with their roots in the general hostility to the Beresfords, and some from the effects of disasters abroad, beginning with the gradual breakdown of the society in which he lived.

The Four Courts rose slowly and painfully. Colonel Burton Conyngham died in May of 1787,[114] but the opposition to Gandon which he had organised remained. Whatever feelings of relief Gandon may have felt at the death of the colonel were soon counteracted by the death from drink of the viceroy, the Duke of Rutland, on 24th October.[115] There is a miniature of the duke in the National Gallery in Merrion Square which reveals a friendly and affable man. The artist, without omitting the high colour of his cheeks and nose, has rendered it with such skill as to make it appear almost natural. The next viceroy was without any culture, had no interest in architecture, and so Gandon was left without support from the castle.

From the death of the Duke of Rutland in 1787 to the appointment of the Earl of Westmoreland in 1790, while work continued slowly on the record office, the Four Courts was left derelict. Its progress now became a matter of party politics, and on 29th January 1788, a Colonel Hayes, very much in the spirit of Malton, introduced the matter, somewhat hypocritically, in the House of Commons. He did this at the instigation of the anti-Gandon party which was anxious to try its strength against the new administration of the Marquis of Buckingham. Gandon says:

> A motion was made ... for me to attend at the bar of the House with the designs and estimates of the expense of the new Courts of Law. Having been apprised (by whom?) that it was intended to revive the old objections to the situation, together with the supposed smallness and confined dimensions of the new Courts, I made a parallel between the dimensions of each of the old Courts with the new ones, together with the hall, in order to show by how many feet square the old Courts were exceeded; these facts were distinctly ascertained, and written on cards, which I gave to the Lord Chancellor, the Chief Judges, and some of the members of both Houses, in order that they might refute the misrepresentations made by clamour, and show the business in a just light. This measure produced the desired effect with all who were unprejudiced and defeated the malignity of the parties.
>
> On my attending the House of Commons, Colonel Hayes came and sat down by me, and said 'he hoped I did not think his motion proceeded

from anything invidious to me, but as the Courts had been a subject of much conversation, and were attended with considerable expense, it was right to have the particulars before the House'. It is is curious to observe that this was three years after the commencement of the works, and £12,000 had been expended. I replied, 'he was best acquainted with the motives which induced him to bring me before the House; that if he required any information could have satisfied him, without such a mode being adopted; that I was aware misrepresentations had gone abroad, by some through ignorance, by others through malice, of which he might be convinced by the statement I gave him; that the Judges, who, I supposed, would best know what would answer their purpose, had expressed themselves highly satisfied with their intended accommodations'. We then separated, and Colonel Hayes went out, I believe, to read the card I had given him, and to consult with other members, which was the cause of his silence afterwards, for I was only called upon by the Speaker to present the papers at the Bar, and, no questions being asked, I withdrew.[116]

It is hard to see any other motive for the colonel's approach other than ordinary politeness, and he did not deserve to have been lectured by Gandon. At the same time, Gandon must have known very well that he had, by this time, been replaced as architect for the extensions to the House of Commons – with which Colonel Hayes was involved, despite his later profession of ignorance – for the building community was then a tight one, and such items of news were immediately known to all involved. It was his first rejection in his new country, and he cannot have been happy about it.

In 1790, a further attempt was made to stop the work. Gandon says:

As the Marquis of Buckingham had left the Government, (replaced by the Earl of Westmoreland, 5th January, 1790), this was to lead to another attempt to have them (the Courts) removed. Colonel Conyngham had asserted, in a conversation in the House, that this might be done at a small expense. Accordingly, at the instigation of this gentleman and some others, Sir John Parnell, then Chancellor of the Exchequer sent for me and gave me the following queries, which for singularity, at such an advanced period of the building, will not easily be paralleled.[117]

Query 1: What expense would attend removing the centre of the building of the Courts of Justice?

Query 2: What would be the value of the ground to be purchased in the rear in order to set the building back?

Query 3: What are the sizes of the Courts on each side and are they damp?

Query 4: Is the quay sufficiently wide from the wall of the Courts to the wall of the river?

Query 5: What will be the expense of finishing the buildings as they are now?'

I went fully into detail in the answers to these questions because I had been informed of the expressions used in the House of Commons by Colonel Conyngham, who, notwithstanding he had been foiled in every attack on a former occasion, and driven from trench to trench, yet, like a gallant soldier still broke new ground. The last objection made use of was, that as the army passed by every day from the barracks to the Castle, the fifes and drums would disturb the Courts. To which it was replied, that in summer, to avoid the sun, they frequently went on the opposite side of the river, which, if found necessary, they might be directed to do always in future.[118]

Again we find two different occasions compressed together, for Colonel Conyngham had died three years before this last attack. Gandon continues:

I cannot but observe in this place, the injurious tendency of repeated attempts of this kind on any of the works of which I had the management. Whenever the stopping of them became in this manner a subject of conversation, impediments to their future progress immediately took place; every articifer was apprehensive that the materials prepared or ordered would be thrown on his hands, and that his bills might remain long unpaid. This directly gave a check to every exertion on their parts by withdrawing their men, and counter ordering the materials which came from any distance; so that when the business was to recommence the season was nearly lost by the delays, which circumstance occasioned considerable injury to the works. Indeed the frequent opposition given to this work had so harassed and disgusted me, that I did not like to go near it, and it prevented me from constructing the inner dome with brick, which for the sake of expedition, and to save expense, was done in carpentry.

But to return: the answers to the queries proposed by the Chancellor of the Exchequer so satisfied him of the absurdity of removing or pulling down the Courts, that in order to get rid of being annually worried, a grant was made of £30,000 of the suitors' in Chancery and Exchequer, of which £10,000 only was to be expended annually. The works now went on until the session of 1793, when another application became necessary, and a grant was made of £6,000. The building was now so far advanced that some part was covered in, and the rest, except the dome, in a state of being so; preparations were likewise making for this, which would have been soon accomplished, but the war now broke out, which, together with an accident that occasioned great difficulty in obtaining columns, &c., from Portland caused an interruption in this part of the works.

On the 15th. of February, 1792, I received a letter from Mr. Stewart who is the owner of the principal quarry in Portland, which, among other circumstances, contained the following curious one:

> On Sunday morning a part of the island of Portland began to crack, and appeared convulsed; it soon began to move forward with a grumbling noise, not very loud, but when interrupted by the falling of enormous rocks; a great part of the island, more than a mile in length and half a mile in breadth, is now in motion, destroying everything in its way. Our pier, a body of solid stone blocks of 4,000 tons made not the least resistance, but is now sunk in thirty feet of water, and rocks that were that depth are now in some places ten feet out of the water. At least £5,000 worth of stone that was brought to the waterside is irretrievably lost, and such a check put to the trade that I fear that it will be out of my power to do much the ensuing summer. A similar accident befell my predecessor in the trade in 1695, as recorded in the third volume of the Philosophical Transactions.' [119]

The session of 1794 was nearly over when it was again rumoured that the works were to be stopped. This, at first, I did not regard, but as the session was drawing to a close, and no mention had been made as usual at the time of granting public moneys, I was led to apprehend that the rumour was too well founded, and that the parties who had opposed the business from the beginning had at last succeeded; which indeed was the case, but however unpopular the works had been made by the cabal, as the building advanced, the public opinion changed more and more in its favour.

The statues had been placed on the pediment of the portico, and four of the columns, complete with their entablature, were raised and set around the drum of the dome, so that some idea could be formed of what was intended: from this circumstance I was in hopes to secure the completion of the design whenever it was resumed. The dome, from its eminence was now become the most conspicuous feature of the public of Dublin, and from many adjacent parts of the country was seen with imposing effect. I had the pleasure to hear the work mentioned with general commendation, and that it would be reckoned a misfortune not to have it completed.

The House, I heard, was to rise in a fortnight; I had now very little interest at the Castle, for the frequent changes of the Lord Lieutenant rendered it impossible for anyone in my station, without family or political connection, and engaged entirely in the profession which called me into public notice, to seek for any new interests; even those Right Honourable personages who had first invited me over, and to whose friendship I owe so much; even they did not find their situation the most pleasant at every change. However, I had not long to hesitate, and therefore concluded the shortest way was to draw up a report of the state of the works, which I showed to the Archbishop of Cashel, whose family was much interested in their completion. This report I afterwards presented to the Lord Chancellor, and to the Chancellor of the Exchequer, Sir John Parnell, as the only person who could see the necessity of the case.

Gandon gives us the report, and continues:

[This] ... representation produced the effect beyond what I could possibly have expected; a grant was made for £16,000, £2,500 of which was by King's letter, and £13,500 out of the suitors' money in the Chancery and Exchequer. In consequence every exertion was made, and the remaining columns round the dome, with the entablature, were completed and the roof covered; in the meantime the internal scaffold was raised for finishing the vault of the internal dome; all the foliage, with the medallions being cast, and afterwards repaired by carvers, which added greatly to their boldness of relief, and every department went on with the same expedition. The Courts were ready for the reception of the Judges, who held their first term therein on Monday, the 8th November, 1796, being ten years and eight months from laying the first stone. But it must be remarked that the works were suspended nearly three years, while the south eastern portion of the offices were being erected.

It was not until the year 1798 that the foundations were laid for the east wing of the remaining offices; nor, owing to the political events which then convulsed society, was it until 1802 that the screen arcade, and wings of offices were finally completed.[120]

* * * * *

ARCHITECTURAL NOTE

If it is fitting to describe the Custom House as a palace, we must view the Four Courts as a temple within which was served not necessarily the god of justice, but the god of law, and in practical terms, the god of property. In the eighteenth century, the social order was based on the ownership of property, for property brought with it power. It was handed down and consolidated by an orderly and preordained descent in the family line from generation to generation.

The law dealt essentially with property, its ownership and inheritance, recognising land as real property, the possession of which brought with it political and social influence. Everything else was defined as personal property. Thus, the great landowners made the laws, and these laws were their mainstay, the sacred mystery by which their position was maintained and perpetuated. They were acutely aware that this body of law must be preserved at all cost, and rendered sacrosanct by ritual display and a high level of public respect. Therefore, the courts of law had to reflect the law's pre-eminence in their appointments and dignity.

Many of the architects of today who regard themselves as unaffected by traditional ideas unconsciously display this attitude in their work, and in so doing, reflect the philosophy, or lack of it, of the society in which we live. Gandon was no less a child of his time, and held the law in deep respect, especially as an unwelcome change was taking place: the centre of gravity was moving from the monarch and the nobility towards the parliament, and also towards the cities with their own dangerous, liberal culture. Already the first shadows of the industrial revolution, though yet faint, were dark upon the horizon. But the law still remained stable, and Gandon was, by conviction, fit to lavish his art on the temple of this god.

It is clear he appreciated the link between property and the law in his society, perhaps more so than his clients did, for he had started life without it. Therefore, it is no surprise when we stand within the domed hall which dominates the interior of the Four Courts to find we are reminded of the Pantheon of Rome. Alternatively, we are brought back to the Nottingham courthouse, for we are looking at a circular development of one side of the central hall there. In the Four Courts, the major axis is marked and emphasised by calumniated recesses, and the secondary axis is defined in a similar way but in a quieter manner. Height is gained by the attic storey, lighting the interior dome and suspending it at a suitable remove, and the central vertical axis pierces the eye of this interior dome and continues upwards, with striking effect, to the ceiling of the distant exterior dome.

This central concourse is not large relative to others of its kind, but it holds an effect of space quite, due to Gandon's skill in the planning of the entrance system, out of proportion to its size. Firstly, the rear wall of the entrance portico is concave. This is our introduction to the shape within, and not, as Richardson would have it, to respond to the external dome in the baroque manner. In Gandon's original design, the portico was much deeper and would have masked this feature. Then, having passed under the portico, we enter a vestibule with a pronounced lateral axis, emphasised by an apse at each side behind columns, which force us to look from side to side and unconsciously to absorb the

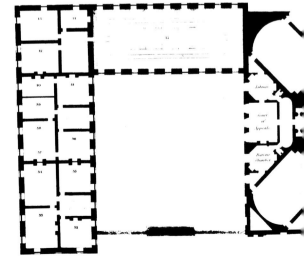

The Four Courts, 1785-1802
– elevation and plan
(courtesy Irish Architectural Archive)

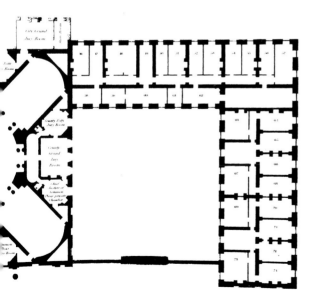

199

diminished scale of this vestibule. We are, in fact, passing through a device which adjusts our sense of scale. If we were to enter directly from the open air into an enclosed space, however large, it would lose scale in comparison with the unlimited space we have just left. Here, however, our sense of scale is compressed to the domestic level, and then, when we enter the concourse, we have been conditioned to appreciate its true size.

Once inside, we are not hemmed in by a solid circular wall. The space in which we stand is bounded by a variety of recesses, but in Gandon's original building it was far more interesting and impressive, for then the entrances to the Four Courts were not built up, but were defined merely by pairs of columns. Then, as well as the central vertical axis reaching up to the outer dome, one could look diagonally from corner to corner of the whole building, the courts becoming a part of the concourse. This dimension is now destroyed, greatly to the loss of the whole interior.

In Gandon's sectional drawing, the circular colonnade appears too high for the enclosed floor area; in fact, it is just right. This is one more example of his fine judgment in matters of proportion, a rare faculty among architects of every era. The reconstructed internal plaster dome is laid out in panels unsympathetic with the structure, and out of scale, and the effect is both weak and incongruous.

Having seen the interior, we can the better appreciate the exterior, which is dominated by the dome. Here too the post Civil War reconstruction was both mean and insensitive: mean in that the circular course above the entablature was replaced by concrete, and insensitive in that, it is said, the true Gandon silhouette was lost. It is worth noting how the dome sits on a massive drum without competing with it. It has been remarked that the dome was derived from that of St Paul's in London, but if we remember Gandon's preoccupation with the romantic compositions of Piranesi, we will find it more probable to have been inspired by some of his imaginings.

As the building stands today, the river front has the effect of an applied façade, out of character with the main central block. This is largely due to the sharp contrast to the fenestration of the side walls with the solidity of the front, but Gandon had no windows in these walls, showing only the stone architraves of blank windows as a concession to the pattern of the other two faces of the intermediate courtyards. This was in accordance with Gandon's expressed preference for blank wall spaces. Again, the frontal screens connect the central façade with the river-ends of the wings, but some twelve feet has been chopped off these ends, destroying the original effect of framing the central block. Gandon had taken the Cooley building on the west, modified it, and constructed a mirror image to the east so as to form a frame for the courts, which stood happily dominant within the neutral background thus created. His frontal screens serve to unify a rather extended complex, and he gave a settled air to the flanking wings

The Four Courts

The Four Courts

by setting a flattened ridge on the pitched roofs, another feature which has disappeared. If, however, there was in the original Gandon building some effect of a façade, we must keep in mind that Gandon introduced a sense of horizontal recession by creating his own horizon with the background buildings. In contrast, the open arcade at the rear of the courtyards added a lateral direction. These arcades have since been closed in.

In this building, Gandon may be said to have demonstrated his mastery of his art in fusing into the composition a vigorous life and an uncommon virility. It may be a flight of fancy to detect in its character echoes of a similar character in the stronger parts of Beethoven's symphonic music. They were both children of the neoclassical movement, inheritors of a common European culture, and even though Beethoven was much younger, their lives overlapped by half a century. It is curious that genius expressed through music receives universal recognition, while the same qualities built into a structure go unnoticed by the majority.

CHANGING TIMES (1788-89)

While the Four Courts was in jeopardy, Gandon still had plenty of work to keep him busy; even though the castle and the viceroy had come to feel that the volume of public building in the city was excessive. On the 8th May 1788, the *Dublin Evening Post* tells us that the viceroy, the Earl of Buckingham, disapproved of the prodigality of the expenditure on public building, and of the Custom House in particular. This building was approaching the finishing stages, and must have taken up much of Gandon's time on essential matters of detail. Coolbanagher church had been finished by March 1785; in May, work started on the House of Lords, and in July of that year, the foundation stone for the Rotunda Rooms was laid.

The work on the House of Lords proceeded rapidly, and in the autumn of 1788, Gandon's designs for the new Carlisle Bridge were ready. We read in the *Freeman's Journal* for Saturday, 20th September, that 'Wednesday, proper persons were appointed to examine the bed of the Liffey in that quarter opposite the space where Achmet's Baths heretofore stood, for the purpose of ascertaining the nature of the bottom, as the intended new bridge will be proceeded upon, it is said in the ensuing spring.'

Dr Achmet Borumbarard, a tall, dark man in Turkish dress, had made himself known to the city by proposing to set up hot and cold sea baths for the aristocracy, and others for the sick and poor, and thus by appealing to both ends of the scale, he managed to extract money from Parliament for his schemes. His first establishment was close to the river, as mentioned above, but he subsequently moved to Lincoln Place, where the minaret-like pinnacles of his baths still stood until the middle of this century.

He knew the rules, and became popular with the Members of Parliament by providing them, from time to time, with lavish banquets in Lincoln Place. Unfortunately, one evening, for some reason, he left the festivities, and while he was out of the room, the inebriated Members began a follow-my-leader game, each hanging on to the coat tails of the person in front. The leader opened a door and led them into a dark space, where he fell into the baths and the others followed blindly. Dr Achmet returned in time to fish out the more incapable Members before they drowned. The Members felt they had made fools of themselves, and after that, they did not know Dr Achmet. Dr Achmet was eventually found to be a confidence man from Kilkenny.

So far, perhaps, the native Irish had not impinged in any significant way on Gandon's consciousness. On his travels outside Dublin, he had seen from his coach the straw-thatched and mud-walled hovels along the roads and on the sides of boreens, with ragged children playing in the ditches and around the near-by potato patch. That three-quarters of the population lived under these conditions may have surprised him at first, but the disdain of Beresford and his friends for the intractable superstitions of these people, and their stubborn refusal to appreciate the superior culture offered by the aristocracy would have satisfied him as to their naturally inferior status.

However, the native Irish were beginning to have an influence on national affairs. The more active and desperate of them were banding together in various parts of the country as 'Whiteboys'; wearing white sheets, they attacked, at night, the property and herds of their persecutors. At the same time, those few Catholic families who had quietly managed to become traders in the larger towns, and in ports such as Cork and Waterford, had formed a Catholic Committee, which included those Catholic noblemen such as Lord Fingall and Lord Kenmare, with others of the aristocratic classes who had managed to survive. The Committee came into the open when, on 25th February 1788, it presented a memorial to Pitt, the English Prime Minister, asking for relief. From this time on, the Catholic question assumed more and more importance.

In the country, the outrages continued sporadically throughout the year, but now another problem faced the Irish parliament. George III had, while driving in Windsor Park, descended from his coach and addressed a tree in an affable manner. News of his insanity reached Dublin on 25th October, and soon the 'Regency Crisis' was occupying the minds of the Members. At the advent of the crisis, Pitt and the Tories were uneasy with and distrustful of the Prince of Wales, for should he become regent (and for this there was no other choice), he was likely to dismiss them and replace them with the Whigs whom he favoured. So they introduced a Regency Bill to limit the powers of the regent. But in Ireland, the Parliamentary Patriots had been conspiring with the Whigs and hoped to replace Pitt. On 16th February 1789, both houses of the Irish parliament invited the prince to become regent for Ireland, with the same powers as a king, thus underlining, at the same time, their devotion to the House of Hanover and their independence of the English parliament. The viceroy, the Duke of Buckingham, refused to transmit the invitation, so the Duke of Leinster and the Earl of Charlemont were sent to London to present it. While they were travelling, the king recovered his wits, and on their arrival they received the thanks of the prince for their pains. However, the incident upset Pitt and the English government, who were unwilling to tolerate an Ireland which might have the power and the will to defy the imperial parliament in such important matters. They determined to undermine the Irish parliament through the castle and the viceroy, but they looked around for strong allies in the Irish parliament, and, on 20th June 1789,[121] they appointed John Fitzgibbon as Lord Chancellor. He was, with the Beresfords and others, fully committed to maintaining the Protestant tradition, and all had strong connections with the English Tories.

Gandon, through his work, had become an associate of that powerful group which would in the end destroy the Irish parliament, and he had come to identify himself with it. It comprised his close acquaintants and clients, John Beresford, John Fitzgibbon, Frederick Trench, Sackville Hamilton, Lord Clonmel, and others of like mind, leaving his old friends, Lord Charlemont and Lord Portarlington with the opposition. We are told that at one time, Lord Charlemont, who was fond of bathing at Fairview, would continue on to Mecklenburgh Street to call on Gandon, and discuss with him current matters of culture, and also the designs for his Rockingham Library which he was about to have added to the rear of his house in Parnell Square. Perhaps these visits petered out as Gandon became absorbed into the Beresford party.

The year was scarcely half over when, on 14th July 1789, the Bastille was attacked and taken, and the French Revolution was under way. Belfast was en fête at the news, and the progress of the Revolution was watched with interest and approval by many in Ireland. No doubt Gandon avoided the subject, as he probably had no wish to draw attention to his Huguenot ancestry which he had left behind him.

In March, Gandon had been instructed to commence work on Carlisle Bridge, and now had to direct the tedious work of finding foundations for it. As the new docks were incomplete, the shipping on the river had to be free to pass up to the old Custom House, so for the time being, there was no particular urgency towards the completion of the bridge. However, the House of Lords extension was completed on 29th April 1789.

FRANCIS GROSE

The year 1790 started with the swearing in of a new viceroy, in the person of the Earl of Westmoreland. He was acquainted with Pitt's plans to curb the Irish parliament, and he agreed with them. Then, on 20th February, Grattan, who appreciated Pitt's new objective, proposed a select committee to look into the sale of peerages and the purchase of votes in the House of Commons. If Grattan had had the support of the Members, Pitt's schemes would have been largely frustrated, and the Union might, at least, have been delayed. The Members, including professed Patriots, with an eye to the future, turned down the proposal by 144 votes to 88. The ambivalence of the Patriots was noted, and on 11th March a proclamation was issued against the Volunteers.

For Gandon, it was a pleasant year, although on the 6th January,[122] the secretary of the Royal Academy wrote to him to tell him he was entitled to be a candidate for His Majesty's pension, which would allow him to travel abroad as a student of architecture. It was a curious communication, and Gandon rejected the doubtful offer. His financial arrangements with Paul Sandby were still current. On 26th January, Sandby wrote to him from London:

> I have again wrote out my account and I fancy you will find it right. If so, please send me a Dt. for the balance due to me. Payne's Michaelmas and Christmas (the two last quarters, I mean) are paid out of the interest of the money you have in Stock at my cousin Sandbys I have drawn more out of it on my own account...

So we see that the quarterly payments to Mrs. Payne were still current.

No attacks – perhaps it is better to say, no overt attacks – were being made on him, but he had been replaced as architect to the extension to the House of Commons. He must have realised, too, that the high successes of the 1780s were at an end, but here there was no parallel with his London disaster. Things were different now. He had status and also a comfortable fortune behind him, and his old friend, Captain Grose, was to visit him that autumn. Grose had spent the previous two years in Scotland in pursuit of material for his work on the antiquities of that country, while also hobnobbing with the poet Burns. Now he was going to start work on the antiquities of Ireland. Gandon procured lodgings for him with his next-door neighbour in Mecklenburgh Street (off Marlborough Street, but no

Francis Grose by N. Dance
(courtesy National Gallery of Ireland)

N. Dance delin.

FRANCIS GROSE ESQ.ᴿ F.A.S.

W.ᵗ Ridley sculp.ᵗ

Published by J. Sewell Cornhill. June 1 1797.

longer existing), and although Grose may have spent some time visiting different institutions in Dublin while collecting basic information for his work, it is probable that both took the opportunity to pass much of the time in the convivial company of Gandon's artist friends in the city. *The Life* describes the visit, and includes a letter from Grose, written on his return to London, which gives us some idea of the hazards of travel in the eighteenth century:

212 High Holborn, London, November 30th. 1790
   Dear Sir, – I arrived here only on Thursday last, after a variety of adventures. I left Dublin on Monday evening, the 8th.; embarked on board the Dartmouth at the Pigeon-house, whence I did not set my foot on shore till the following Saturday evening, during which period we experienced storm, calm and every other intermediate kind of weather. On the second day we picked up a shipwrecked sailor, riding on some spars and yards; the sea ran so high we could not put out our boat, but threw out several ropes, two of which he laid hold on, one with his hands, the other with his teeth; by these he was drawn up on deck, but such was his fear, that it was above five minutes before he could be persuaded to let go the rope out of his mouth. To mend the matter, our pilot got out of his track, though we had no foggy weather, so that another packet which sailed a few hours after us, got into the Head (Holyhead) twenty hours before us.
   After beating about several hours in Caernarvon Bay, we landed at the back of the Head, three long Welsh miles from the inn: there were however, coaches to convey us there at free cost, though it was evident by our bills that this service was not forgotten. I remained at the Head all the next day, and on Monday morning was whirled in the small coach to Holwoell; from thence Mr. Pennant's coach fetched me to Dowling, where I spent a very pleasant week, and proceeded to Litchfield by post-chaise: there I halted another day, and dined with my friend Green, and on Wednesday morning took another spell in the mail coach and arrived in London by six on Thursday.
   I am sorry to acquaint you that I heard on good authority that the King read his speech in such a manner as alarmed his friends and gave hopes to his enemies. I was informed that he stopped frequently in the wrong place, and pronounced what he read in a crying tone; you know he was always famous for reading well, for which Quin, the player, took all the merit
   I hope you and all your family are well; do let me hear from you, with directions how I shall forward a small parcel to you. Adieu. Compliments to all friends
      Yours sincerely, Francis Grose [123]

At this time, Mary Anne Gandon had returned from London. She was now about nineteen years old.

Winter passed, and with the spring of 1791, on 5th March, work started on Carlisle Bridge. But for Gandon it was to be a sombre spring. His friend, Captain Grose, was back again, and together they indulged in the social life which was so essential to them both. However, it was too much for Grose, who was then sixty years old (to Gandon's forty-nine). Gandon's son describes the occasion in *The Life*:

> On his return to his friend's house, after three days festivity at Lord Avonmore's he seemed dull, and at dinner, disinclined to take any wine, admitting that he had been 'going it too hard' for the last three days. After dinner, in order to shake off his lethargy, Mr. Gandon proposed to Captain Grose a visit to their mutual friend, Mr. Horace Hone, at that time residing in Dorset-street.
>
> The writer of these memoirs accompanied Captain Grose and his father to the residence of Mr. Hone. In passing Rutland-square they met Dr. Harvey, then an eminent physician, and in practice in Dublin, to whom Grose was introduced.
>
> Arrived at Mr. Hone's residence, Grose, on ascending the stairs, seemed to labour under great difficulty of breathing, and in endeavouring to address Mr. Hone in his kind, good hearted manner, a great change was evident in his countenance. Mr. Hone, perceiving this, requested him not to speak, but to sit down; which he had scarcely time to accomplish, when he sunk back in the chair – to breathe no more.
>
> Every exertion was immediately made; burned feathers and other stimulants resorted to, but all in vain, and Dr. Harvey, to whom but a few minutes previously he had been introduced, and who was immediately in attendance, pronounced all further applications useless. Thus terminated the active life of this artist and celebrated antiquary.[124]

He died on 12th May, and his funeral took place on 18th May at Drumcondra churchyard. His work was continued by his friend, Dr Edward Ledwich.

During the year, the question of relief for Catholics was much to the fore. In Barclay's Tavern in Belfast on 14th April, those present had resolved 'to form themselves into an association to unite all Irishmen to pledge themselves to their country'. It was the first move, and was followed in the autumn by a visit to Belfast by Theobald Wolfe Tone, now secretary to the Catholic Committee. Then, on 14th October, the Society of United Irishmen was founded by Robert Simms and Samuel McTier, and practical Irish republicanism was born.

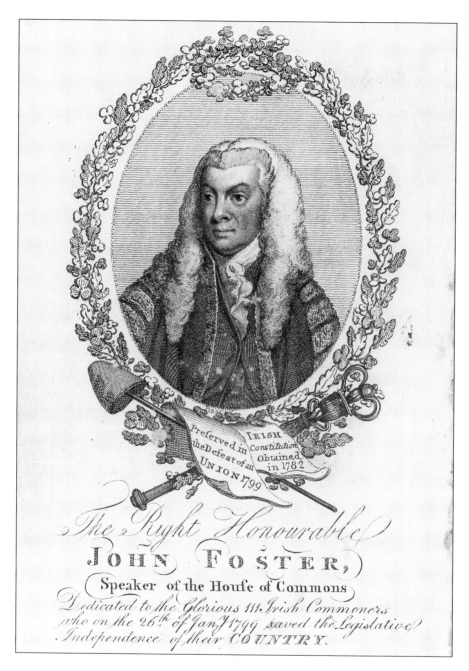

Preferved in the Defeat of an UNION 1799

IRISH Constitution Obtained in 1782

The Right Honourable
JOHN FOSTER,
Speaker of the Houfe of Commons
Dedicated to the Glorious 111 Irish Commoners
who on the 26th of Jan.y 1799 saved the Legislative
Independence of their COUNTRY.

John Foster by G.C. Stuart
(courtesy National Gallery of Ireland)

SMOKE DOCTOR (1792)

Throughout the 1780s Gandon had been active, and was largely in control of the major events which affected himself, but now, in the 1790s, the pattern was reversed, and he was to be the impotent observer of occurrences which would seriously impinge upon his life. In 1792, there were occurrences which might have afforded him, at first, a quiet satisfaction, perhaps even a mild malicious pleasure, such as many of us have felt from time to time in similar circumstances.

On 20th February, Lord Norbury (otherwise John Toler, the Attorney General) publicly referred to Napper Tandy's appearance in an insulting manner. Napper Tandy knew quite well that he was no oil painting. He took umbrage at the remarks and challenged Lord Norbury to a duel. For this he was found guilty of a breach of privilege and put in gaol. It was an unexpected outcome for Gandon's first tormentor, but oddly enough he managed to escape and went into hiding.

No doubt the Members of Parliament were amused by the situation into which Napper Tandy had been led. But a week later they faced a different situation themselves. The Speaker, John Foster, although a government man, was neither a Gandon enthusiast nor in favour of the Union. He had been persuaded, unwisely, that a Mr Nesbit, who called himself a smoke doctor, had perfected a method for enhancing the heating of a building by diverting the hot smoke from the fires into pipes let into the walls, and all this without increasing the amount of fuel consumed. Mr Nesbit was allowed to cut ducts into the walls of the Commons chamber for his copper pipes, which he took up to outlets at the corners of the dome. Naturally, these pipes became coated internally with soot, which had the habit of going on fire from time to time, but the extra heat was a bonus which added to the comfort of the Members in the chamber. However, the householders in the vicinity became alarmed at the rain of particles of burning soot thrown out by the pipes around the dome, and which were blown by the wind over their houses. There were continuous complaints from them, but typically these were ignored until, on 27th February, while the windows of the dome were open, burning soot was blown in and set the woodwork of the dome on fire while the Members were sitting in debate. They were forced to leave, and had the doubtful pleasure of watching their Commons chamber burn down as they stood in the street outside.

The work of reconstruction was given to the architect, Waldre, under the direction of the Board of Works. He was forced to replace the dome with an ugly wagon vault on top of a high brick wall, due to the interference of one of the

Members who was in a position to have him replaced should he refuse. The work on the additions to the House of Commons continued under the architect Robert Parke. As for Napper Tandy, he seems to have found his absence from the public eye little to his taste, for he surrendered himself on 17th April, but was released after a few hours. From such small beginnings, James Napper Tandy went on to become a personage of European consequence.

FITZWILLIAM DUEL (1795)

There now occurred an incident – short, sharp and decisive – which precipitated the suspended passions of the eighteenth century, and crystallised them into the enduring shapes they still hold in some measure today. In July 1794, the leaders of the Whigs in England joined Pitt's government to support the war with France. They were the Duke of Portland, Lord Fitzwilliam, Lord Spencer and Windham. In Pitt's dealings with them there were misunderstandings, undetected at the time, which lay like mines between them. Lecky, the historian, says:

> It is a significant fact that at the very outset of the coalition, a grave misunderstanding arose between Dundas and Portland about the limits of their respective provinces, but it is at least certain that Ireland lay within the department of Portland; it is equally certain that the Whig leaders believed that Portland was to have the chief direction of Irish politics, that Westmoreland was to be replaced by a Lord Lieutenant belonging to the Whig party, and that some change of system favourable to the Catholics was to be effected.

Lord Auckland wrote to Beresford, and in confidence told him something of this secret agreement; afterwards, Pelham, a Tory, denied the whole thing. However, in the event, nobody wanted to go to Ireland, and it was only after much persuasion that Lord Fitzwilliam reluctantly agreed to become the next viceroy. As soon as the news reached Ireland, the hopes of the Catholics rose immediately, for it was well known that both Portland and Lord Fitzwilliam favoured emancipation. A great number of resolutions in support of emancipation flowed into the Irish parliament from every part of the country, and it was in this excited atmosphere that Fitzwilliam landed on a Sunday afternoon, 4th January 1795. For him the crossing had been unpleasant, and he spent the next day in bed, but on the 7th

William Wentworth, 2nd Earl Fitzwilliam by Joshua Reynolds
(courtesy National Gallery of Ireland)

he sent Daly, the well-known Dublin gambler, to Beresford to tell him that he was dismissed from his position of Chief Revenue Commissioner. Although dismissed, he was to be left with all his salaries and income. This act of Fitzwilliam has been described as 'hasty, curt and probably injudicious'.

John Beresford retired quietly to Abbeville and set out to undermine Fitzwilliam. As a professional intriguer, he has had few equals, and certainly Fitzwilliam was no match for him. He canvassed his influential friends in Ireland and England; he got at the noble families allied to him by marriage; he harassed Pitt and the Tory politicians with his complaints; he inserted his influence into the Court of George III, and here Fitzgibbon lent his powerful support. The old arguments of the regency were resurrected and given a polish. George III was reminded that it would be a breach of his coronation oath to countenance Catholic Emancipation in Ireland, and his stubborn mind closed on this argument. This was decisive: no matter what Fitzwilliam might do now, it would come to nothing without the royal consent.

On 9th February, Pitt wrote to Fitzwilliam concerning the dismissal of Beresford, but did not mention emancipation. The scheme for emancipation had been sent to England at the time of the opening of the Irish parliament. Fitzwilliam had agreed with Grattan that it would be best to postpone the measure for a while, until the English cabinet had seen it and commented on it. At the time of Pitt's letter, the cabinet had seen the scheme, but had neglected to do anything about it. Now events moved mysteriously and swiftly: on 18th February, the cabinet decided to censure Fitzwilliam, and on the 19th they dismissed him.

It is instructive to follow Beresford's movements during this time. On 22nd January, the day of the opening of Parliament, he sailed from Dublin, bound for Bath. For some time now, his wife Barbara had been in poor health, and this seemed a suitable opportunity to take her for a course of 'the waters'. As soon as she was settled in Bath, he went to London, arriving there probably early in February. From this time on, Pitt and the English cabinet started to show concern for affairs in Ireland. Beresford's campaign in London must have been extremely efficient, for, as we have seen, Fitzwilliam was recalled on the 19th. The news of the recall brought great satisfaction to Fitzgibbon and to the Beresford party; now there was no doubt as to who governed the country. For Gandon, the whole occurrence must have been a severe shock. He had come to be identified with the Beresford party, the dominant force in the country, and although trouble of some sort had not been unexpected, the suddenness and scope of the dismissal was a disaster. He wrote to Beresford, perhaps a little belatedly. Beresford's reply was as evasive and optimistic as ever:

> Dear Gandon, – Many thanks for your kind letter. I could not have a
> doubt of your sentiments as to me. I see great inquiries on foot, but they

will all end to the confusion of those whose malice has dictated them. As things have turned out, I shall not have occasion to remove.

You may imagine that my mind is at present in a state of uncertainty, as I cannot, for a few days at least, foresee what may be the consequence of the turn things have taken. I shall, therefore, look to Abbeville as my great object, and make it as comfortable as I can afford to do. I cannot say more on this subject at present. I have received my letters from Ireland, by which I find you are to be deprived of Lord Fitzwilliam's presence.

Yours sincerely, J.B.[125]

Fitzwilliam now made preparations to return to England, but the Irish government, fearing a disturbance, persuaded him to postpone his departure for some weeks. When he left on Wednesday 25th March, just six days before Lord Camden arrived, Dublin put on mourning; the shops were shut and all business was suspended. His coach was drawn to the quayside by a body of prominent citizens, and he left behind a gloomy and apprehensive city and a resentful country.

Before he left, he had allowed his letters to Portland to be published, and in one of these he said that the Beresford's conduct in the sale of a public lease had been scandalous, and that extraordinary measures had been taken to baffle inquiry. A copy was sent to Beresford, and he stored it away for future use.

If the day of Fitzwilliam's departure was one of gloom, the day of Lord Camden's arrival was one of anger. The mob missed Lord Camden, for his route to the castle had been changed, but its anger was then turned towards Fitzgibbon. His sister, a voluble lady who lived in Blarney Castle, had this to say:

On the day Lord Fitzwilliam was recalled, when my brother, (as Lord Chancellor) was returning from the Castle after having assisted at the swearing-in of the newly arrived Lord-Lieutenant, a ferocious mob of no less than 5,000 men, and several hundred women, assembled together in College Green and all along the avenue leading to my brother's house. The male part of the insurgents were armed with pistols, cutlasses, sledges, crowbars, and every other weapon necessary to break open my brother's house, and the women were all of them armed with their aprons full of paving stones. This ferocious and numerous mob began to throw showers of stones into my brother's coach, at his coachman's head,and his horses; they wounded my brother in the temple, in College Green, and if he had not sheltered himself by holding his great square official purse before him, he would have been stoned to death before he arrived (through the back-yard of his own house); where with several smithy sledges, they were working hard to break into his hall door, while some others of them had ropes ready to fix up to his lamp iron to hang him the moment they could find him. When I arrived, disguised in my kitchenmaid's dress, my blue apron full of stones, I mingled with this murderous mob, and addressed a pale, sickly man, saying: 'My dear jew's, what ill become of hus! I am after running from the Castle to tell you all that a regiment of Hos is galloping down here to thrample hus, etc., Oh! yes,yes,where will we go?' Then they cried: 'Hurry, hurry, the hos is coming to charge and thrample hus – hurry for the Custom House'. And in less than a moment the crowd dispersed. I then procured a surgeon for my brother and a guard to prevent another attack, and thus I saved Lord Clare's life at the risk of being torn limb from limb if I had been recognised by any of the mob.[126]

The riot spread rapidly through the city to the houses of the primate and the speaker. The old hostility brought the crowds to the Custom House, where they gathered under the north portico, breaking the windows of Beresford's rooms on the first floor. They may have attacked Lord Waterford's house in Marlborough Street, and if Gandon was at home that day, he could have heard above the roaring of the mob, the smashing of the windows and the tinkling of the glass as it fell to the ground. He would remember the start of that other riot in London before he left it, and realise that he was now a marked man. This he was unlikely to forget in the years ahead.

In the afternoon, the troops were called out, and the rioters dispersed, but not before two men were killed. Meanwhile, the author of the trouble had returned to Bath, and to his wife. Her health was indifferent during March and April. Early in May, she seems to have got worse, and Beresford decided to risk taking her to London. The trip soon proved too much for her, and at Marlborough she died. For a few weeks Beresford mourned, but after this respite, again took up his quarrel with Fitzwilliam, whom he had already defeated politically. Now he attacked him personally. On 22nd June, he sent a carefully composed letter to Fitzwilliam, politely telling him he was a liar. There was no word from Fitzwilliam for the rest of the week, but on Sunday morning, the 20th, Beresford was knocked up at eight o'clock by Lord George Cavendish, who brought him a letter from Fitzwilliam:

Sir, – I have the honour to announce to you my presence in town. As I could not misunderstand the object of your letter, I have only to signify that I am ready to attend your call, and have the honour to be,
sir, your most obedient servant.
Wentworth Fitzwilliam [127]

Lord George told him that he was sorry to come on so disagreeable a business, and that Fitzwilliam was waiting for him in a hackney coach nearby. Beresford, according to himself, made one of those short Greek-like speeches beloved of eighteenth-century gentlemen, and added that as he was expecting to hear from Fitzwilliam, he had arranged for Lord Townshend to accompany him. Sir George Montgomery, Beresford's half brother-in-law was with him, and he sent him off for Lord Townshend.

While he was away, Lord George showed Beresford a letter which a police magistrate named Ford had written to Fitzwilliam. It was marked two o'clock, Sunday morning, and said that Ford had information that Fitzwilliam intended to fight a duel with Beresford, and his duty would oblige him to prevent it. Because of this letter, Lord George said, Fitzwilliam had had to get up before seven, and leave his house by the back door. Sir George now returned to tell Beresford that Lord Townshend could not come out before eleven. They decided to go out immediately, in order to avoid arrest, and Sir George agreed to accompany Beresford. Sir George then went off with Lord George to arrange the meeting, and when they were alone, Lord George, according to Beresford, suggested that they might interfere. They agreed that Fitzwilliam should attempt an apology, and Lord George went on, with Sir George following in another coach with Beresford. When they came to the ground, Lord George and Fitzwilliam made several drafts of an apology, but Beresford turned them down. It was obvious what they were up to, and soon a crowd gathered to see the fun, and they had to move off. They drove through Paddington, out into the country for about a mile-and-a-half, and went into a field where another apology was attempted and failed. Then, as Beresford tells us:

> Sir George measured the ground, dropping a glove where he set out and another where he stopped; I went directly to the latter with my pistol, and his Lordship was walking to the former and within two yards of it, when a magistrate called out to him by name: 'Lord Fitzwilliam, I desire you will keep the peace, I am a magistrate'. His Lordship turned about, much agitated, when he was arrested, his pistol taken from him. I then walked to them and gave my pistol to Sir George. Lord Fitzwilliam then turned to me and said: 'Now, Mr.Beresford, that we have been prevented from finishing this business in the manner I wished, I have no scruples to make an apology', which he did and hoped it would be satisfactory to me ... And considering that it was he who called on me, for my expressions in my letter to him ... I thought it right to accept his apology to me and put an end to the business ... He then hoped I would give him my hand, which I did, and he said 'Now, thank God, there is a complete end to my Irish Administration', and said something civil, purporting that he hoped we should meet again on more pleasant terms.' Beresford added 'The report and conjecture of the town you will hear from others; I have only to add

that I do not wish to publish my letter, but have no objection to its being shown.[128]

Like all Beresford's activities, there is a curious smoothness in the sequence of events, leading to a conclusion which was very closely timed. Shortly afterwards we hear: 'By desire of Mr. Pitt and with the approbation of the Sovereign himself, Mr. Beresford returned in July to Dublin and was restored to his various offices.'

Politically, 1795 was a crucial year, and the embellishment of Dublin became of secondary importance. For Gandon, the first part of the year was marked by the uncertainty of the possible completion of his major projects. The sequence of events was ominous; Grattan's Relief Bill for Catholics was defeated. The significance of this was understood, and five days later, on 10th May, the United Irishmen was converted into a secret and oath-bound society. This too was noted. The Ascendancy was now on a collision course, and its anchor, John Fitzgibbon was, on 12th June, created Earl of Clare.

GANDON'S PRACTICE

Gandon's practice during the 1790s had shrunk to finishing work on the Custom House, where Beresford's influence sustained it, and to the completion of the Four Courts, which was helped on by Beresford's links with Lord Clare. The work on the Four Courts struggled on in typical legal style into the beginning of the nineteenth century. There had been Carrickglass, where Gandon's designs for the main house were abandoned, leaving only the stables extant; there was the Rotunda and Carlisle Bridge; and there was Emo.

Since 1785, when Coolbanagher church was completed, or perhaps from a later time, when the extension to the House of Lords was completed, there seems to have been a gradual drifting apart between Lord Carlow, now Earl of Portarlington, and Gandon. This may have been due to Gandon's growing identification with the Beresford party, or more probably, to Gandon's own inattention. We find Thomas Sandby's entrance gates for Emo, and after 1796, when Gandon drew up a design for the portico, Dr McParland traces the progress of Emo through Lewis Vulliamy into the next century and on to obscure Dublin architects, such as the Williamsons. The completion of this building appears to have received little attention after Lord Portarlington's death during the rebellion of 1798. His son became busy dissipating the wealth so carefully nursed into being by his father, and is reported to have remarked on occasion that he could not see

Carrickglass, Co Longford, 1792-1804
(drawing by Michael Craig)

Carlisle (O'Connell Street) Bridge, Dublin, 1791-95
(engraving showing original obelisks; rebuilt 1880)

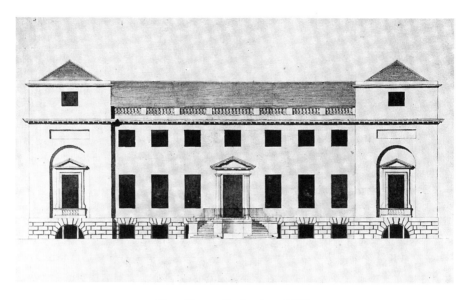

Emo Court, Co Laois, c.1790
above Unexecuted elevation
below Garden (north) elevation, by Gandon and others
opposite Ground-floor plan (*courtesy Denis Looby*)

what difference an extra nought made to his extravagances.

Lords Charlemont and Portarlington had seen to it that the extensions to the House of Lords were completed by Gandon. It was a different matter with the work to the House of Commons. After Gandon's designs were approved by the building committee, he heard no more from them. The work was given to Parke (otherwise Parks), and even if the builders' grapevine failed to apprise him of this, Gandon, in his daily business around the city, must have seen the work going on. This was an experience which had been common enough in his London days, but was new to him in Dublin, and cannot have been a pleasant one. The *Life* however, pretends that he was ignorant of the fact for some years, until the Penrose auction in 1793. Penrose was one of the architects consulted by the building committee, and had died the previous year. At the auction, Gandon found his designs and drawings for the scheme up for sale. He was naturally affronted, and wrote to John Foster, the Speaker, and to Samuel Hayes about it. Hayes replied to Gandon for them both on 31st July, concluding in a rather condescending manner:

> You had trouble, no doubt, and we have no idea of availing ourselves of any gentleman's professional abilities without compensation. The Speaker desires me to refer you to him, and he will, I dare say, act on this, as he does on every occasion, with honour and propriety'.
>
> I am, Sir, Your very faithful, And most obedient servant
> Sam. Hayes
> Hume Street, 31st. July, 1793.[129]

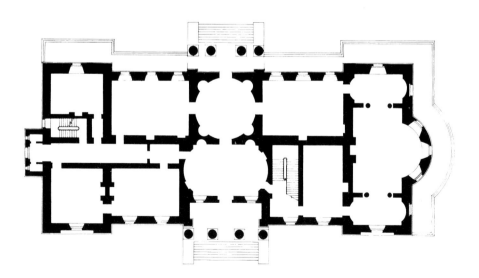

What Gandon thought of the mention of honour and propriety we can only infer.

Gandon's curious reluctance to extend his practice is noted several times in *The Life*; each time it is attributed to an overabundance of work in hand. But one is led to suspect that once the Custom House was well advanced, Beresford's pressure began to tail off, and Gandon tended to revert to the style of life which had ruined him in London. By the 1790s he had become familiar with the group of artists practising in Dublin, and could once more indulge in the pleasure he found in their company.

Although Gandon was only in his early fifties at this time, and ideally placed, with his powerful connections and their wide influence, to promote his art and extend his practice, he seems, as before, to have done nothing to help himself. It was not as if he wished to attend personally to the designing of every part of his work. He now had plenty of time for that, but we have to remember that he suffered from fairly frequent attacks of gout, which could be brought on by stress, and that he was also of an anxious disposition, but we can only conclude that without pressure from determined clients, he was reluctant to exert himself and to limit his desire for convivial company. During the 1790s, other architects, such as John Soane, Robert Adam and James Wyatt, could pursue and obtain commissions in Ireland, and as well as this, the younger Dublin architects were acquiring clients under Gandon's nose, and making inroads into areas where he should have been paramount. Dr McParland points out that about this time, November 1793, he wrote to Henry Holland in a tone which suggests that he felt his work as an architect was coming to an end. The extraordinary self-confidence which had been such a feature of the Ascendancy during the 1780s was gradually weakening as the 1790s progressed. The triumphalism of this body was turning out to have been self-destructive, for it had infected the Dissenters and the Catholics, and as they began to make their presence felt, the certainties of the previous decade began to fade. For the Ascendancy was flawed by an internal weakness. R.F. Foster describes it:

> Increasingly, the Ascendancy were prey to fears that England would let them down by breaking their monopoly: resentment of English pressures toward liberalising the laws against Catholics and Dissenters remained a constant irritant, and would eventually work, with other pressures to create polarization in the 1790s.

There were also the effects of the Regency Crisis, the French Revolution, and the execution of Louis XVI in Paris on 21st January 1793. This act panicked and unsettled the Ascendancy, and when, on 1st February, France declared war on England, they saw that their future was dependent on the outcome. Nobody expected that the war was to last, on and off, for over twenty years.

There were disquieting happenings throughout the country. One of particular interest to Gandon was the disappearance of Napper Tandy. He had been arrested on 16th February 1793, but discovered he was to be tried for taking the Defenders' oath. He escaped, only to surface in Philadelphia in 1795. The various ominous occurrences of the time, and especially the war with France, induced a certain frugal spirit into the allocation of public moneys, and the work Gandon had in hand slowed down. A further potential source of work for Gandon was taken from him when, during 1793, the Chief Secretary asked the Wide Streets Commissioners to stop spending. The prosperity of the country began to dry up. In Dublin, the difficulty in letting houses was noted in the *Dublin Evening Post*. Troubles too, became more frequent and more serious. There was a riot in Belfast on 9th March when the 17th Dragoons came into conflict with the Volunteers, and in April, Hobart's Catholic Relief Bill fuelled the spread and determination of the Orange Order.

Events in Europe, too, were to have an effect on Gandon's personal life, although at that time he could have had no hint of this. By now, the French armies were under the command of a military genius. Napoleon Bonaparte had arrived on the scene, and in time was to make himself emperor of the French and tyrant of Europe. Germany and England were left in the field, and Germany made peace with Napoleon by the Treaty of Luneville in February of 1801, followed by England in the Treaty of Amiens in 1802.

INSURRECTION (1797-1798)

On the national stage there were trends which forecast the abandonment of constitutional methods for the eventual use of force. On 1st February 1796, Wolfe Tone arrived in France and met Carnot, the president of the Directory, which governed France. He had in mind help from France for the United Irishmen.

At home, an Insurrection Act was passed on 24th March. It was overtly meant to deal with the Defenders, and gave magistrates far-reaching powers to proclaim a district. It became a capital offence to administer illegal oaths. By 12th July, there were ninety lodges of the Orange Order, and now they held their first 'Twelfth' demonstration. It was several thousand strong, and was not without incident: a soldier in Lurgan killed a marcher who had struck him.

On 8th August, Robert Stewart was created Earl of Londonderry, and his son became the notorious Lord Castlereagh. Then, in September, the Viceroy, Lord

Camden, agreed to establish a yeomanry, for the regular Crown forces were now drained by the war with France. The yeomanry was made up of armed Protestant volunteers, in units recruited by the landlords.

On 26th October, the Habeas Corpus Act was suspended until 1st June 1799. This was a remarkable forecast of the length of time felt to be necessary for the suspension of the Act, and some have seen in it a clear plan already in mind for the provoking of an insurrection and its suppression. The unrest caused by regular confrontations between the Orange Order and the Defenders and the United Irishmen was cited as the reason.

On 15th December, Admiral Lazare Hoche with forty-three ships and fifteen thousand troops set sail for Ireland. The attempt was frustrated by fierce gales and storms on the Irish coast, and the admiral had to sail back to Brest. While the Government felt easier following the failure of this attempt, the new year brought a scene of social and financial chaos. The French war caused the banks of Ireland and England to suspend gold payments. Then General Lake proceeded with the disarming of Ulster. From March to October of 1797, the Ulster Presbyterians were exposed to the ferocity of the troops and the militia. The troops, in many places out of control, exceeded even their brutal orders, and freely hung, raped and burned as they pleased. There were protests in the Irish and English parliaments, but as is usual in time of war, there was a reluctance to censure the troops. Some fifty thousand muskets and seventy thousand pikes were taken in, and this satisfied the government that the threat posed by Ulster had passed.

Fitzgibbon now believed a general rising was imminent, and the military throughout the country were ordered to flog any such tendency out of the people, or, as it is thought, to provoke a premature rising. Seeing no reason to change the methods which had proved so successful in Ulster, General Lake now applied them to the rest of the country. Shootings and hangings, floggings, rapes, and burnings with torture were commonplace, and the victims comprised both the so-called guilty and the innocent. As was to be expected, the savagery of the Crown forces evoked a corresponding reaction when the rising eventually got under way, and acts of desperate savagery were perpetrated. In Geneva Barracks, since well before the rising, torturing and hanging were daily occurrences. Anybody thought to have been connected with the United Irishmen could face being flogged to death. An early method was the 'pitch cap'. Twigs were threaded through the men's hair, hot pitch was poured over them and then set on fire. The Irish began to crop their hair to frustrate this, and became known as the 'croppies', hence the song 'The Croppy Boy'. The dragging of pregnant women from their homes, and the tossing of them in a blanket was a barbarity which the Scottish troops, to their honour, refused to have anything to do with. Such was the reign of terror during and after the rising that the silence of the people following 1798 about what they endured was noted by a number of observers.

During the French Terror, it is estimated that some 2,500 people went to the guillotine. Many times that number perished at the hands of the Crown forces in Ireland.

CENTURY'S END (1798-1799)

For seventeen years in Ireland, Gandon had served the aristocracy, the greater number of his clients being noblemen, but the barriers were still there between the landed classes and those who worked for a living. Now Gandon was to become a satellite of the aristocracy, for, on 12th March 1798 his eldest daughter, Mary Anne, was married by special license to Robert Annesley of the 3rd Regiment. The wedding took place in Mountjoy Square, and by it, Gandon could now aspire to the rank of gentleman.

The Annesley family lived in a large house in Marlborough Street, opposite the home of Lord Waterford (a Beresford), with whom they were connected by marriage. We must suppose that for some time before the marriage, Gandon was received into the withdrawing rooms of the Annesleys. The father of the Hon Robert held down a position in the revenue under John Beresford, and was in effect one of the Beresford party. Gandon, who would seem to have followed his patron in his political opinions, fitted well into this branch of society. The marriage should have given Gandon satisfaction, for no longer could the question be asked 'Who is Mr. Gandon, Sir?' He was to find out, as time went on, that the Irish nobility could exact their price.

Gandon was a member of the Dublin Library Society. The aim of the society was to provide a library of books which were too costly for an individual to acquire, and it took rooms in Eustace Street. A start was made on the library, but soon a large part of the funds, amounting to £140 a year, was diverted to supplying the members regularly with three Irish and two English newspapers. In effect, the society became a political club.

In March 1792, the Earl of Charlemont was elected its president, which would indicate the Volunteerist and Patriotic tone of the members. It says much for Gandon's affability in congenial company that he, closely identified with the Beresford party as he was, could take his place in such a society. The *Life* tells us:

Amongst others who were in regular attendance at those reading rooms was a gentleman, who was afterwards implicated in being one of the principal persons involved in the unfortunate rebellion of 1798. This gentle-man asked Mr. Gandon on evening to accompany him into an adjoining room, where he thus addressed him: 'Mr. Gandon, you are a liberal man, and a great favourite with the subscribers; you will permit me to give you a little private advice, feeling as I do a confidence that the communication I make to you will proceed no further. I recommend you to absent yourself for some time from Ireland, and bring your family with you to England.' Coupled with passing events, which every day at this period developed some new feature, in no manner contributing to the public peace or the security of property – coupled with the artificers leaving the public works he was conducting, and other outbreaks that too evidently announced that some great commotion was rapidly approaching, Mr. Gandon consid-ered this friendly communication as a warning of an impending danger, not to be slighted; he, therefore, broke up at once his establishment in Dublin, forwarded his library and papers to Liverpool, where they remained in cases until his return in 1799, and left Ireland with his family for London. Here he took a ready-furnished house in Great Portland-street, where he continued to reside during this unhappy period of distur-bance.[130]

That Gandon was singled out for such a warning indicates how egregious his opinions, which he was too honest to hide, appeared to the members. It also implies that personally he was respected. Probably the actual warning was couched in a more pointed manner than that reported by his son. He certainly responded to it with dispatch, for he could move when his personal, as distinct from his professional, preoccupations were threatened.
While in London, he sought out his old friends of the artistic community he had left behind so long ago. His disappointment must have been deep when he found them scattered and many missing, and a younger and unknown crowd in their place. Paul Sandby and his family naturally became the focus of his attention, but he liked to take morning walks during which, perhaps, he hoped to meet some of his old friends. The *Life* mentions one such encounter. James Barry was a histori-cal painter. He was of an age with Gandon, but as a protégé of Edmund Burke, he had studied for four years in Italy. Like Gandon, the 1780s seemed to have brought him success, for he was appointed Professor of Painting to the Royal Academy in 1782. His temper was uncertain; he quarrelled with everybody, and was eventually expelled from the Academy, so that by 1798 he was beginning to feel the pinch.
About one o'clock one afternoon, Gandon and his son found themselves in Castle Street and decided to call on Barry, which is an indication of Gandon's desperation of making any contact with those of the old days. Barry himself

opened the door. He was poorly dressed. We are told that Gandon said: 'How do you do, Mr. Barry; I have taken the liberty of introducing my son to you, and to request your permission to see your paintings.' They had arrived at his door at the same time as an old woman carrying a jug of porter. Barry grabbed the jug of porter with one hand, and while closing the door with the other, barked 'sir, this is a very inconvenient time.'

While in London, Gandon met Farrington who mentions this in his diary:

> November 18 – Gandon, the architect, met on the Hampstead Road & talked with him of the affairs in Ireland – The Chancellor (Earl of Clare) is an able man of great courage. He has conducted the business of the Court of Chancery, with such attention and dispatch as was never known before & he has watched the mode of proceeding of the Attorney and in consequence of ignorance or imposition, dismissed so many as counteracted their evil designs with so much integrity that there is no business in that court at times for him to decide upon – In Gandon's opinion if Lord Cornwallis had not gone over the measures pursuing by Ld. Camden wd. soon have effectually crushed the rebellion. The plan of lenity adopted by Lord Cornwallis gave occasion to many difficulties and treacheries. Gandon has long been of opinion that an Union of England and Ireland would be attended with very beneficial consequences to that country. The evil owing to men of property being absentees would be trifling in comparison with the benefits arising. Napper Tandy is a tall man with a down look and 51 or 2 years of age.
>
> Gandon went to Ireland in March 1781. At that time beef was sold in Dublin at twopence farthing a pound and Port Wine at £30. a pipe. He is now preparing for publication an account of the works he executed in Ireland, to which will be added a narrative of the difficulties attending his undertaking from (armed) opposition & in the erection of the buildings from the nature of the situations of them. About 70 plates would be required: the engravers ask high prices. it would cost £1,600. to have them engraved. If he does not adopt this mode, he will have them executed in Dublin in Aqua-tinta. He is 56 years old.

No doubt Gandon absorbed the thinking of Beresford and his friends concerning whatever leniency Lord Cornwallis may have shown, which was relative to the savagery current before, during and after the rising. But there may have been other considerations at work in Gandon's mind: the Irish peasantry had destroyed the golden years of the 1780s when commissions were continually on offer to him. Remembering Gandon's self-absorbed reaction to his father's bankruptcy, one is inclined to wonder if a similar emotion may not have been at work here.

We know too, that Napper Tandy still occupied his thoughts, being perhaps a sort of 'objective correlative', a symbol in his person of that alien Ireland which had destroyed the close and comfortable world of the Ascendancy for him.

Gandon was now in comfortable circumstances. He had done much of which he could be proud, and should have been a happy man, yet in his plans for publishing and describing his works, his mind still dwelt on the difficulties and the many oppositions, even armed, which he had encountered on the way. Dismayed by the oppositions of daily life, he seems to have been happy only in the company of artists – a class that tended to shun responsibility and consider only the practice of their art. In his depreciation of the 'leniency' towards the defeated Irish, Gandon could scarcely have been unaware of the methods used against them. Beresford's notorious son, Claudius, had given over the grounds of his house to the torture and hanging of captives, on the boundary wall of which someone had inscribed the message, 'Mangling done here'.

JAMES NAPPER TANDY (1798-1802)

While all this was going on, the opening scenes of the drama of James Napper Tandy were taking place. The previous February he had arrived in Paris from Philadelphia, and he had lost no time in letting the French know that he was an experienced officer, a man of extensive property in Ireland, and had at his command thirty thousand United Irishmen. Obviously, he understood the principle that the greater the lie, the better the chance it would have. Whether the French believed him we do not know, but they were anxious to hold down as many English troops in Ireland as possible, and felt that constant threats from the sea would have this effect.

The Directory gave him the title of general, which cost them nothing. They also gave him command of a swift sailing corvette named the *Anacreon*, loaded it with arms for the United Irishmen, and added a contingent of troops. The *Anacreon* sailed on 4th September, and General Napper Tandy and his soldiers landed on Rutland Island off Donegal on the 16th. On sight of them, the local people fled, but in the post office, Napper Tandy found news of the surrender of General Humbert. It was a considerable shock for him, and later his troops carried him back to the *Anacreon* extremely drunk. In fear of capture, they sailed northwards as far as Bergen, and then south to Hamburg, where they arrived in a snowstorm on the evening of 22nd November. Tandy was arrested two days later at the request of the English.

James Napper Tandy by James Gillray
(*courtesy National Gallery of Ireland*)

He now became the object of international speculation, for the French minister immediately demanded his release as he was an officer of the French army. The senators of Hamburg found themselves in an invidious position, literally between the devil (Napoleon) and the deep blue sea (the English fleet). They temporised, and kept him in prison, but not in irons. Then, in 1799 when the Directory fell, and since most of their trade was on the seas, they handed him over to the English.

On his arrival in London, Tandy was taken to Newgate prison. Great crowds turned out to catch a sight of him. By now, the whole of Europe was interested in his fate, for he had, as a passive prisoner, become a crucial pawn in the quarrel between Napoleon and the English. He was sent to Dublin on 12th February 1800, and was tried for treason, but the charge failed. He was then rearrested for invading Rutland Island; he pleaded guilty and was sentenced to be executed on 4th May.

Napoleon, however, did not take lightly to such treatment to one of his generals. He fined the city of Hamburg four-and-a-half million francs for handing Tandy over to the English, and, it is said, created difficulties about signing the Treaty of Amiens while Tandy was in jeopardy. The English now found Tandy a serious embarrassment. They eventually let him free.

He arrived at Bordeaux on 14th March 1802. The continent of Europe was delighted at his liberation, and he received a public ovation in Bordeaux, and also in Paris. Immediately he was raised to the rank of General of Division, and he settled in Paris, full of honours, but not for long. He died on 24th August of the following year, and received a magnificent military funeral. Enormous crowds marked his passing.

INNS OF COURT (1799-1805)

Most buildings of any considerable size have, from their inception, a history of indecision and change. Generally the indecision centres on the details of the proposed accommodation, and, in rare cases, on the precise purpose of the building itself. Change is mostly associated with fits of panic when the probable cost is mooted. But in the matter of the Inns of Court, these considerations received little attention. The states of mind in which this building was conceived and brought into being were quite unusual, and difficult to define. From the beginning, there were the eccentric aspirations of one man, and at the end, the mischievous meddling of another. To obtain a coherent view of the whole affair, we must go back over ten years.

On 23rd May 1789, William Caldbeck became treasurer to the Honourable Society of the King's Inns. He had been called to the bar in 1755, and was a gentleman with estates in Clondalkin and Whitechurch in Co. Dublin. The gunpowder factories at Clondalkin were owned by his family, as was a Merchant House in Bishop Street. These business concerns did not preclude a flirtation with the nobility, for he acted as squire to James Hamilton, Lord Clanbrassil, on the occasion of the earl's installation as a Knight of St Patrick. The new treasurer was, therefore, a man of wealth and position. That he was influential is apparent, for Bartholemew Duhigg, in his *History of the Kings Inns*, tells us that in one year, when the fees accruing to the new office of Under Treasurer exceeded the average by some £250, 'the Treasurer named to that office his eldest son. This gentleman dying in 1790 or 1791, his stepson, then under age, was named in a similar manner; both assisted by an office clerk, also appointed by the Treasurer.' As we shall see, he was a man of some resource, but beneath all this lay a curious ambition (one might say, almost a craving in one so placed) – the treasurer wanted to be an architect.

His taste in this direction had already been whetted by the construction of his new gunpowder factory near his Clondalkin residence, Moyle Park. The foundation stone for this undertaking was laid by Lord Charlemont in May 1792, in the presence of a detachment of Volunteers, thus securing the financial success of the factory well before it came into production.

The amateur architect is a familiar figure. The practice of this elusive and subtle art appears to many to be a simple matter. It is, if one may use the adjective, so concrete, so amenable to the exercise of common sense, and so obviously mishandled by professional architects, that the thoughtful amateur can at times scarcely contain himself. The professional is sure to notice as he grows experienced how many able architects are lost to the profession, and how ill-equipped they are for the professions they have chosen. This is not to say that the gifted amateur has no value; on the contrary, but without experience he is no match for even a mediocre professional. Lawyers as quasi-architects are rare; perhaps they see enough of the results of benevolent meddling to be able to resist the temptation, and we can only be thankful this is so.

The Honourable Society had grown wealthy since 1782. Buoyed up by this new found affluence, the benchers felt free to indulge themselves in an extravagant manner, such as the appointment of some thirty tipstaves. From time to time, they discussed the construction of a hall, a library and a chapel, as well as a square of houses where the barristers could take chambers. Here the new treasurer found his opportunity, and determined to put these schemes in hand himself. The society owned a plot of ground at Inns Quay, adjacent to the new Four Courts, and here was obviously a suitable and convenient place for the projected buildings. But the treasurer thought otherwise. His line of thought can only be inferred from his subsequent actions. Perhaps he felt a ready-made site denied him opportunities for patronage. There was also Gandon's Four Courts nearby, in an advanced stage of construction and already much admired. Maybe he suspected the Lord Chancellor would put the work in Gandon's hands. He smothered any such possibility by leasing out the Inns Quay ground in perpetuity, thus putting it beyond the reach of its owners forever, and he looked around for a more remote site. He and his friends in the building committee settled on a plot of ground at Galway's Walk on the south side of the river, which is now occupied by a part of Guinness's brewery. On 21st July 1792, this ground was approved and the treasurer was ordered to purchase it. However, he showed a strange reluctance to do so, and for over a year nothing happened. There were, necessarily, meetings to discuss the scheme, but from February 1793, no entries were made in the treasurer's book, not until 17th November when the committee approved a site at Henrietta Street and ordered the treasurer to rent it.

Henrietta Street was at that time a street of large early Georgian houses, some with palatial interiors, where the ruling families lived. The Protestant primate, Richard Robinson, Baron Rokeby, had a house at the top of the street on the left-hand side, in which he did not live, but where he was waked in an elegant state in 1794. On the other side, facing the primate's house, lived Luke Gardiner himself, Viscount Mountjoy, who gave his name to one of Dublin's major squares and to Dublin's central prison, but at that time was famous for, among other things, the magnificent wakes held there for his wife and his daughter-in-law. It was a residential street of the highest class, deliberately remote from the noise and stench of the city, and leading nowhere.

So, on 17th November, he was ordered to rent the plot beside Lord Mountjoy's house and garden. The law's delays were cast aside, and by 14th December a lease was taken from Richard Trench, later Lord Clancarthy, who was Lord Mountjoy's trustee. There were some curious features in this transaction: the rent was £514 per annum, although Duhigg considers fifteen guineas would have been reasonable, but apart from this, any development of the site to the east was prevented by Lord Mountjoy's property, and to the west by Lord Palmerston's estate. Where it was open to the north, a strip was reserved by Lord Mountjoy which might show a profit as building land if the scheme went ahead; indeed, it was remarked that the Honourable Society would have done Lord Mountjoy a favour if they had taken the ground for nothing. Oddly enough, this plot had, at one time, been the property of the Honourable Society, but a previ-

---

Luke Gardiner, Irish School c.1778
(courtesy National Gallery of Ireland)

ous chancellor had passed it on to his son as his own in the confusion of one of the periodic bouts of confiscation in the seventeenth century. At this time, no comment was passed on the signing of the lease by the treasurer as if he were the representative of a corporation, an act which was later held to be illegal. But while these negotiations were going on in a relatively open manner, the treasurer was dealing secretly for the nearby primate's garden. During the Hilary term of 1794, he was authorised by a bench rule to treat 'with a certain gentleman' for the ground, but it had already been settled that rent would start from December in 1793. In February of 1794, the garden was taken at a rent of £650 a year, bringing the combined rents of the plots to the considerable sum of £1,164 per annum. There were surprising features about this plot too: it was restricted on two sides, while the actual position of the third side was doubtful, and although the primate did not live there, it was a condition of the lease that no building was to be carried out there during his lifetime. Afterwards it was pointed out that the 'certain gentleman' was a bencher and a trustee of the Honourable Society, and it was felt that in these dealings the treasurer, Caldbeck, had betrayed his trust.

The treasurer was busy in another way too. He was enjoying himself designing the new buildings. At last the tiresome problems of the site and the threat of professional interference had been resolved, and now he could express his personality with freedom. Characteristically, the work was put in hand before we find any mention of plans, while for the better recording of this work he had three books printed, and bound in soft leather. On the front of each was a panel of scarlet, and in fine gilt lettering, his name and the date, '14th. Decbr. 1793'. Two were composed of blank pages – one for the entry of his contracts – and the other for expenses. The third book, of more than three-hundred pages, carried three engraved and stamped receipts to a page, almost one thousand in all, each reading, 'RECEIVED from the Honourable Society of King's Inns by the Hands of WILLIAM CALDBECK, Esq., their Treasurer, the sum of...' These books are still preserved in the society's archives, and we find that his activities started on 16th December 1793, with the purchase of padlocks, staples, ropes and a hatchet. Perhaps he felt that, for completion, he might as well be the builder as well, for in the first half of 1794 he spent as much as £1,188 on excavations, sand, rubble, stonework and cartage, partly for the erection of a porter's lodge, and also for the serious work of the new inns. In July he started to call in the accounts, at the time when his plans were first approved by the benchers (but which approval was almost immediately cancelled), and he continued to pay off the workmen's accounts until November, to the amount of £506. He had a final fling that November on the death of the primate, when he spent £60 knocking down walls and rooting up trees in the primate's garden. After this, the amounts shown are for the taxes on the property and for the porters' wages. They are relatively small amounts, in keeping with his diminished hopes and plans. Duhigg gives us an ironic description of his fall, but it should be remembered that although Duhigg is very conscious of the irregularities of others, he does not mention the censure passed on himself by the society for gross irregularity during his period of office as librarian. He tells us:

> In July, 1794, that gentleman's (the Treasurer) plan and elevation of a Dining Hall and Library was approved in Council; nor is it easy for me to forget the transport with which he communicated the intelligence and the satisfaction apparently visible when I hailed him as the legal Vitruvius, a character more permanent and respectable than what accrued from the fleeting mark of artillery Captain or Squire of St. Patrick.
>
> A day was even fixed and nearly approached for laying the founda-tion stone, but sudden clouds frequently interrupt ambitious prospects, the seemingly unalterable order yielded to over-ruling influence. I was present at the interesting opposition when a young Bencher, Mr. Marcus Beresford joined to his opinion the strength of an ascendant party. In vain the Treasurer and his partisans pointed out the oeconomy of his approved plan, in which architectural profit was disclaimed, and a recompense only looked for in the generous commendations of contemporaries and the juster applause of posterity. In the true spirit of professional debate these reasonings formed a basis for opinions of the opposite party; that of disin-terested oeconomy was ridiculed as the harbinger of ruin; if such a building should be committed to any person's guidance who was not a professed architect. Why, it was added with warmth, vary in an expenditure of large amount and public trust from the established practice of mankind. Though an unanimous assent was not given to the apparent integrity and obvious good sense of the preceding observations, the Treasurer's building party shrunk into a diminished minority, and in that respect, blasted his official activity for ever.[131]

William Caldbeck, we remember, had the foundation stone for his factory laid by Lord Charlemont, the Commander-in-Chief of the Volunteers and one of the leaders of the Patriot Party. While this may have been a smart business move with profit in mind, it placed him in opposition to the Beresfords, and when it came to party influence, he had no chance against the Beresfords, nor against Gandon, who was the Beresfords' favourite, and whom, we have noticed, seems to have been regularly tipped off by them concerning matters of mutual interest.

The work slowed down and finally stopped. For a year or so, the treasurer was to be fully occupied with unpleasant legal matters. There was an outburst of activity within the Honourable Society, and an examination of the treasurer's various dealings was made. The legality of the leases of the new ground was questioned, and counsel's opinion was taken. He was also preoccupied with troubles nearer home, for two men had been killed when his new gunpowder factory blew itself to pieces. So violent was the explosion that it was reported to have caused the collapse of a chimney stack on Usher's Quay, many miles away. His troubles with the Honourable Society continued, but he hedged. The rising shelved the matter, and the Honourable Society paid £1,188 in rent for the abandoned plot at Henrietta Street for the next six years, but a temporary hall was erected on it in 1798. With the inception of the rising, the treasurer turned his mind to another profession of almost equal attraction for amateurs: he took up soldiering. He made himself colonel of the Lawyers' Artillery Volunteers, and it would not be surprising if he were not behind the choice of weapons, with his family business in mind.

Some time in the summer of 1799, Gandon decided it would be safe to return to Ireland. His family travelled with him, and before they reached Anglesea, they made a short tour through Wales. They stopped at Caernarvon for a few days, and resumed their journey in a coach drawn by two horses, both of which were blind. Near Bangor, the horses bolted, ran off the road, and smashed the carriage to pieces in a quarry hole about eight-feet deep. Gandon and his family were taken from the wreckage bruised and badly shaken, but not seriously hurt. The shock of this mishap lingered in Gandon's mind for some time, and a year later it was still a subject for comment in his letters to Beresford.

Back in Dublin, he found the city still recovering from the rising and the preparations for the Union under way. The Custom House and the Four Courts were almost complete, the boom in building was over, and the only serious scheme in contemplation was the new King's Inns. No doubt he was asked to prepare designs by the Beresfords or by Lord Clare. Certainly he was in possession of the requirements of the Honourable Society, and it is probable that some of the benchers were familiar with his proposals. Two other architects were at work that autumn on the same scheme. One was Richard Morrison, a former pupil of Gandon, and the other was the ubiquitous Myers.

On 23rd January 1800, a new building committee was appointed. It consisted of Lord Clare and Lord Clonmel, Lord Carleton and the Right Hon Barry Yelverton, with two others. The treasurer was pointedly excluded, but was ordered by the committee to write to Gandon and Morrison and ask them to send their designs to his office. He swallowed the pill and did so, and at the end of the month he notes the receipt of plans from Morrison and also from Myers. Gandon, perhaps on advice, knew better than to trust his plans to chance or to the treasurer, and replied with a short note: 'Mr. Gandon presents his compliments to Mr. Caldbeck and will do himself the Honour of waiting on the Committee with his designs for the new Inns whenever they signify their desires.' [132]

Nothing is recorded for some months, but the result was in no doubt. The committee met again on 13th June 1800, and approved of Gandon's plans. They recommended that work should start, and ordered the treasurer to pay Gandon £2,000. Of this, Duhigg dryly remarks:

> As no premium was given to disappointed candidates, nor their designs ever reviewed the reader will naturally conceive that the approbation was preconcerted and the Society of Benchers gravely assembled to sanctify such resolutions. The report of the Committee conclusively ascertains that important fact: nor was the present respectable architect fully informed on the proceeding indispensable subjects, whereby a princely structure has been planned, disproportionate to necessary use, and superior to any expenditure which the income of the Society could suggest or warrant. Whether that concealment was premeditated or accidental, the error was extremely natural ... A universal opinion prevailed that where so much money was visibly misapplied, the income must be great and capable of immediate increase.[133]

Once again, the ground at Henrietta Street was invaded by workmen. This time, however, they knew their job. Many of the names are familiar: John Semple, bricklayer; Fred Darley, stonecutter; John McKenzie, smith; John Stuart, carpenter, and, of course, Edward Smyth, sculptor. The Clerk of Works was Richard Louch. The treasurer looked on impotently, but not for long.

The committee soon held another meeting. They wanted to have the ground for the new chambers marked out, and plans and elevations drawn up. The treasurer was ordered, or perhaps he ordered himself, to 'receive proposals from persons willing to take such ground or any part thereof'. The fragmentation of responsibility which this produces is the nightmare of every architect, and Gandon put a stop to it for the time being. The records say: 'Mr. Gandon objected thereto, as he said, of many inconveniences likely to arise from the workmen of different employers working at the same time within the gates, and the danger of encouraging combination and rise of wages by setting so much building on foot at once.'[134] The next entry by the treasurer says: '1st August, 1800; Be it Remembered that On this day the first stone of the new Buildings for the Societie's Dining Hall and Library was laid by the Right Honourable the Earl of Clare, Lord High Chancellor of Ireland.'[135]

Nothing is recorded for nearly a year, but at a meeting on 12th June 1801, the committee ordered Gandon to furnish plans, elevations and sections of the library and dining hall. This is an odd request as he had already discussed his plans with them. He may have got the originals back, prudently, to keep them out of the hands of the treasurer, and he must have suspected the motives behind this order, for, perhaps on advice, he did not comply with it. At the same meeting, he was again ordered to prepare plans for the chambers, and it was resolved when these further plans were approved to advertise the plots for building. The old trouble was starting again, and again Gandon procrastinated. There must have been other considerations on his mind of which we are ignorant, for it was a time of dramatic change, and the old order, from which Gandon had had his main support, was now in disarray. He must have realised that his own life and professional practice would have to change too.

He obtained a year's grace, for the next meeting of the committee took place on 18th June 1802. It was a new and very different committee. Caldbeck was now a member, for, in the meantime, Lord Clare had died. Having done their work, the English were finished with him. He quickly fell into ill-health and it soon became clear that he was about to die. He ordered his papers to be burned, as did most of those who were concerned in the bringing about of the Union. (It was thought that this wholesale destruction was necessary to suppress the evidence of the measures taken to foment the rising, and it is reported that for years afterwards agents of the British government were still searching for and suppressing any papers which might reveal the conspiracy.) At his death, a great crowd of people gathered in front of his house, hooting and shouting, and they followed his funeral to his grave in St Peter's churchyard, where dead cats were thrown on his coffin to show that the people had not forgotten his promise at the height of his power to make the Irish Catholics as tame as cats.

On the 9th February 1802, a new chancellor had been appointed. He was John Freeman Mitford, 1st Baron Redesdale, and an Englishman, for one of the advantages of the Union was that the best jobs could be given to Englishmen. He was described as 'a sallow man with round face and blunt features, of a middle height, thickly and heavily built, and having a heavy drawling and tedious manner of speech', and without a sense of humour. He took his seat in the Irish Chancery Court on 5th May, and settled down to a career of mischief in Ireland.

The Beresfords too had, with the Union, suffered an eclipse, so Gandon was now left to face a very different committee without their support. He seems to have felt that shock tactics would be appropriate, for on 3rd June, he wrote to the treasurer:

> Sir, you will please to inform the Honbl. Lords on the Committee for the Temple that a further sum of £3,000 is necessary for carrying on the said works in order to take the first opportunity to purchase a proper assortment of Deals and Timbers to Season. The sum hitherto granted not being sufficient to allow for that purpose. I am, sir, your humble servant, J. Gandon.

He also submitted plans for their approval.

The new committee appointed a committee to decide on how much money to allow Gandon and to examine his plans. No doubt, Caldbeck formed the backbone of this sub-committee, and now it was found that Gandon's plans for the chambers encroached on ground not in the possession of the Honourable Society. Duhigg did not mistake the reason for this:

> The Treasurer was averse to the appointment of Mr. Gandon and needed no instructions from the keenest statesman how to render enquiries for such a man, so far troublesome as to make the information incomplete. The situation of the western side was entirely unknown to the architect who conceived it to belong to the Society, or to be reducible to immediate possession by the nature of its tenancy. Under this impression, the front has been moved so far to the westward as to approach within a few yards of cowhouses, a Racket Court, and a few obscure tenements inhabited by the poorest class of people.

The committee decided it would be unwise to purchase more ground, and continued to debate the matter for the rest of the year. It was suggested that the building be pulled down, as was only to be expected since Gandon was the architect. This suggestion might well have come from Redesdale, now the Lord Chancellor, who was busy making himself unpopular with the Irish lawyers by his arrogance and his instinct for meddling during his term of office. An uneasy tension existed between him and the legal profession. William Caldbeck died on the 6th September 1803, but whatever relief this may have brought to Gandon, it was more than outweighed by the activities of Redesdale.

The work at the Inns continued throughout 1804, but more slowly. It appears to have been starved of money and confused by the interference of Lord Redesdale. Gandon went to London during that year, and on his return, Redesdale adopted the habit of visiting the site and leaving written complaints for Gandon. These wore Gandon down, and after putting up with them for about a year, he wrote to Redesdale resigning his appointment. He defends his workmen, points to the difficulties placed in his way, and concludes:

> I hope I may be allowed, without the appearance of vanity, to assert, that the works already erected under my inspection, in Dublin, are equal in magnitude and importance to any construction in this part of the United Kingdom, and I trust I have conducted them with credit to myself, as well as satisfaction to those who honoured me with their confidence, and I cannot but regret the misfortune of not being enabled to give equal satisfaction to your Lordship. Under this impression, I consider it my duty to decline being any longer employed as architect to the King's Inns, and I

am convinced that your Lordship will adopt such speedy measures for completing the works as may be necessary.

Mr. Baker will do himself the honour of attending on your Lordship as usual, to receive your direction to regulate the further progress of completing the building, as the funds of the Society may enable him. Mr. Baker is in possession of all my drawings for this building, to assist him, and his abilities are fully equal to the undertaking.[136]

Following a change of ministry in England, Redesdale was dismissed, and left the Irish bar on 4th March 1806. Gandon may have reflected that he should have been patient for another few months, but on the whole, he was probably just as pleased to be out of a situation which, given the deteriorating financial position of the Honourable Society and with Caldbeck's legacy of confusion, had every sign of gradually grinding to a halt.

* * * * *

ARCHITECTURAL NOTE

In Gandon's time, Henrietta Street was perhaps the most socially desirable street in the city, but in siting the Inns of Court, he chose to ignore it, and faced his building out towards the west and towards the poorer houses along Glasmainogue Road. He did not even place it on the axis, apparently using the street merely as access to an area of greater importance. This we can understand when we read what Duhigg has to say:

> An oblong enclosure including the western front may be built round the new King's Inns which will contain twenty two-houses and form an elegant interior of 497 feet by 224; each house may be fifty three feet eight inches in front, by thirty seven feet six inches, and from three to four storeys high, with apartments underground. This plan gives six rooms to each floor; the landing leads to a small lobby, a door from which encloses three apartments. the above houses will have rears. But if the adopted plan be to build Chambers without such conveniences, nine additional houses may be erected on the south and north sides. Should Glasmainogue Road be entirely excluded from the intended interior, an iron railing is to form the western boundary. A plan of one house has been given in and is estimated to build for 'five thousand five hundred pounds', thus, 'one hundred and twenty one thousand pounds' would be required to build the square.

Here Duhigg is discussing a concrete proposal which has been gone into suffi-

Inns of Court, 1800-1803
above Elevation of the principal (west) front
(courtesy Irish Architectural Archive – RIAI Murray Collection)
below View of the proposed square

241

ciently to determine the size of the houses which would act as chambers for the
barristers. The dimensions he gives will fit twenty-two sets of chambers around a
square of 497 feet by 224 feet. This is no random proposition, for they fit exactly,
with scarcely any tolerance, and we must infer that quite an amount of thought
and work went into this scheme to produce so precise a result. He describes a
plan which can be set out, and which provides a moderate six rooms for each
floor. He is doubtful as to the number of floors, but four have been shown in the
accompanying sketch. With four storeys, the height of the terraces approximates
to the height of the Inns, and the Inns now serve as the central feature for the
whole square, uniting it around a developed centrepiece in the London manner
to which Gandon was accustomed. Three storeys only would have the effect of a
too violent change of character between the central feature and the rest of the
square. In our sketch, the house style of Beresford Place has been followed – the
London style of building where individual houses are united by horizontal bands.

The proposed square of barristers' chambers makes sense of Gandon's placing of the Inns of Court as the focal point of an enclosed area. Because this
scheme was abandoned, it leaves his building standing there like a stranded ship.
Even if it had been left like that it would still be impressive, but later symmetrical
extensions echoing his elevations for the hall and library were added. These have
destroyed the force of his design, diminishing the thrust of his original building,

Inns of Court
Plan of proposed barristers' chambers
opposite *Elevation to square and ground-floor plan*

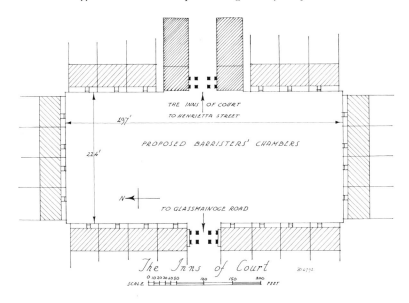

ELEVATION TO SQUARE

The Inns of Court

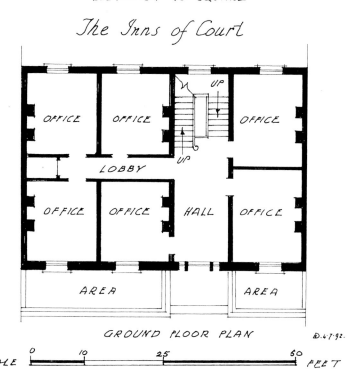

GROUND FLOOR PLAN   D.4.7.92.

SCALE   0   10   25   50   FEET

Inns of Court

Inns of Court

and the added mass constricts his central feature so that the cupola appears to have been added to strengthen a central weakness. It would be difficult to think of a more destructive method for extending the building. If these extensions had even been set back two or three yards from the face of the Inns, much of the thrust of Gandon's building would have been preserved.

When we consider Gandon's original building, we are faced with a major surprise. One of the tenets of the neoclassical theory of design was that significant columns should rest on the ground or on a low podium. Here they are placed as Palladio would have placed them on his urban buildings, raised on a rusticated base or ground floor, or, as they then called it, a basement.

Internally, perhaps the only major example of Gandon's work which has survived unaltered and unspoiled is the benchers' hall. It is an impressive interior, and nothing could be said about it here which would equal Dr McParland's description in his remarkable book:

> The formula Gandon uses for this hall is one he had used earlier at Coolbanagher and Waterford. There is a high blank lower zone, straddled by the giant Ionic aedicule at either end, but above this on the side walls his favourite niched piers separate arched openings or recesses, and from them spring the transverse arches of the barrel-vault: this upper zone, with its reiteration of an astylar triumphal arch theme, is a transcript of the internal elevation of the Waterford Court House. Gandon, in other cases had stressed the continuity of articulation across all four walls of an interior despite the problems this raised when the bays of the end walls came to be continued above the cornice. Here he introduces on the short walls his giant orders,[137] bound to the other walls only by the entablature. It is interesting, too, to see him in this late building opening his walls with windows instead of confining the openings – as he frequently did – to the area above the cornice (at Coolbanagher, they come below the cornice but are placed above a high impost). It is likely that he would have considered top lighting as insufficient, on its own, for the library range opposite, and symmetry would then have dictated corresponding opes on the hall elevation. These could of course have been blind, though such large scale deception at piano nobile level would have been odd. And so, ignoring the convenient top-storey circular windows of the exterior which were ready to light his hall above the cornice, he blanked these off with his unbroken barrel-vault and allowed light to come in through his tall southerly windows. This produces its own interest, for when one is in the hall one can see, beyond the laminations of the repeated triumphal arches of the interior, and through the windows, to the façade of the nearby library wing with its answering window arcade and gradation of surface layers.

THE DETENUS (1803-04)

The year 1803 was not a tranquil year in Ireland. Throughout the country there were isolated outrages, and a palpable undertone of violence existed. Then, on 18th May, England went to war again with France, a war which was to last until 1815. In Dublin there was an explosion in an unofficial munitions factory, which may have forced the premature Emmet rising. Recent research has shown that this was a more organised affair than had appeared likely, when, on 23rd July, Robert Emmet and about thirty followers marched down Thomas Street to capture Dublin Castle. It was an unlucky day for Chief Justice Lord Kilwarden and his son-in-law, the Rev Richard Wolfe, who were going the other way. They were dragged from their coach and killed. The Crown forces moved in and the rising collapsed, but not before a Colonel Brown met his death in a confrontation in the Coombe. Emmet went into hiding on the outskirts of Dublin, but was arrested on 25th August. On 24th August, Gandon's *bête noire*, Napper Tandy, had died, aged sixty-three. In the meantime, the Habeas Corpus Act was suspended and trials under martial law resumed, while the Lord Mayor of Dublin imposed a curfew on the city from 9pm to 6am. All houses were required to display a list of the occupants on the front door, and, no doubt, checks were made on suspect houses during the night. Emmet was tried in Green Street courthouse on 19th September, where he made his famous speech from the dock. He was hanged the next day and his head cut off.

All of these activities must have been viewed with alarm by Gandon, in particular the murder of Lord Kilwarden, who had been a member of the group which he had served now for over twenty years, and which, with the start of the new century, was fast disappearing. Lord Portarlington was dead, as were lords Charlemont and Clonmel, and John Claudius Beresford. The Hon John Beresford had retired to his place in Derry, and washed his hands of affairs in Dublin while writing friendly letters to Gandon telling him not to worry.

These were all Gandon's friends and clients, and they had protected him throughout his life in Ireland. Now he was virtually alone, and known to the public as an associate of those who had so ruthlessly put down the rising of 1798. Such considerations must have possessed his mind, reinforced by the memory of the warning he had received before 1798. The imposition of the curfew, too, may have convinced him that the authorities knew more than had appeared at the time, and that another countrywide rising was imminent. So, once again, he packed up and left for London.

He was not the only one to seek asylum there: Farrington writes in his diary for 14th February 1804:

Mrs. and Miss Hone called. They are come from Bath & have taken lodgings in Piccadilly & Hone is to follow them next week being determined to try what London will do as the state of Dublin is now so dangerous – The price of living in Ireland is now equal to that of England, formerly they cd. live there for a 3rd the expense – Gandon + has a son and 2 daughters. The son has been proposed to be an architect but has not been peculiarly brought up to anything and is now a weight upon his father. The eldest daughter, a beautiful woman, is married to a Mr. Annesley son of a commissioner of excise, an extravagant young man, deeply in debt, who had a commission in the army which he sold & went to France where he is now a prisoner. His wife and three children are with him. Gandon is peevish under these circumstances. He has purchased a house at Lucan 6 miles from Dublin where he does not dare to live on acct. of the bad disposition of the Irish people. He proposes to come to England.

But it was no longer the London Gandon had known twenty-five years previously. He was now sixty-three, and the familiar faces and places of his younger days were changed or gone. Despite his inclination to return, he might have found himself even more alone in London than in Dublin. Chambers was gone, as was Thomas Jones, and of the Maltons, Thomas, the father, and James, his former apprentice, were both dead, and the other son, Thomas, died on the 7th March while Gandon was in London. Only Sandby remained, and the empty house, which had been for so long a centre where artists and those noblemen interested in cultural matters could meet, was now, perhaps, only a reminder for Gandon of a social group which had disappeared.

His son was thirty-two-years old by then, and apparently dependent on his father. The house in Lucan was also on his mind. But his prime worry must have been the position of his daughter and her husband, with his grandchildren, who were now prisoners in France. Within a week of war having been declared, the French issued a decree of 23rd May 1803. It was conveyed to all the English in France at that time in the form of a letter from the local prefect. For example:

The Prefect of the Department of the Somme to M Soames, Englishman at Amiens. I inform you sir of the Decree of the government of the Republic dated 2nd. Prairial, 11th. year of the Republic of which a copy is below.

Saint Cloud, 2nd. Prairial, 11th. year of the Republic. All the English enrolled in the Militia, from the age of 18 to 60, holding a commission from his Britannic Majesty, who are at present in France, shall be made Prisoners of War, to answer for the Citizens of the Republic who have been arrested by the vassals or subjects of his Britannic Majesty before the declaration of war. The Ministers, each as far as concerns him, are charged with the execution of the present Decree.

Bonaparte, the First Consul

B. Marot, the Secretary of State.

Consequently, within the space of 24 hours from the present notification, you will please to constitute yourself a Prisoner of War at the house of the Town Major of the City of Amiens. I tell you beforehand that no pretext, no excuse, can exclude you, as, according to the British laws, none can dispense you from serving in the Militia. After having made this declaration within 24 hours, you will be permitted to remain a prisoner on Parole. In case you have not made your declaration within 24 hours, you will no longer be allowed to give your Parole, but will be conducted to the control point of the military division that will be fixed upon by the Minister of War

I salute you.[138]

The English should have foreseen French reaction when they began to detain French subjects. However, they took the opposite view, that their own subjects had been detained while travelling on French passports, and so they considered the decree as a breach of faith. Since they held to this view up to 1814, all negotiations to have the captives, or, as they were known in France, the *detenus*, released, were nullified.

There were twelve depots set up for the detention of the *detenus*, but it was to Verdun that English officers and gentry were sent. Those of the captives lacking blue blood were dispersed among the other eleven depots. It was possible in Verdun for the *detenus* to lead a moderately normal if somewhat circumscribed life, depending on what each could afford. A *detenu* could chose a room or a house, and could live alone or with his family, and although the town was locked up at night, he could move about in it freely.

In Verdun, there is a lower town and an upper town. The upper town became the fashionable quarter. Here social gatherings took place. There were several clubs, and one of these was accommodated in the Bishop's Palace as, since the revolution, he no longer lived there. There were even gambling houses and a cock-fighting ring. These relaxations were approved of by the authorities in the person, at one time, of a rapacious commandant called General Wirion and his more rapacious wife. Scarcely any activity was possible unless the commandant got his cut. In spite of this rather heavy type of taxation, extravagant fêtes and balls were held from time to time.[139]

If Gandon's daughter and son-in-law were indulging in these displays, he had reason to be worried. It is likely that his daughter looked to him for support, since the Hon Robert was, as we have seen, deep in debt, and nobody could have foreseen how long the war was going to last. We cannot blame Gandon for his

his peevishness, surrounded as he was then by so many intractable problems, including his troubles with Lord Redesdale and the Inns of Court, and all this, especially, at a time of life when he should, with reason, be able to look forward to some relaxation from domestic and professional cares.

RETIREMENT (1806)

Gandon had other worries during the progress of the Inns of Court. In 1803, the works in connection with the Custom House were still going on, but a new board made difficulties for him. These became such that he resolved to complain to the viceroy, but the ever-cautious Gandon first turned to his patron for advice. Beresford replied shrewdly, warning Gandon that such complaints might lead to an enquiry in which Gandon would fill the role of accuser, and that it would be better to acquaint the authorities in an indirect way of the irregularities going on. This was a typically devious Beresford ploy. At the same time, the old blackguard did not forget to congratulate both Gandon and himself on their dedication and honesty in managing the huge outlay on the Custom House 'when the public lost not a sixpence by either of us'. He recommended Gandon to his own family and grandchildren, of which there was now John Robert, born in 1799 (who was to become British Consul to North Holland), Mary Anne, born in 1800, and Catherine, born in 1802. During his life, Gandon was to see both girls grow up, be married, and to die before him.

Another year passed, but Gandon was not yet rid of the troubles connected with the Custom House. An accounting clerk had replaced him as architect, a man who had been brought over from London by Gandon himself and who was later dismissed for improper practices. Now Gandon faced a commission of enquiry into the whole project, and again appealed to Beresford. Beresford was not impressed, commiserated with Gandon on his sufferings from gout, and in a later letter said: 'I think Morgan's acknowledgements are your quietus. I am sorry to hear that your head is out of order: avoid business, take exercise, get into Irish post-chaises, and come and visit me, they will give you a good shaking.'[140]

The next news of Beresford was that he had died on 5th November 1805. This was a severe shock for Gandon, and was followed by a serious and prolonged attack of illness. His doctors advised him to get out of Dublin, so he finally moved out to Canonbrook, his new house in Lucan, to begin his long period of retirement.

Gandon's oldest and best friend Paul Sandby was the next to go. In a letter

James Gandon, 1805, by Comeford
(*courtesy Dublin Corporation Public Libraries – Gilbert Collection*)

to Gandon in 1806 he says, 'You commence your letter by mentioning increasing years, and croak like a banished mortal in a foreign land.' He also refers to the scarcity of food during the war:

> Though you get not a slice of John Bull's loaf, which is very difficult to obtain by us poor souls, yet you have this consolation to bid defiance to famine, for you not only have land to plant, but also good potatoes, which latter are most certainly preferable to John Bull's bread, with alum and lime, to screw up our mortal bodies.

Then he adds a most ambivalent paragraph. Is he referring to his dalliance with his brother's wife?

> I really am delighted with your planting, it is the best hobby a reasonable man can mount: in the juvenile part of my life, I put a few acorns in my brother's garden at Windsor, and found great pleasure in viewing the opening buds. My son Thomas, has been a great planter also, having ten living instances of his nurseryship.[141]

Paul Sandby died on the 7th November 1809. Apart from his family, Gandon was now virtually alone.

Of his personal life, we can imagine his winters relieved by simple social occasions, such as evenings spent with his remaining children and with the friends he had made locally. But the summers, perhaps, brought him face-to-face with his essential loneliness. He might of a morning amble down the path to his summerhouse, where the air was balmy and the birds busy around him in the trees, and as he watched the dappled sunlight on the ground, inevitably his thoughts must have returned to those early days of perennial sunshine when being young was an enchantment in itself. But the lilac was long lost, and the sea smell and the granite shore belonged to another century and another place. Now he lived on in a changed world where nothing with which he had been familiar had survived. Gregarious by nature and affable by habit, his enforced exile in the little village of Lucan, with the river moving in the valley below the hill on which his villa stood, and the strangeness of the silence of the countryside would only have exacerbated his longing for the life of the noisy and smelly cities in which his life had been spent. Silence and loneliness he had always avoided, and it would have been strange if now they did not bring up to the surface of his mind the memories of those disappointments and indignities which had marked his life. He wrote accounts of his experiences, and throughout those which have survived we find him searching for self-justification, a silence where memories were too painful, and a very human effort to show himself in a superior light.

And so, the years of his retirement began to pass, quiet years, as far as we know, after the stresses of public life and the strains of the early years of the new century when the protection of powerful clients was taken from him. His friends in high places, and his enemies too, had vanished with the old regime, but his interest in the arts was unimpaired. His mind now rested not on the problems of large and costly schemes, which are in essence a matter of organisation, but on that most difficult of all architectural problems – the design of dwellings. His villas, or the few designs which have survived, have been dealt with by Dr McParland, but it is within the restricted compass of these that the architect's ingenuity is fully tested, and here Gandon found his last and most abiding interest.

However, he was not totally cut off from his Dublin acquaintances. The Royal Dublin Society, dealing as it did with art and artists, had a natural attraction for him. He served on various committees and was a 'very regular attendant'. The status of the society was high, and apart from members of the Irish and English nobility, the honorary membership was extended to some surprising Europeans, such as Baron Barintrinsky, chamberlain to the Empress of Russia; the archdukes John and Lewis of Austria; the Grand Duke Michael of Russia; the princes Nicholas and Paul Esterhazy; Prince Victor Metternich, and others of that ilk.

Gandon was a member of the Committee of Fine Arts of the RDS, and in 1809 he was involved in framing comprehensive recommendations for the organisation of the society. Many of his friends among the Society of Artists of Ireland had connections with the RDS, such as Edward Smyth, Thomas Kirk, George Papworth, George Petrie, William Sadlier, and of course, William Ashford, for whom he designed a villa. In 1813 he was party to further resolutions, and in 1815 he was a member of a select committee which included Francis Johnston, by now the leading Irish architect. The committee was set up to consider the necessary alterations to Leinster House, which the society had bought from the Duke of Leinster.

By the end of the nineteenth century, Leinster House had become the centre of an enclave which included the National Gallery, the National Library, and the two National Museums. It was a unique centre of art and culture of which any nation could be proud. It was destroyed when the Free State government insisted on making Leinster House its headquarters. The National Library and the National Museum are now barred in by immense railings which diminish these buildings, and the gardens in front of Leinster House have become a car park, in the centre of which a peculiar structure, reminiscent of a riverside quay, complete with bollards, puzzles the visitor.

* * * * *

In 1816, Gandon wrote to Lord Castlereagh suggesting the embellishment of Westminster Bridge as a memorial to the British Navy. The proposal was in line with his original scheme for Carlisle Bridge. He received a reply to the effect that Lord Castlereagh had no time for his proposal. He then turned his mind to a scheme for a triumphal arch at the entrance to the Phoenix Park as a memorial to Wellington. This too came to nothing, but in July of the following year, the foundation stone was laid for the present Wellington Monument in the park. The architect was Robert Smirke, and it was completed in 1820.

* * * * *

In June of 1820, Gandon made his will. At that time, a married woman to whom property was given for her separate use had the sole disposition of it. Everything else she had at the time of her marriage became the property of her husband, and he could use it as he wished. This was the general position until the Acts of 1870 and after, and Gandon may have been on doubtful ground when he signed his will on 23rd June, for in it he left property and allowances to his unmarried daughter Elizabeth, who was forty-four-years old at that time: '...all my title and interest in or to my dwelling house and its appurtenances situate in Mecklenburgh Street in the County of the City of Dublin, together with the entire furniture therein contained ... however without the interference or control of any husband she may hereafter marry.' He also left her an annuity of £300 a year: '...my will and desire that such her annuity or any part thereof shall not be subject to the debts intermeddling or control of any husband she may hereafter marry...' The Hon Robert Annesley was not mentioned, and Gandon's attempts to secure Elizabeth's property from husbandly rapacity may well have had for its source his experiences with the Hon Robert. The bulk of his estate he left to his son, James, with £50 to his daughter Mary Anne Annesley, 'having already amply provided for her on her marriage'. No mention is made in *The Life* of the return of his daughter with her family from their imprisonment in France. There is a note of the positions held by the grandchildren in later life in the cities of Europe. Apparently they made good connections during their enforced confinement. He also left £30 each to his two servants, and an annuity of £100 to his sister, Mary Handyside.

A few weeks later, two of his granddaughters were married: Catherine, aged eighteen, married the Rev J. Mahon, and Mary Anne, aged twenty, married Sir John Stepney Cowell Stepney.

———

GEORGE IV (1821)

On 19th July 1821, George IV was crowned King at a ceremony which surpassed other coronations in its splendour and magnificence. He had married Caroline in 1795, and left her after the birth of their daughter, Charlotte, to pursue a life of vice. She had lived abroad since 1814, but when George succeeded to the throne, she returned, and received a royal welcome from the people of London. George tried to get rid of her by having a divorce bill brought in, but he had to drop it, being unwilling to face the public hostility it provoked. Caroline tried to take her place as Queen at the coronation, but was excluded, with needless brutality, from Westminster Abbey.

After the coronation, George decided it was time to visit Ireland. He boarded at Portsmouth, and from there he made his way along the south coast of England and up the Irish Sea to Holyhead, where his ship and the accompanying vessels dropped anchor and waited for news of the queen, who was, at that time, dying. She soon succumbed to the ministrations of her doctors, and on the 9th August, express dispatches from the Earl of Liverpool brought news of her death.

George was thus enabled to gratify his often expressed wish to land in Ireland on his birthday, 12th August. Also the matter of whether he should make a public landing at Dun Laoghaire or a private one at Howth, and which had agitated the minds of his companions for some time, were now solved, and transferring himself and his suite to the packet boat, *Lightning Steam Packet*, he set sail for Ireland. On this Sunday, 12th August, Sir Benjamin Bloomfield paid a number of visits to Howth from his yacht in the harbour, and the local people guessed that something was about to happen. A large crowd gathered on the pier during the morning, and by quarter-to-three, the packet boat was sighted. By four o'clock it was close to Ireland's Eye, and Sir Benjamin had the royal coach taken down to the pier. By half-past-four the boat had reached the end of the west pier, and the crowd caught sight of George IV on deck. They cheered wildly, and the king cheered back. He was dressed, it was reported, 'in a blue frock, blue pantaloons, Hessian boots, a black cravat, white silk gloves and a foraging cap with gold lace.' With him were the Marquis of Londonderry, the Marquis of Thomond, Lord Mount Charles and Lord Francis Cunningham.

A ladder was run up from the deck to the top of the quay wall. Some of the gentlemen mounted the ladder and then George IV climbed up. Now, a slight contretemps occurred, for the pier was so crowded that none could move without spilling somebody into the sea. The king waited patiently at the top of the ladder until sufficient room could be made for him to step ashore. The first person he noticed was the Earl of Kingston whom he greeted loudly: 'Kingston, Kingston, you blackbearded good natured fellow, I am happy to see you in this friendly country.' By this time it was obvious that he was drunk. A number of his companions were also drunk, and in the general excitement, some of the gentlemen fell into the water.

George IV next recognised Denis Bowes Daly, and shook hands with him. It was a moment Daly was to remember, for in the act of shaking hands he was deprived of his watch, valued at sixty guineas, and of his wallet also. Many others in the crowd suffered the same fate. George, however, continued to shake hands with those nearest to him, and seemed prepared to work his way through the whole crowd. At last, Sir Benjamin, who had been waiting for this moment, got the door of the coach open. George IV entered, and stretching out his arms, exclaimed, 'God bless you all, I thank you from my heart.' He then collapsed in the back of the coach as it started with a jerk, the horses in the having become restive. They brought him to the Phoenix Park by way of the North Circular Road, and here he retired, exhausted, to drink bumpers to his Irish subjects.

The following weeks saw a round of banquets and meetings, and it is doubtful if His Majesty fully appreciated where he was for much of the time. But it is his visit to the Curragh races which is of interest to us. This took place on Friday, 31st August. At eight in the morning, the High Sheriff and the gentlemen of Co Dublin assembled in the Phoenix Park, and at half-past-eight, George appeared, attended by the Marquis of Conyngham, the son of Gandon's old enemy. They set out at a sharp pace on the lower road to Lucan. We have two accounts of what happened at Lucan. *The Life* tells us:

> On the occasion of George IV passing through Lucan, on his way to the Curragh, preparations were made by the inhabitants of the village and neighbourhood to demonstrate their loyalty by a triumphal entrance. Mr. Gandon expressed his anxious wish to be present, and had invited some friends to escort him in his Bath chair to witness the royal passage. Some passing illness or change of purpose, defeated the intention, and Mr. Gandon expressed his regret to his friends afterwards, at dinner, that he had not been able to see the King, whose father he had seen crowned full sixty years before. This circumstance is also to be regretted, as it was known to have been His Majesty's intention, on this occasion, to have conferred on Mr. Gandon the mark of distinction to which his preeminent talents and useful career so well entitled him.[142]

The reporter of the *Dublin Evening Post* tells us:

> His Majesty's carriage drove up to Colonel Vesey's gate precisely at half past nine, attended by a guard of honour; the residing Magistrate, Colonel Vesey, Governor of the County, and Mr. Gandon were in attendance; the

George IV, King of England by Henry Brocas, the Elder
(courtesy National Gallery of Ireland)

fine Band of the Co. Dublin, stationed at Lucan, with the Staff, were also in readiness, and on His Majesty's arrival immediately struck up 'God save the King', while the shouts and cheers of the assembled Peasants added to the general enthusiasm displayed on this gratifying occasion. A beautiful triumphal arch was thrown between the fine Lombardy poplar and the principal Inn, the whole covered with laurel evergreen with festoons of blue and pink silk, a beautiful gilt crown surmounting the centre, with banners of various colours. As this arch was constructed in a few hours it showed the enthusiasm of all Classes, however humble, to welcome their beloved Monarch. It displayed the following motto: 'George IV, Ireland's Glory'. Here His Majesty changed horses. An immense concourse of People assembled to greet him, and almost every window displayed a banner ... after a delay of a few minutes His Majesty drove forward, taking the road to Celbridge.

The son's account is curiously evasive. One would suppose that he, if anyone, should have been aware of the sequence of events, even if he were not actually present. His hint of the proposed honour to be conferred on his father ignores the party with which he was associated and the long memories of those in power.

George IV had his day at the races in the pouring rain. He was afflicted at that time by a distressing looseness. For his visit to the Curragh, a specially prepared sanitary engine followed his cavalcade. It had been tailored to fit his bulk, the Member of Parliament for Clonmel, Mr Massey Dawson having been measured *in loco regis* for it. Whenever His Majesty felt the need for its solace, a little procession formed, led by the Duke of Leinster carrying a white wand and followed up by the royal doctor, and then marched off to the cabinet of easement.

The royal visit came to an end on 3rd September amid scenes of unbelievable alcoholic bathos.

THE LAST YEAR

On 12th August 1822, Robert Stewart, Viscount Castlereagh, killed himself. His had been the hand that forged the Union, and this was not forgotten. His passing was celebrated in verse, none complimentary; the mildest ran: 'They say he cut his throat at last. 'Why so – 'He cut his country's long ago'.

* * * * *

On 5th August 1822, the Royal Hibernian Academy received its charter. The members do not seem to have felt any urgency for organising themselves, for it was not until 1823 that William Ashford and William Cuming, both painters, with Francis Johnston, the architect, drove out to Gandon in Lucan to offer him the distinction of representing the nation's architects jointly with Johnston in the new Academy. Cuming tells us:

> ...the summer occasionally allowed a visit to Lucan, and it was always productive of the highest gratification. He was fond of the Fine Arts and its professors, and impressed those who conversed with him with the same feeling. I sometimes met him in his Bath chair, sitting out under the shade, enjoying his Tivoli, as he called the scene about him; sometimes I found him confined to the parlour, suffering from gout, but always cheerful and communicative.[143]
>
> When his late Majesty granted the charter to the Royal Hibernian Academy, your father and the late Mr. Johnston were nominated the representatives of architecture in that body, the latter the well known benefactor of the Institution. In consequence, I accompanied Mr. Johnston and Mr. Ashford in a visit to Lucan. Your father, as was usual with him, made our morning very pleasant; he showed us a variety of sketches and designs, the production of intervals of cessation from gout. He liberally imparted his store to his brother architect, which, became the topic of observation and praise from Johnston during our drive to town.[144]

Gandon, now in poor health, refused the honour.

As Christmas approached, 'having experienced a slight attack of his old tormentor, accompanied by want of rest, his physician prescribed a narcotic mixture. The lethargy caused by the medicine continued so long as to alarm those about the patient, the medical attendant was again sent for; Mr. Gandon was raised, by his directions, to a sitting posture; in the act of change, he seemed to rouse, and, uttering some hurried words of surprise in a loud voice, seemed for a moment to recognise those around him; then, instantly falling back in his attendants' arms, expired.' He died on Christmas Eve, 1823, having lived for eighty-one years, ten months and four days. He was buried in Drumcondra churchyard, beside his old friend, Francis Grose.

* * * * *

Gandon's had been a long and eventful life, fruitful, but tinged by the misfortune of perennial disappointment: the high promise of the early years frittered away in an unavailing search for the security of stable friends; the expectation of professional success based on the private conviction of an ability which went unrecognised through inattention; a marriage which seemed to have languished, perhaps through insensitivity; all leading to a desperate clutching at a doubtful opportunity. Then, the alien land, and the irresistible will of a patron which encouraged him, at last, to exercise his latent talents for ten triumphant years against extreme and ever present opposition; the gradual relapse; the return to the city of his early life only to find it too had vanished with the years; the retirement and the resignation to endure his now-inevitable exile; and lastly, the years of waiting, which, even with their loneliness and illness, seem in the end to have brought to his uneasy soul a measure of peace.

———

APPENDICES

APPENDICES

————————

ARCHITECTURAL WORKS

The dating of these has been greatly assisted by the work of Dr McParland in the appendix to *James Gandon, Vitruvius Hibernicus.*

1767	NEW WING, THE WODEHOUSE, Wombourne (unexecuted)
1768	GARDEN TEMPLE, The Wodehouse, Wombourne, for Sir Samuel Hillier, as a memorial to Handel (since taken down)
1768-69	ROYAL EXCHANGE competition, Dublin: awarded second premium (design untraced)
1768-72	SHIRE HALL, Nottingham, completed 1772 and rebuilt in 1876 after a fire
1768	THE DEANERY, Killaloe, Co Clare, for Rev Joseph Deane Bourke (design untraced)
1770-73	WINDMILL AT EASTBOURNE, conversion to living quarters for Mortimer senior (eroded by sea in last century)
1771	HEYWOOD,Ballinakill, Co Laois, for Frederick Trench (since demolished)
	MILL AT LLANGEDWYN, Denbighshire, for Sir Watkin Williams-Wynne (a mill has survived)
	WINGS FOR DUFF HOUSE, Banffshire, for Earl of Fyffe (unexecuted)
	(*Vitruvius Britannicus*)
	20 ST JAMES'S SQUARE, designs for Sir Watkin Williams-Wynne (unexecuted)
1771-72	THEATRE AT WYNNSTAY, Denbighshire (since taken down)
1777	ST LUKE'S HOSPITAL, London (designs unexecuted and untraced)
	WARLEY PLACE, Essex, for Captain Adarns (bombed during last war)
1778-80	ALTERATIONS TO BROOM PARK for Sir Henry Oxendon (untraced)
1780	MONTAGUE HOUSE, 22 Portman Square, for Mrs Elizabeth Montague, when assistant to James Stuart
	CLASSICAL SCREEN (gate piers survive at Kenwood, Middlesex)
*c.*1780	CHAPEL AT ROYAL HOSPITAL, Greenwich, while assistant to James

Stuart (Dr McParland has pointed out the similarity between design features here and in the King's Inns, Dublin)

1781-83   SLANE CASTLE (unexecuted designs)

1781-85   CHURCH AT COOLBANAGHER, Co Laois, for Lord Carlow

1781-1800   CUSTOM HOUSE, Dublin
              1781   Foundation stone laid on the 8th August
              1791   East Dock, work commenced.
              1795   Stores designed
              1800   North stores designed
              (The dock has been filled in and the stores taken down)

1783   TOWN PLAN FOR NEW GENEVA, Co Waterford

1784-87   WATERFORD COURTHOUSE AND GAOL (since demolished)

1784-91   THE ROTUNDA AND ASSEMBLY ROOMS, Dublin (altered plans for Assembly Rooms and largely rebuilt the Rotunda)

1784-95   CARLISLE BRIDGE, Dublin (designing and building)

1785-1802   THE FOUR COURTS, Dublin (following Cooley's Law Offices)
              1786   Foundation stone laid on 13th March
              1798   Foundations for east wing
              1802   Completed

1786   SACKVILLE STREET, Dublin, elevations for Wide Streets Commissioners (unexecuted)

1786-93   ADDITIONS TO HOUSE OF LORDS, Dublin

              ADDITIONS TO HOUSE OF COMMONS, Dublin (unexecuted)

              ROYAL INFIRMARY, Phoenix Park

1787-89   HOUSES AT CAVENDISH ROW AND GREAT BRITAIN STREET (Parnell Street)

1788   VILLA AT SANDYMOUNT, Co Dublin, for William Ashford

1788-90   HOUSES AT BERESFORD PLACE, Dublin

1789   ROCKINGHAM LIBRARY for Lord Charlemont

c.1790   EMO COURT, Co Laois, for Lord Carlow

1790-96   ABBEVILLE, Co Dublin, for the Hon John Beresford

1792-1804   VILLA AT CARRICKGLASS, Co Longford (unexecuted); farm-yard, stables and entrance extant

1800	CHURCH TOWER AND VESTRY at Maryborough, Portlaoise
1800-03	KING'S INNS, Dublin
1801	A SQUARE proposed with Chambers
1801	CANONBROOK, Co Dublin, sold to James Gandon junior
1802	CHAPEL FOR DUBLIN CASTLE (unexecuted designs)
1804	WALWORTH, Co Derry, alterations for the Honourable John Beresford
1815	WELLINGTON TESTIMONIAL (unexecuted designs)
1816	WESTMINSTER BRIDGE, London (unexecuted designs)
1823	LUCAN CHURCH, Co Dublin (uncorroborated)

James Gandon's name has been associated with quite a few buildings in addition to the above, such as:

> BISHOPSCOURT, Co Kildare
>
> PHILIPSTOWN COURTHOUSE (Daingean), Co Offaly
>
> FERNS PALACE, Co Wexford
>
> DUCKETTS GROVE, Co Kilkenny
>
> ANNAGH'S HOUSE, near New Ross.

The CASINO AT MARINO received much of his attention while he was with William Chambers. During that time, while working on it, he became friendly with Lord Charlemont. Later, when Lord Charlemont and Gandon were in Dublin, Lord Charlemont, who liked sea-bathing, would continue on into the city after his bathe and call on Gandon, where they would discuss the position of the arts, etc. While with Chambers, Gandon clearly had something to do with the WILTON ARCH, which is different in style to any other arch executed by Chamber's office.

There is no written evidence that he designed YORK COURTHOUSE, but it is clearly not by Carr and it is very much in Gandon's style. They had become friendly while Gandon wa with William Chambers.

ASPECTS OF GANDON'S ARCHITECTURE

1 The avoidance of windows: wherever circumstances allowed, Gandon, by careful planning and design, dispensed with windows and introduced either high-level or top lighting

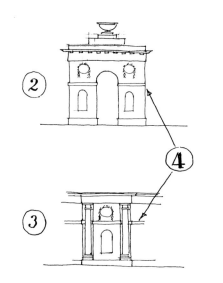

2 The triumphal arch: this feature, in various guises, was one of Gandon's favourite motifs

3 The niche with columns.

4 The horizontal band.

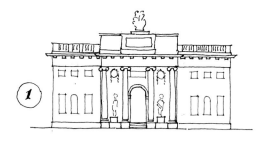

5 Entablatures without architrave, and, in places, only a cornice.

6 The simple Classical screen.

7 The double reading: where a unit may be read as pertaining to either feature.

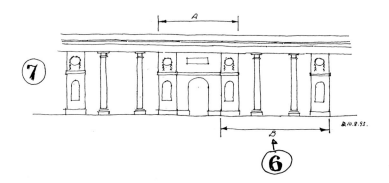

ABBEVILLE

Parts of the building date from about 1700 with further extensions before about 1740. It was bought by Beresford in 1760 from a Kildare landowner, Edward Beover, and he renamed the property 'Abbeville' for his first wife, who came from a town of that name in northern France. Gandon's additions have given distinction to the building. The only clue we have of the probable date of his work comes from a remark by Beresford during the Fitzwilliam affair that he intended to see to Abbeville. This would date Gandon's work at about 1796 or 1797. Percy Reynolds, who bought the property in 1948 had the Gandon rooms restored by Michael Scott. The fine Gandon dairy has been neglected.

Ground-floor plan showing changes to Abbeville over time
(courtesy David Griffin)

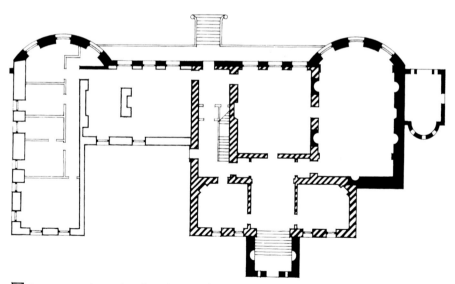

☐ Late seventeenth or early eighteenth century house

▨ Alterations or additions of c.1720-1740

■ Alterations or additions attributed to James Gandon, late eighteenth or early nineteenth century

CARRICKGLASS

During the 1790s, Gandon designed a house and stables for Carrickglass, which lies two or three miles north-east of Longford. The house was not built, but his stables remain. They are interesting in that Gandon articulated the central block so that one is always conscious of the adjoining open space.

Carrickglass, Co Longford, 1792-1804 (unexecuted)
Front elevation
opposite, top Ground-floor plan *opposite, bottom* First-floor plan
(courtesy Dr Edward McParland)

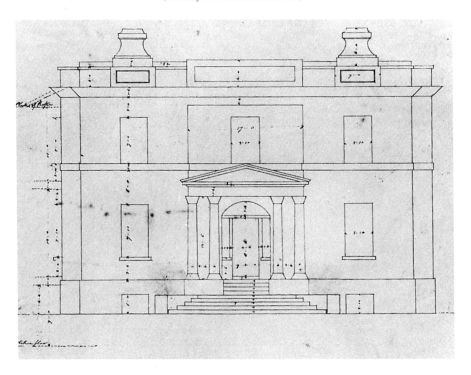

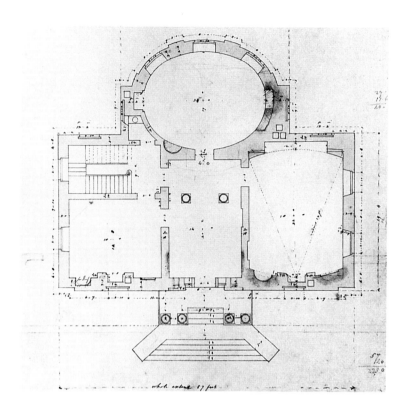

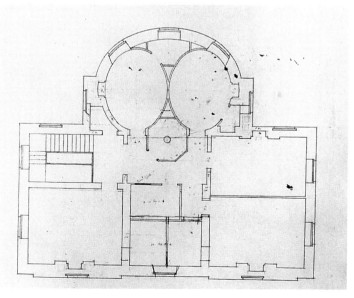

A Gandon Drawing

This drawing [page 85], after Clerisseau, was discovered in Dublin by Dr Hugh Maguire, and was published in *Irish Arts Review Yearbook 1995* (vol. 11). It falls below the standard of his other drawings, but even from these, we sense that Gandon was not happy with the principles of perspective drawing. Here we have the Escher-like effect, where the base of the nearest column seems to fall in line with the columns at the rear.

Gandon's Central London

1   No. 21 Broad Street (later Broadwick Street), Soho: James Gandon, 1771-81.
2   No. 58 Poland: Street William Chambers, 1758 to 1765; Paul Sandby, 1766-72; Thomas Malton, 1772 and after.
3   Cornaby Market, Dufours Court, Broad Street, Soho: Paul Sandby, 1760-66.
4   No. 13 Berners Street: William Chambers, 1765 and after.
5   No. 16 or 18 Russell Street, Covent Garden: William Chambers, 1755-58.
6   No. 4 St George's Row (later 11 Hyde Park Place): Paul Sandby, 1772-1809.

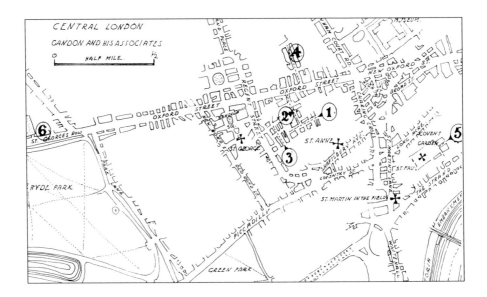

SIGNIFICANT DATES

Date	Age	Month	Event
1742		20th Feb	James Gandon is born
1743	1	May	Mary Gandon is born
1749	7		Gandon sent to school
1751	9		Gandon sent to another school
1752	10		The eleven-day riots
1754		April	Gandon's father bankrupt
			Gandon taken out of school
1754?	12		Gandon's mother dies
1756	14		Brooks becomes a bankrupt
		January	a Peter Gandon dies
			At Shipley's (for two years)
1757	15	May	Paul Sandby married
1758	16		Chambers takes on Gandon
		May	an Elizabeth Gandon dies
1765	23		Gandon leaves Chambers; starts in practice
			Said to have employed Thomas Malton
1767	25		Designs for Sir Samuel Hillier
			Sir Henry Oxeden's residence
			Volume IV of Campbells's series published
1769	27		Plans for the Royal Exchange, Dublin
		January	wins Royal Academy Gold Medal
			Sea trip with Mortimer and Jones
1770	28		Volume V of Campbell's series published
			Building started at Nottingham
		26th July	Gandon is married
			Trip to Eastbourne at Christmas
			Designs for Ballinakill, Co Laois
1771	29	July	a daughter, Mary Anne, born
			Bought house in Broad Street
			Lessons to Sir Watkin Williams-Wynne and design for his theatre at Wynnstay
1772	30		Nottingham Shire Hall completed
		August	a son, James is born
1774	32	March	a daughter, Eleanor, is born
1775	33		Exhibited drawings in style of Clerisseau
		April	a daughter Anne, is born; dies shortly after

271

Date	Age	Month	Event
1776	34	July	a daughter, Elizabeth, is born
			Gandon fails to obtain election to the Royal Academy
1777	35		Designs Warley Place
			Enters competition for New Bethlehem (St Luke's) Hospital
1778	36		Wins, but another is appointed; suffers nervous breakdown.
1779	37		Mortimer dies
1779-80 ?			Stuart employs Gandon
1780	38	November	Mary Gandon marries Captain Handyside
			The Gordon Riots
1781	39		The Hon John Beresford brings Gandon to Ireland
		April	Gandon arrives in Ireland
			Visits the Hon Burton Conyngham at Slane
			Work starts on Custom House
		August	Foundation Stone of Custom house laid
		December	Gandon visits Dawson Court (Lord Carlow)
1782	40		Work starts in Coolbanagher church
			Death of Mrs Gandon; Gandon goes to London
			Gandon returns to Ireland with his son and two of his daughters
		June	plans for House of Lords approved
1784	42		Courthouse and jail in Waterford
		February	Charles Manners, Duke of Rutland, is viceroy
1785	43	March	Coolbanagher church consecrated
		December	the Malton letters published
1786	44		A severe winter
		March	foundation stone of the Four Courts laid, Hon Burton Conyngham offended
			At work on the Rotunda
1787	45	May	Hon Burton Conyngham dies
		October	Duke of Rutland dies
1788	46		Designs prepared for Carlisle Bridge
1789	47	May	King's Inns: William Caldbeck becomes treasurer

1790	48	November	Gandon's houses for Beresford Place approved
			£30,000 granted for Four Courts
			Visit by his old friend, Francis Grose
1791	49	January	received Royal Academy offer of royal scholarship
			Paul Sandby sends in another account
			Work starts on Carlisle Bridge
			Death of Francis Grose
1792	50	February	Portland Island partly destroyed
			House of Commons burned down
1793	51	January	execution of Louis XVI of France
			Gandon's drawings for sale at Penrose auction
		February	King's Inns: Caldbeck rents ground at Henrietta Street
1794	52		Further opposition to Four Courts; grant of £16,000 made
		July	King's Inns: Caldbeck's plans approved and later abandoned
1795	53	January	Lord Fitzwilliam is viceroy
			Hon John Beresford is dismissed
		March	Lord Fitzwilliam leaves
		March	John Fitzgibbon attacked during riot
		June	Beresford writes to Lord Fitzwilliam and calls him a liar; the Fitzwilliam duel follows
1796	54	August	Robert Stewart, father of Lord Castlereagh was created Earl of Londonderry
		October	Habeas Corpos Act suspended until June 1799
		November	Four Courts opened
			Wolfe Tone arrives in France
		December	Admiral Lazare Hoche turned back by storms
1797	55	March to October	General Lake disarming Ulster
1798	56		General Lake harassing the rest of country
		March	Mary Anne Gandon marries Hon Robert Annesley
			Rising of '98 imminent; Gandon packs up and leaves for London

Date	Age	Month	Event
		November	Lord Portarlington dies while with troops
		November	Gandon meets Farrington
1799	57		Gandon returns to Ireland in summer
		August	Lord Charlemont dies
1800	58		Act of Union passed; end of Irish parliament
		January	King's Inns: new building committee appoints Gandon
		June:	King's Inns: Gandon's plans approved and work starts
		August	King's Inns: foundation stone laid
1801	59	February	Thomas Malton senior dies
1802	60	March	Napper Tandy arrives at Bordeaux
			King's Inns: new committee appointed; Lord Clare dies
		February	Baron Redesdale appointed chancellor
1803	61	August	Napper Tandy dies; given magnificent funeral
		July	James Malton dies
		September	King's Inns: William Caldbeck dies
			The Emmet Rising
			Gandon leaves again for London
1804	62	March	Thomas Malton junior dies
1805	63		King's Inns: Gandon resigns and retires
		November	Hon John Beresford dies; Gandon suffers breakdown
1809	67	November	Paul Sandby dies
1815	73		Gandon on committee to recommend on Leinster House
1820	78		Gandon makes his will
1821	79	July	George IV crowned
		August	George IV lands at Howth
			George IV passes through Lucan
1823	81	December	James Gandon dies on Christmas Eve

FAMILY TREE

THE GANDON FAMILY

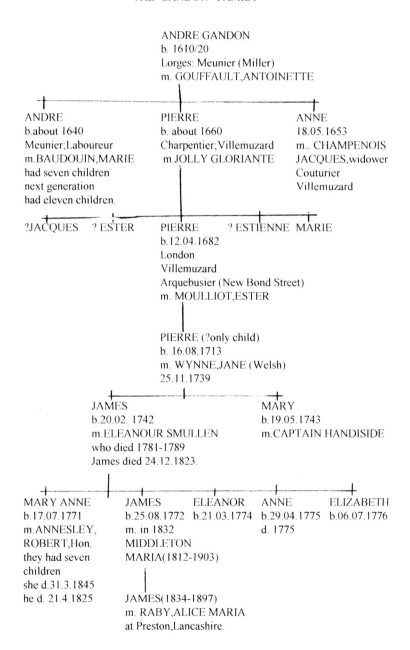

ANDRE GANDON
b. 1610/20
Lorges: Meunier (Miller)
m. GOUFFAULT,ANTOINETTE

ANDRE
b.about 1640
Meunier;Laboureur
m.BAUDOUIN,MARIE
had seven children
next generation
had eleven children.

PIERRE
b. about 1660
Charpentier;Villemuzard
m.JOLLY GLORIANTE

ANNE
18.05.1653
m.. CHAMPENOIS
JACQUES,widower
Couturier
Villemuzard

?JACQUES   ? ESTER   PIERRE
b.12.04.1682
London
Villemuzard
Arquebusier (New Bond Street)
m. MOULLIOT,ESTER

? ESTIENNE MARIE

PIERRE (?only child)
b. 16.08.1713
m. WYNNE,JANE (Welsh)
25.11.1739

JAMES
b.20.02. 1742
m.ELEANOUR SMULLEN
who died 1781-1789
James died 24.12.1823.

MARY
b.19.05.1743
m.CAPTAIN HANDISIDE

MARY ANNE
b.17.07.1771
m.ANNESLEY,
ROBERT,Hon.
they had seven
children
she d.31.3.1845
he d. 21.4.1825

JAMES   ELEANOR
b.25.08.1772 b.21.03.1774
m. in 1832
MIDDLETON
MARIA(1812-1903)

JAMES(1834-1897)
m. RABY,ALICE MARIA
at Preston,Lancashire.

ANNE   ELIZABETH
b.29.04.1775 b.06.07.1776
d. 1775

NOTES AND REFERENCES

———

The Irish historical background has been culled mainly from:

J.A. Froude, *The English in Ireland in the Eighteenth Century* (1881)

W.E.H. Lecky, *History of Ireland in the Eighteenth Century* (1892-6)

E. Curtis, *A History of Ireland* (1945)

E.M. Johnston, *Ireland in the Eighteenth Century* (Dublin 1980)

J.H. Plumb, *England in the Eighteenth Century* (London 1979)

The Dictionary of National Biography (*DNB*)

and the European background (Napoleon) from *The Illustrated Chambers Encyclopaedia* (new edition)

1 Parish registers, St George's, Hanover Square, London
2 Court books of the Gunmakers' Company, London
3 *ibid.*
4 *ibid.*, f.57
5 *ibid.*, f.167
6 *ibid.*, ff.78, 79
7 *ibid.*, f.82
8 Parish registers, St Martin in the Fields, London
9 MS 135, Gilbert Collection, Dublin
10 Parish registers, St Paul's, Covent Garden, London
11 *ibid.*
12 West India Reference Library, Institute of Jamaica
13 James Mulvany (ed.), *The Life of James Gandon, Esq.* (Dublin 1846), 3
14 Ministry of Education, Curzon Street, London
15 Records of the Bankruptcy Court, index 22646, f.102
16 Parish registers, St George's, Hanover Square, London
17 John Harris, *Sir William Chambers*, 5-6 (London 1970)
18 *ibid.*
19 John Fleming, *Robert Adam and his Circle* (1962)
20 J. Rickman, *Life of Thomas Telford*
21 Harris, *op. cit.*, 7
22 Fleming, *op. cit.*, 202
23 *ibid.*, 211
24 Mulvany, *op. cit.*, 13-14
25 Harris, *op. cit.*, 10 (note)
26 *ibid.*, 10
27 *ibid.*, ch. 1
28 *ibid.*, 11
29 Mulvany, *op. cit.*, 16
30 *ibid.*
31 *ibid.*
32 *ibid.*, 21

33 *Lord Harvey's Memoirs*, ii, 346; Lady M.W. Montague, *Works*, ii, 196; Horace Walpole, *Letters*, i, 342; vii, 434
34 *The Dictionary of National Biography*
35 *ibid.*
36 *ibid.*
37 *ibid.*
38 *ibid.*
39 *The County Records of the Eighteenth Century Nottingham*, 46
40 *ibid.*, 55
41 Mulvany, *op. cit.*, 23-4
42 T. Jones, *Memoirs of Thomas Jones*
43 William Thomas Whitley, *Artists and their Friends in England* (1928)
44 *Dublin Evening Press*, 19 Apr 1967
45 *Freeman's Journal*, 6-10 Aug 1785, 387a
46 *ibid.*, 18-22 Nov 1766, 91a
47 *ibid.*, 26-30 July, 1768, 379b
48 *ibid.*, 6-10 Sept 1768, 11c
49 Mulvany, *op. cit.*, 26-8
50 *ibid.*, 30-32
51 MS 135, Gilbert Collection, Dublin
52 *Freeman's Journal*, 21-25 Feb 1769, 201b
53 Knight of Glin, *Malton's Dublin* (Dublin 1978) viii
54 *Freeman's Journal*, 24-26 Oct 1769, 70c
55 Jones, *op. cit.*
56 *ibid.*
57 Parish registers, St Paul's, Covent Garden, London
58 Jones, *op. cit.*
59 Parish registers, St Paul's, Covent Garden, London
60 Parish registers, St James's, Piccadilly, London
61 *ibid.*
62 *ibid.*
63 *ibid.*
64 *The Essex Countryside*, June-July 1959
65 Edward McParland, *James Gandon, Vitruvius Hibernicus* (London 1985) 31
66 Mulvany, *op. cit.*, 38-9 (note)
67 Mrs Elizabeth Montague, Letters 1710-85, Hist MSS Comm.
68 *ibid.*
69 Parish registers, St Bennett Grace church, 15 Nov 1780
70 Mulvany, *op. cit.*, 40
71 *ibid.*, 42
72 *ibid.*
73 *ibid.*, 43
74 *ibid.*, 44-5
75 *ibid.*, 46
76 *ibid.*, 49
77 *DNB*
78 *ibid.*
79 Mrs Godfrey Clark (ed.), *Gleanings from an Old Portfolio*, 3 vols (Edinburgh 1895-98)
80 Mulvany, *op. cit.*, 49-51 (note)
81 *ibid.*, 49
82 *ibid.*, 51-4
83 *ibid.*, 54-5 (and note)
84 *ibid.*, 55-6
85 *ibid.*, 56-7
86 *ibid.*, 58
87 *DNB*
88 *ibid.*
89 Mrs Godfrey Clark, *op. cit.*
90 *ibid.*
91 *ibid.*
92 Mrs Godfrey Clark, *op. cit.*
93 *ibid.*

94 *Dublin Historical Record*, vol. xv, no. 3
95 Thomas Drew, contract drawings, Irish Architectural Archive
96 Mulvany, *op. cit.*, 58
97 *ibid.*, 59-63 (note)
98 Mulvany, *op. cit.*, 72
99 *ibid.*, 69
100 *ibid.*
101 *ibid.*, 70
102 *ibid.*, 71
103 Hubert Butler, *New Geneva in Waterford*
104 McParland, *op. cit.*
105 Mulvany, *op. cit.*, 67 (note)
106 *ibid.*, 88
107 *ibid.*, 65
108 *ibid.*, 64 (note)
109 King's Inns, Public Moneys Receipts Book
110 Mulvany, *op. cit.*, 95-7
111 *ibid.*, 97-9
112 *ibid.*, 100
113 James Malton, Letters to Parliament, 1785-86. Edward McParland has pointed out that the copy in the National Library of Ireland is the only copy known
114 *DNB*
115 *ibid.*
116 Mulvany, *op. cit.*, 101-2
117 *ibid.*, 102-3
118 *ibid.*, 103-4
119 *ibid.*, 104-5
120 *ibid.*, 105 (note)
121 *DNB*
122 Mulvany, *op. cit.*, 120-1
123 *ibid.*, 125-7
124 *ibid.*, 133
125 *ibid.*, 160
126 Constantine Fitzgibbon, *Miss Finnegan's Fault*, 109 (London 1953)
127 The Beresford correspondence
128 *ibid.*
129 Mulvany, *op. cit.*, 116-17
130 *ibid.*, 170-1
131 Bartholemew Duhigg, *An Account of the Honourable Society of the King's Inns, Dublin, 1806*, 477
132 King's Inns minute book for 1792-1803, 156
133 Duhigg, *op. cit.*, 509
134 *ibid.*
135 King's Inns minute book
136 Mulvany, *op. cit.*, 218-19
137 Edward McParland has pointed out that Stuart's chapel at Greenwich shows Gandon's hand at the altar end, in a design similar to that in the hall of the King's Inns. Gandon was with Stuart at the end of his time in London.
138 MS 135, Gilbert Collection, Dublin
139 Michael Lewis, *Napoleon and his British Captives* (London)
140 Mulvany, *op. cit.*, 182
141 *ibid.*, 185-6
142 *ibid.*, 230-1
143 *ibid.*, 228
144 *ibid.*

Edmund Curtis (A *History of Ireland*, 350) tells us that the Irish parliament was sold to the English for forty-eight creations and promotions to the peerage, and £1,260,000 for the buying-out of pocket boroughs and compensation for all office holders for the loss of their positions.

BIBLIOGRAPHY

———

Viola Barrow, Dublin Historical Record, xxv, no. 2

Reginald Blunt, *Mrs Montague* (London 1923)

H. Butler, 'New Geneva in Waterford', *Journal of the Royal Society of Antiquaries of Ireland*, lxxviii (1947)

R.M. Butler, 'The Custom House, Dublin, and its architect', *The Architect*, cvi, nos 1743, 2747

Colin Campbell, *Vitruvius Britannicus*, 3 vols (London 1715-25)

Nicholas Carlisle, *A Topographical Dictionary of Ireland* (London 1810)

William Chambers, *A Treatise on Civil Architecture* (London 1759)

Charlemont, *The Manuscripts and Correspondence of James, 1st Earl of Charlemont*, 2 vols (HMC, London, 1891-9 4)

Mrs Godfrey Clark (ed), Gleanings from an Old Portfolio, 3 vols (Edinburgh 1895-98)

Howard Colvin, *A Biographical Dictionary of British Architects 1600-1840* (London 1978)

Maurice Craig, *Dublin 1660-1860* (London 1952)

Maurice Craig, *The Volunteer Earl* (London 1948)

Maurice Craig, 'James Gandon, Custom House and Four Courts', *The Bell*, xvii, no. 1 (1951)

James Culliton, 'The Four Courts, Dublin', *Dublin Historical Record*, xxi, no. 4 (1967)

C.P. Curran, *The Rotunda Hospital, its architects and craftsmen* (Dublin 1945)

C.P. Curran, 'Edward Smyth', *The Capuchin Annual* (Dublin 1948)

C.P. Curran, 'Cooley, Gandon and the Four Courts', *JRSAI*, lxxix (1949)

Dictionary of National Biography

Dublin Historical Record

Dublin Evening Press

Bartholemew Duhigg, *History of the Kings Inns* (Dublin 1806), and other publications

Edward Edwards, *Anecdotes of Painters* (London 1808)

The Essex Countryside, June-July 1959

Constantine Fitzgibbon, *Miss Finnegan's Fault* (London 1953)

W.J. Fitzpatrick, *The Sham Squire*

John Fleming, *Robert Adam and his Circle* (1962)

R.F. Foster, *Modern Ireland, 1600-1972* (London 1988)

Freeman's Journal

James Anthony Froude, *The English in Ireland in the Eighteenth Century*, 3 vols (1871-74)

James Gandon (jr) with Thomas Mulvany, *The Life of James Gandon, Esq* (Dublin 1846)

John T. Gilbert, *A History of the city of Dublin*, 2 vols (Dublin 1854-59)

Gilbert Collection, Dublin, MS 135

Daniel Gillman, Lucan Church Papers, Co Dublin

Knight of Glin, *James Gandon's work at Carriglass, Co Longford*

Knight of Glin, *Malton's Dublin* (Dublin 1978)

James Greig (ed.), *The Farington Diary*, 8 vols (London 1922-28)

Francis Grose, *The Antiquities of Ireland*, 2 vols (London 1791-95)

Francis Grose, *The Olio* (London 1792)

John Harris, *Sir William Chambers* (London 1970)

Lord Harvey's Memoirs

Peter Hughes, 'Paul Sandby and Sir Watkin Williams-Wynn', *Burlington Magazine*, cxiv, no. 832 (1972)

Irish Builder and Engineer, 'The Four Courts', lviii, no. 15; lxiv, no. 14; lxvii, no. 5; lxvii, no. 15

Irish Builder and Engineer, 'The Custom House', lviii, no. 18; lxiii, no.13; lxiv, no. 4; lxvii, no. 6

Irish Builder and Engineer, 'James Gandon,' lviii, no. 16

Journals of the House of Commons, 19 vols (Dublin)

Journals of the House of Lords, 8 vols (Dublin)

William Kent, *The Designs of Inigo Jones* (London 1727)

Kings Inns, The benchers' minutes and others

Harold Leask, 'Dublin Custom House, the riverine sculptures', JRSAI, lxxv (1945)

William Edward Hartpole Lecky, *History of England in the Eighteenth Century*, 8 vols (1892-96)

Samuel Lewis, *Topographical Dictionary of Ireland*, 2 vols (London 1837)

R.B. McDowell, *Ireland in the age of Imperialism and Revolution, 1760-1801* (Oxford 1976)

? McDonagh, *The Viceroy's Post-Bag*

Edward McParland, *James Gandon, Vitruvius Hibernicus* (London 1985)

Edward McParland, 'The Wide Streets Commissioners', *Quarterly Bulletin of the Irish Georgian Society*, xv, no. 1 (Dublin 1972)

Edward McParland, 'James Gandon and the Royal Exchange Competition', *Journal of the Royal Society of Antiquarians of Ireland*, cii (1972)

Edward McParland, 'Emo Court, Co Leix', *Country Life*, clv, nos 4012, 4013 (1974)

Edward McParland, 'The Early History of James Gandon's Four Courts', *Burlington Magazine*, cxxii, no. 932 (1980)

Edward McParland, *Castle Coole, Co Fermanagh* (1981)

James Malton, *A picturesque and descriptive view of the city of Dublin* (Dublin 1779)

James Malton, *Letters to Parliament by an Admirer of Useful and Necessary improvements* (Dublin 1787)

Constancia Maxwell, *Dublin under the Georges* (London 1936)

Constancia Maxwell, 'James Gandon, Architect of Georgian Dublin', *Country Life*, civ, no. 2701 (1948)

Niall Meagher, 'A Gandon Drawing of the Portico at Emo', *Journal of the Co Kildare Archaelogical Society*, xiv, no. 4 (1969-70)

Mrs Elizabeth Montague, Letters 1710-85, Hist MSS Comm.

George F. Mulvany, The Gandon Memoirs', *The Athenaeum*, no. 1012 (1847)

Nottingham, The County Records of the Eighteenth Century

A.P. Oppe, *The Drawings of Paul and Thomas Sandby at Windsor Castle* (Oxford and London 1947)

A.P. Oppe (ed.), *Memoirs of Thomas Jones*, 32nd vol of Walpole Society

J.H. Plumb, *England in the Eighteenth Century* (1979)

Robert Pool and John Cash, *Views of the most remarkable public buildings in the City of Dublin* (Dublin 1780)

Public Records Office, Gandon's will

P.J. Raftery, 'Who was Malton?', *Dublin Historical Record*, xix, no. 4 (1964)

J. Rickman, *Life of Thomas Telford*

Colin J. Robb, 'James Gandon, his patrons and friends', *Irish Builder and Engineer*, xciv, no. 13

Walter G. Strickland, *A Dictionary of Irish Artists*, 2 vols (Dublin 1913)

John Summerson, *Architecture in Britain, 1530-1830* (London 1953, etc)

Horace Walpole, *Letters*

J. Warburton, J. Whitelaw and R. Walsh, *History of the City of Dublin*, 2 vols (London 1818)

James White, 'Tilly Kettle (1735-1786) and William Cuming's (1769-1852) portrait of James Gandon, architect (1742-1823)', *Quarterly Bulletin of the Irish Georgian Society*, ix, no. 1 (1966)

William Thomas Whitley, *Artists and their friends in England* (1928)

John Wolfe and James Gandon, *Vitruvious Britannicus*, iv, v (London 1767, 1771)

Michael Wynne, 'Tilly Kettle's last painting', *Burlington Magazine*, cix, no. 774

INDEX

Loop Line, Dublin 146
Louch, Richard 237
Louis XIV 18
Louis XVI 222, 273
Low, Mr 191
Lowry (artist) *99*
Lucan (*see* Canonbrook)
Lucan church 265
Lying-in Hospital (*see* Rotunda)

McKenzie, John 237
McParland, Edward 11, 15, 44, 64, 96, 97,
    100, 151, 154, 218, 222, 246, 253, 264
McTier, Mr 209

Magdalene College, Oxford 171
Maguire, Hugh 270
Mahon, Rev J. 254
Malton, James 9, 73, 76, 77, *136-137*, *149*,
    159, 160, *164-165*, 166, 170-171, 176,
    182-183, 184-186, 189, 190, 192, 248,
    272, 274
Malton, Thomas (the elder) 52, 76, 77, 170,
    248, 270, 271, 274
Malton, Thomas (the younger) 76, 77, 248,
    274
Malton, William 76
Manners, Charles (*see* Rutland, Duke of)
Marchant, Mr 56, 84, 85
Marot, B. 249
Maryborough, Portlaoise, church 265
Mason, William 55, 102
Meara, Mr 128
Metternich, Prince Victor 253
Michelangelo 41
Military Academy, Woolwich 52
Mill House, Eastbourne *89*, 90, 263
Mitford, John Freeman (*see* Redesdale,
    1st Baron)
Moira, Countess 122
Montague, Elizabeth 98, 99, *99*, 263
Montague House 263
Montgomery, Barbara 122, 123
Montgomery, Sir George 217
Montgomery, Sir William 122
Moore, Catherine 31, 32
Morgan, Mr 250
Morrison, Richard 236
Mortimer, John Hamilton 55, 56, *56*, 57,
    81, 82, 83, 84, 85, 88, 90, 271, 272
Mortimer, Mrs 154

Mosse, Bartholomew 163
Mount Charles, Lord 255
Mountjoy, Lord 122, 232 (*see also* Luke
    Gardiner)
Moyle Park, Co Dublin 231
Mulvany, Thomas J. 15, 18, 19, 20, 23, 49,
    50, 51, 67, 99, 153, 154 (*see also* Gandon,
    James: *The Life*)
Murphy, James Cavendish 162
Myers, Mr 236
Mylne, Robert 73

Napoleon Bonaparte 223, 249
Napper Tandy, James 132, 178, 180, 211,
    212, 223, 227, 228, 228-230, *229*, 274
'Nat' 56, 85
National Gallery of Ireland 192, 253
National Library of Ireland 253
National Museum of Ireland 253
Nesbit, Mr 211-212
New Assembly Rooms, Dublin (*see* Rotunda)
New Bethlehem Hospital 95-98, 100, 272
    (*see also* St Luke's Hospital)
Newcastle, Duke of 38
New Geneva, Co Waterford 161, 170, 264
New Ross (*see* Annagh's House)
Norbury, Lord 211
North, Frederick, 8th Lord 37, 88, 104
Norton, Mr 24
Nottingham (*see* Shire Hall)
Nottingham Courant 57

Oak Boys, The 117
O'Donovan, John 67
O'Dwyer, F.M. *167*
O'Dwyer, W.M. *167*
Office of Works, London 38, 51
Old Brown 82
Old Slaughter's Coffee House, London 21,
    26
Oppe, A.P. 92
Opsdell, Mr 58
Orange Order 223, 224
O'Toole, Shane 9
Oxendon, Sir George 50
Oxendon, Sir Henry 50, 263, 271

Palladio, Andrea *40*, 41, *42*, 246
Palmerston, Lord 232
Papworth, George 253
Parke (Parks), Robert 162, 212, 221